mums on
babies

mums on
babies

**Rachel Foster, Carrie Longton
and Justine Roberts**

mumsnet.com

CASSELL
ILLUSTRATED

First published in Great Britain in 2003
by Cassell Illustrated,
a division of Octopus Publishing Group Limited
2–4 Heron Quays, London E14 4JP

A CIP catalogue record for this book is available
from the British Library.

ISBN 1 84403 071 7

Printed in Spain

Cover and inside image: Getty Images/Tim Flach

Dedication

To the Mumsnet mums, the real authors of this book. In the words of one member, 'On Mumsnet there is always someone who can be bothered. All too often in real life, most people can't.'

Acknowledgements

We'd like to thank Steven (Tech) Cassidy. Without his gargantuan brain, technical wizardry and endless patience Mumsnet would not be. Tif Loenhis, our agent, has been fab and Rebecca Nicolson, Chris Malloy, Justin Walters and Steve Hilton endlessly supportive. Mumsnet has been sustained by the goodwill and encouragement of our thousands of members, some of whom have been kind enough to volunteer their time in research for this book. Thanks in particular to Valerie Goedkoop and Rhona Westrip. Special thanks to Ian Katz for his boundless enthusiasm and to the rest of our families. Without their help and tolerance nothing would have got done.

Contents

Introduction

It was all so much easier once. For a generation who became parents in the 50s and 60s, the toughest bit about choosing a parenting manual was locating the 'S' section of their local bookshop so they could pick up a copy of Benjamin Spock's *Baby and Child Care*. It was hardly surprising that new mothers and fathers embraced the Californian doctor's exhortation to 'trust yourself' by the million – until then the leading dispensers of parenting advice were chilly figures like the psychologist John Watson, who warned parents to 'never hug or kiss your children, never let them sit in your lap' and to 'shake hands in the morning.'

These days new parents and parents-to-be are blessed – or cursed – with an unimaginably wider range of choice. In the smallest of small town bookshops, you'll find several dozen titles dispensing every brand of advice from 'tough love' to 'baby knows best' and every shade in between. So do you plump for a Spock-style 'go with the flow' approach, an authoritative medical-sounding type, or one of the voguish new disciplinarians, who people seem to be discussing a lot over dinner parties? And what if you make the wrong choice? Might you be scarring your child for life by opting for a hawkish, routine-driven regime? Or laying the foundations for a selfish and indulgent adult by choosing to demand feed?

The chances are that when it comes to selecting a parenting manual, you will employ a time honoured research technique: ask a friend or relative what worked for them. But what if you could do the same for any parenting dilemma, from what kind of nappies to use to when to stop breastfeeding? After all, that's how new mothers must have got by before parenting manuals (OK, maybe they didn't have to choose between travel systems, three-in-one and two-in-one pushchairs or decide whether to go organic) and it's how plenty of parents still survive in those corners of the world amazingly not yet colonized by Spock, Leach, Stoppard and co.

But in our increasingly atomised modern western world, what are the chances that even the most sociable of us will know someone whose child has exhibited precisely the same pattern of sleep-defying behaviour as our own, or, for that matter, who will take our call at four in the morning? That's where Mumsnet.com comes in. The Mumsnet website is a vast archive of expertise – collected the hard way – by thousands of real parents. Whatever the parenting poser you are facing, the chances are that one of Mumsnet's members will have been there already. Their advice is offered in a rather different tone of voice to the tablets of stone delivered by the parenting gurus: not so much 'do this because it's the right way' as 'this worked for me, maybe it could work for you.'

Though we have produced six children between us (with two more on the way as we write this) since meeting in ante-natal classes five years ago, the three of us are emphatically not parenting experts: Justine is a football reporter, Carrie's background is in TV production and Rachel worked in radio. The initial idea behind Mumsnet was to create a place where parents could pool recommendations on family-friendly holidays. But almost immediately our users began swapping advice on a much wider range of subjects: they shared the pain of miscarriages, helped each other through the first difficult days of breastfeeding, debated the pros and cons of bottled babyfood, fretted over whether to use dummies, colluded on how to get rid of them, agonized over the best type of child care and, when they paused for breath, wondered how they would ever get their figures back.

It was only a matter of time before this frenzied exchange of parenting know-how – frequently in real time – reached its ultimate conclusion: a birth, live on Mumsnet. It came in May last year. Members poured onto our message boards to encourage and reassure one of our users – MalmoMum – who was planning a home birth but worried that her midwife – an hour away by car – would not make it in time and that her partner would not be up to the task. Soon afterwards MalmoDad was online – the contractions were coming every few minutes and the midwife was on the way. A short time later a proud MalmoDad was back to say the baby had arrived nine minutes later: 'The midwife talked me through the delivery much the same way I imagine an aeroplane is talked down!' The news was met with unbridled delight on the Mumsnet discussion boards.

Most contributions to Mumsnet are rather less dramatic but over the three years since the site was launched, they have built into an extraordinary reservoir of experience, know-how and, just as important, wit, covering every parenting conundrum you can imagine – and a few more besides. This book, the first in a series of Mumsnet guides to parenting, is an attempt to distil some of that wisdom in a portable, easily searchable form. Since it is our members rather than us who are the real experts, we have tried to mediate their words as little as possible.

No single piece of advice should be read as 'a Mumsnet way of doing things'. One of the first things we learned from the site is that different folk really do take different strokes. The aim of this book is simply to provide you with a bank of solutions which thousands of our members have found to the countless thorny dilemmas, problems and panics every parent faces in the first year of their child's life. We're confident that, whatever the subject, you'll find someone's advice works for you. And if you can't, or if you'd like to share your own ingenious cure for colic, or if you'd just like to chew the fat about the extraordinary, exhilarating, exhausting business of parenthood, we're just a click away at www.mumsnet.com. Good luck!

Breast and
Bottle-feeding

Introduction

If you've ever visited a doctor's surgery or antenatal clinic you'll know that the health profession believes breast is best – after all it says so on that life-sized poster of a smiling, relaxed, round-breasted mother gazing adoringly at her contented suckling child. With the birth behind them it all looks so simple, and we all know it's terribly good for your child and even – so they say – your figure. What could be more rewarding?

A few weeks and a couple of cracked nipples later, bosoms festooned with cabbage leaves and still trying to work out how on earth the instrument of torture also known as a breast pump fits together, reality bites (it just feels like it's your baby). Given the chance, or indeed the energy, you'd quite like to go back and draw a comedy moustache on that poster – preferably with tears of frustration on the faces of both mother and child. Although for many of the 69 per cent (according to the Department of Health) of women who choose to breastfeed from birth it's a wonderful, life-enhancing experience, for some the reality just doesn't live up to the hype, and for others, particularly in the first few weeks, breastfeeding can be hell.

And once you've finally managed to achieve latching on without clenching your toes, what about where and when you feed; should you stick to a routine or go with the baby's demands? Is it alright to get the equipment out in a restaurant or more daunting still in front of your father-in-law? And what of that cunning plan to express regularly so your partner can share some of the night-time burden? How do you persuade your child to comply and take a bottle, and when is it safe to start trying without scuppering your milk supply?

Supposing you can't or don't want to breastfeed any more, what's the best and most painless way to stop? If you are one of the mothers who for one reason or another opt for formula from the start – how do you cope with the pressure and censure, both real and imagined, from health professionals, friends and family? And how on earth do you manage that military operation of sterilizing and preparing bottles in order to have one ready at just the right moment?

One thing everyone agrees on about feeding a baby is that support for the mother is crucial. We think some of the best support comes in the form of advice from other mothers – who've struggled through feeding problems themselves and emerged, seemingly against the odds, with thriving toddlers.

Demand or routine feeding – what works best?

Trying to follow any kind of routine in the first eight weeks is madness. I had a lot of problems breastfeeding and it took me six weeks to get it established. My baby used to feed hourly during the day and every three to four hours at night. I don't see how anyone can prescribe the 'correct' time interval when babies vary so much in weight, size and ability to feed. Some babies of course will thrive on routines. My friend's baby fed every four hours practically on the dot from birth but that was just the baby rather than the 'routine' he had. Indeed my friend found it rather annoying and predictable!

Eulalia

Feeding routines starting at two weeks don't give many mothers time to establish breastfeeding – six weeks is more the norm. What's more while nearly every mother makes exactly the amount of milk her baby needs over a 24-hour period, each mother's capacity for making milk at each feed is different, so one mum may have to feed every two hours, and the second mother may feed every four. Likewise some babies feed far more effectively than others. Over time, the breasts make more milk at each feed as this is what the baby is demanding and the feeds naturally space out as the baby gets bigger, can digest more at each feed, and feeds more effectively so you reach a 'schedule' in the end.

If you are feeding on demand the baby will feed for as long as he needs to, and as often as he needs to, in order to grow well. But if you are only feeding every three hours for a set amount of time, your baby may go hungry, or you may worry that your baby isn't feeding for long enough.

I had my first babies in the 70s, when the advice was to feed every four hours. By day nine my baby was starving and in despair so we gave him formula. He took 12 ounces and my milk dwindled to nothing by the time he was three weeks. When my second son arrived I'd decided on baby-led feeding, no clock-watching. The midwives would have been horrified to know what I was doing but I successfully fed him for over a year. I find it ironic that scheduled feeding was the norm in the 70s, the opposite became accepted in the 80s and now we are going full circle back to the 70s again!

Baabaa

What the experts say

Whether you breast or bottle-feed there is no point in expecting a 'pattern' to emerge for at least three months

Libby Purves (*How Not to Be a Perfect Mother*)

After as number of weeks – as little as three or as many as eight – you may recognise a pattern for when your baby wants to feed.

Dr Yehudi Gordon (*Birth and Beyond*)

A lot of babies have the occasional feedathon, but constant feeding on an everyday basis when the baby never comes off full is ineffective feeding, not demand feeding! Poor feeding is often amended by attention to positioning and attachment so the baby can remove the milk better. It's wrong to tell people to feed for a set amount of time and imply that all babies will get to hind milk (the rich stuff) after a certain number of minutes – it's more gradual than that. Many women are not 'full' between feeds, especially if the feeds are frequent but this has no bearing on overall production.

If regular or demand feeding is important to you then a sort of flexible, scheduled feeding can work with a baby who is gaining weight and is happy, but I don't think it's a good idea to start off this way. Just ask any breastfeeding counsellor who takes calls from mothers distressed and confused (and sometimes short of milk) who have been desperately trying to follow the routines in a book.

Tiktok

A midwife advised me not to do scheduled breastfeeding because breast milk is so much more easily digested than formula, so the baby gets hungry again more quickly and seems less happy on the routine than bottle-fed babies. The breast-feeding mother starts feeling she can't keep her baby happy and is more likely to give up. I'm suspicious of routines that don't distinguish between breast milk and formula for young babies.

Javarose

I see breastfeeding as being more about my daughter getting comfort from me than being just about nutrition. There's no doubt that there are bad points to breastfeeding but now she's two I realize how fast the first year went and miss that level of closeness like crazy.

Lizzei

> **Mumsnet tip**
> In the early weeks if the baby is sleeping in the same room as you, replace the bulb in your bedside lamp with a twelve-watt night-light strength bulb. It makes getting up in the night a much pleasanter experience for everyone.

It's all a matter of preference. I breastfed my daughter very successfully for seven months using the Gina Ford routine from four weeks, but I also had tons of support from my midwife and the maternity hospital who ran a 'breastfeeding workshop' for mums-to-be, which was absolutely brilliant. In addition I had a lovely mum who had breastfed four babies and was always on hand with advice. All that support probably contributed more to our success than the routine. I know some people who found the whole idea that they were supposed to feed to a schedule for 45 to 60 minutes worrying because their babies were much quicker feeders and they were left feeling worried that they hadn't had enough.

Enid

I didn't have any idea what to do at the beginning and worked on the assumption if it wasn't nappy or sleep, then it must be hunger upsetting the baby. Consequently I was feeding for five minutes at a time (because I did not know any better/any other way). Twenty-three times in one day was our record. It was out of sheer desperation that I discovered scheduled feeding via Gina Ford's *The Contented Little Baby Book* – what a relief! I admire those that can demand feed. I found it a huge invasion, which may sound selfish, but the scheduled feeding sorted out a lot of resentments that I had towards my baby.

Charliesmummy

I am glad that I read a book that gave me the courage not to feed on demand, and to get a routine established quickly with my second child as this meant I had more time and energy to play with my toddler. I wouldn't criticise people who feed on demand, but it wasn't practical for me to be feeding every hour or two. Also the people I know who went with the baby's routine gave up breastfeeding earlier than me because they were so exhausted by having a baby that seemed permanently attached to their boob.

Crunchie

> **Mumsnet tip**
> If you forget which breast's 'turn' it is (as I do), attach a safety pin to your bra to remind you which breast you last used and alternate it each time you feed.

I put my son onto Gina Ford's feeding routines at nine weeks with great success. We didn't get him to sleep at the 'right' times until he was about nine months, but he managed the suggested feeding times without any problems. Sometimes it took us a week or two longer to graduate onto the next routine, but generally the shape of his feeding followed exactly the patterns predicted. It's worth saying routine feeding doesn't mean that a hungry baby must wait – Gina Ford always says to feed them first and then worry about why they're not making it to the scheduled time later. You still feed them when they demand it but you just gently guide them into demanding a feed at predictable times.

Amber1

I am not a Gina Ford person, but having breastfed all four of my children I do think that demand feeding is a misleading concept. I took it to mean 'every time the baby whimpers, stick it on the boob'. However, with my last two I did everything possible to distract them from feeding (without leaving them crying). Obviously this can be difficult in the first few weeks when you have little energy but I used to hold them upright and facing out and dance around the room singing or hold them near to my face and chat – anything to give me five or ten more minutes. If you have friends around let them hold the baby if she is getting grizzly – they often have more patience.

Countrybumpkin

I successfully breastfed my two children for many months and they were both on routines. The trick is not to make the intervals too long. In Gina Ford's case for a baby of less than one month, she actually tells you to breastfeed nine times a day, so they don't usually starve! She also recommends her routine only if the baby gains six to eight ounces a week – so 'problem' babies should not be included.

Pupuce

I fed my first child on demand – sometimes every hour – which in turn meant cracked nipples and agonizing breastfeeding for the first five weeks. My daughter would also feed pretty constantly from about 6 pm to 11 pm every night which meant we had very erratic (non-existent) sleep routines.

With my second child I tried Gina Ford's schedules, but gave up after a couple of days as my son wouldn't stay awake when he was supposed to, or feed at the right time – and there was no way I was waking him at 7 am (as she suggests) after a sleepless night when my toddler was still asleep! I did try and space his feeds, though. The feeding frenzy Gina Ford suggests for the evening just wasn't possible with a toddler to bath and get ready for bed, so often I'd have to leave him to cry downstairs but when I came down he'd be asleep. I think a lot of first-time mums feed a child every time they cry, when they might not be crying because of hunger.

What the experts say
The phrase 'demand feeding' is used time and time again, misleading a new mother into believing that any sort of routine in the early days could deny her baby nutritionally and, according to some experts, emotionally.

Gina Ford (*The Contented Little Baby Book*)

The only thing which seems to help is to institute 'lunch'...there may be three feeds before 'lunch', and one after and vice versa the next day, but at least if you call it 'lunch' you are expressing your faith that one day a sensible and workable routine will evolve.

Libby Purves (*How Not to Be a Perfect Mother*)

It may be that second time around I'm more relaxed, but by spacing out feeds from about three weeks onwards I've had no nipple pain, my son's slipped into a daytime sleep pattern that approximates to Gina Ford's routine and he's generally much easier and more settled. At around 13 weeks he had what I assume was a growth spurt and I fed on demand for a few weeks which was hard, but now he's started solids the routine has returned.

Trying and failing to follow a very strict routine can be more depressing and perhaps even more exhausting than demand feeding. But if you adapt the routines to suit you – even if you just try to space out the feeds a bit – I think most people would be surprised at how much easier a new baby could be.

Biza

Inability to breastfeed – can some people just not do it?

All the breastfeeding courses I went on before the birth suggested everyone can do it. My son took all the colostrum from me but problems started when my milk came in. It poured out of me while my son shook his head violently and got soaked. He really wasn't having any of it. He'd suck my ear lobe, or finger but not my nipples. I tried for five weeks, but had to resort to expressing most of the time as he was losing weight. Only a nipple shield enabled him to feed from me at all. He even fed from two of my antenatal group friends. Having since seen some other women's nipples when breastfeeding, theirs seemed bigger than mine so perhaps he had nothing to get hold of – so to speak. I wish the courses mentioned problems like this so you wouldn't get so depressed when it all goes wrong.

Bj

I found that my nipples were too big and rather flat and my son had difficulty getting the whole thing into his mouth. He was a small baby at birth with a small mouth and a weak suck. I supplemented his feeds with formula milk for the first five weeks and also expressed. After six weeks things got better and I was able to exclusively breastfeed.

He is still breastfeeding at one year and thriving. It is true to say that everyone can do it but with some (like me) it can be a great deal of hard work – sore nipples, sleepless nights, etc. Some people want an easier life so they say 'it didn't work', but, like most things, it will work if you try hard enough.

Eulalia

Mumsnet fact
Only 2 per cent of mothers are not able to fully breastfeed.
World Health Organisation

I had problems breastfeeding my daughter and got very depressed, especially as we were kept in hospital longer due to her weight loss. I fall into the small nipple category. All the assistance from midwives, breastfeeding specialists, etc. did not help and when my health visitor told me I should switch to bottles, I felt a huge wave of relief. I think we should be told more about the potential problems of breastfeeding and that not everyone is able to feed their babies themselves. While I can understand the push by the health professions that 'Breast is Best', it leaves those of us unable to manage it feeling inadequate and guilty.

Viv

I was totally naive about the fact that breastfeeding might be difficult, assuming before the birth that it was the most natural thing in the world. What I didn't realize is that it still needs to be learnt – in many societies women are surrounded by other breastfeeding women who can help them through it. We are not, and the chances are that most of our mothers didn't breastfeed. We get little help from busy professionals so it's no wonder that many people give up.

I was told by hospital staff to use nipple shields to help me feed my son when he wouldn't latch on after two days. This worked but I needed to wean him off them as they can hinder milk production in the long term. At six weeks I spent a miserable week with him screaming and hungry, trying to express then feed him with a cup and trying to get him to latch on. It was hell but eventually he did it and I felt so proud because it was obviously hard for him. He didn't gain the required amount of weight that week and I was told to supplement with formula which I did once before realizing that it might cause a reduction in my milk production. Nine months on we both now enjoy feeding.

Josie

What the experts say

Not everyone can breastfeed. This situation happens for a variety of reasons from not having enough breast milk to a baby simply being unable to nurse. Breastfeeding advocates have a hard time admitting this fact.

Sandra Hardin Gookin (*Parenting for Dummies*)

In fact women can feed twins and triplets, and being physiologically unable to produce enough milk for one baby is a rarity.

Gabrielle Palmer (*The Politics of Breastfeeding*)

I had great problems breastfeeding and didn't get enough support from the hospital midwives. When my son was weighed a midwife finally passed my name to a breastfeeding advisor who held a clinic in the hospital. I don't think the midwives had any idea of the trauma and guilt I went through. It was only after I heard another new mum crying in the bed next to me that I realized I was not an isolated case.

Lj

My first child refused point blank to feed from me, so (with a lot of distress and tears) I expressed for two weeks using an electric pump, then finally got him to latch on using a nipple shield. We then fed like that exclusively for six months and with some supplementation for a further month. I assumed the problem was him, but number two wouldn't feed either and has continued to refuse although she loves breast milk. Six and a half months on I am continuing to express successfully using an electric pump. I thought I would have given up by now because of the hassle, but it has just become a part of life and no bother. I am lucky with my supply, because even back at work I can pump 12 hours apart with no difficulties. It doesn't have to be the end of the world if they won't latch on (although it feels like it and you feel so rejected). Pester anyone until you have access to an electric pump and insist on expert midwife advice.

Loubel

I had a nightmare with breastfeeding. My son would not open his mouth and just chewed my nipples. I had been to all the classes, asked every midwife who visited me for help and had the breastfeeding counsellor round for advice. In the end I expressed milk with a manual breast pump for three months. It was hard work establishing a supply and I expressed every three hours initially, which was a pain because I didn't have much time, but eventually I had it cracked and could express 27 fluid ounces a day in just four sessions. I was even able to put some breast milk in the freezer so that after I stopped expressing my son got one feed of breast milk a day until he was four months old. I also supplemented with formula initially as I was worried that my son might lose weight.

In the great scheme of things, I really do not believe that it's going to make or break your child's life. Neither my husband nor I had a drop of breast milk between us and we have never had an allergy to anything or suffered from poor health.

Molly1

Sore and cracked nipples – what can you do?

Feeding my first child was very painful and I dreaded every feed. I tried nipple shields on the advice of the hospital, but gave them up on the advice of the community midwife! Unfortunately, the tension of the anticipated pain seems to make it worse, so (and I know this is easier to say than do) it's important to try and relax before a feed, make sure you're sitting comfortably, etc. The pain becomes more intense towards the end of a feed because, as the baby falls asleep, she is 'nipple sucking' for comfort, which makes the nipple more tender and more susceptible to cracking so it hurts at the beginning of the next feed as well.

The answer is to take the baby off gently by slipping your finger into her mouth alongside the nipple and break the 'latch'. I then put her down on her play mat. On the first few occasions I did this she bellowed for a couple of minutes, but a quick further cuddle for reassurance and she soon settled. After a week, this was the accepted routine and my nipples were happy once more.

I know I would not have been able to do this with my first child, even if somebody had suggested it, but it has worked a treat with my second.

Helento

I had cracked and bleeding nipples with both my children, to the extent that I used to cringe every time they needed a feed. It got better after about three weeks with the first and about ten days with the second, although I still have scars (literally). What helped me was a completely different position. I fed my first child for the first few weeks by holding her under my arm. I changed position just enough to allow my nipples time to heal and toughen up. I also used nipple shields for a while.

Scooby2

It's the most painful thing I have ever experienced. I'd rather have gone through labour again than the first three months of breastfeeding because I never got the latching on right. I lost half a nipple (and am never going to get it back) but one year on I'm still feeding. I tried a remedy from the US called Lansinoh. It's made of extremely purified Lanolin and is sticky like toffee. It seems to help, despite having no chemical pain relievers in it. I also used a paraffin gauze, which you cut into little squares and put on your nipple between feeds to keep it moist – if you let your nipples dry out they will only crack again when your baby next latches on.

Bruntwig

> **Mumsnet tip**
> To prepare me for the long breastfeeding sessions before my first child was born, a friend recommended I buy two things – no, not a special cushion, or cooling pads – a cordless phone and a Teletext TV.

I tried the old camomile ointment – absolutely slathered it on – and it seemed to help just a little bit. Once my nipples 'hardened up' it was like turning a corner and 13 weeks on I love breastfeeding. I had a C-section so was in hospital for five days and I think that was my saving grace because I had help from the midwives. Incidentally, I was told by my health visitor that each feed should be 45 minutes and I should try breastfeeding standing up (for 45 minutes!) It was only later when speaking to another new mum that I realized this was nonsense.

Janus

Everyone and everything says breastfeeding should be painless with the correct latch. I found it extremely painful at first, settling down to dull pain after about four weeks. I went to the best breastfeeding clinic in the country, and they all agreed the baby was latching on fine. 'But it's still hurting,' I would say. 'Oh well, you've got it wrong then,' they said. It's actually made me pretty cynical. I strongly suspect that for a lot of people it is going to be painful for a long time no matter what, but the breastfeeding advocates don't like to admit it because 'breast is best' and everything about it has to be wonderful.

I should have felt very proud that I was managing to feed through the pain, and instead all they could tell me was that I was doing it wrong.

Amber1

What the experts say
The best course for cracked nipples is prevention. Don't overdo the sucking in the first days, don't pull the firmly attached baby off the breast in mid-suck.
Dr Christopher Green (*Babies!*)

Difficult or uncomfortable breastfeeding is often the result of insufficient feeds or poor positioning of the baby.
Deborah Jackson (*Mother & Child: The Secret Wisdom of Pregnancy, Birth and Motherhood*)

I wish people wouldn't propagate this myth that if you're doing breastfeeding right, it doesn't hurt. I had a lot of unnecessary worry that my positioning must be wrong because it hurt so much – but if you've got sensitive nipple skin and someone's Hoovering away at them six hours a day, they're going to take a while to adjust.

Numbat

I think if the health professionals warned us and said, 'it's bad for a few weeks but then everything will be fine and you will actually start to enjoy feeding', we'd all understand. My friend definitely gave up very early because she 'couldn't get the positioning right' – which was rubbish – and subsequently didn't even try to breastfeed baby number two. No one ever tells about you about the pain, the gritted teeth and watery eyes. If I hadn't had my mum telling me it would get easier, I may well have got out the bottle, which would have been a shame as I enjoyed my 12 months of breastfeeding – except for those first six weeks.

Lizzer

Loads of people said my latching on was fine but when I complained that it hurt, they shrugged and told me it would get better after feeding was established, which was more or less right. However, all the books I read said if it hurts, your baby is not positioned properly and I think that's such a lie. It was such a horrible pain when she latched on, getting a bit better after about five minutes. But have you felt babies' gums? I didn't realize they would be so hard, or the sucking so powerful. No wonder it hurts!

One midwife told me to get a sunlamp on my nipples to harden them – her theory was that the darker the skin, the less it hurts. I got some camomile lotion that seemed to soothe them afterwards. If there's a next time I'm going to use nipple cream pre-birth and I might just sunbathe topless for a while.

Lisa

What the experts say

Don't massage and scrub nipples to harden them. They are made for the job of breastfeeding so they don't need any special preparation.

Penelope Leach (*Your Baby and Child*)

....

If you've got the opportunity, expose your breast to warm sunshine but be very careful not to become sunburnt. Don't however use sunscreen on your breasts.

Nicky Adamson (*Is Breast Best?*)

I found the answer was nipple shields, the very thin silicone ones that are totally flexible and don't get in the way at all. My midwife recommended them as she had used them herself although she told me that I'd get mixed reactions from professionals. I had extremely sore, cracked and bleeding nipples initially – it is very disconcerting to see your newborn regurgitating blood. I was able to stop using them within about five days as the soreness went completely.

Alison222

The main thing is to hold the baby close, so she can get a good mouthful. This means holding the baby on her side with that bottom arm tucked underneath her, or in your armpit. Hold the baby's neck on your wrist and hug her in close so you couldn't even get a piece of paper between you. Once there, check if you are comfortable, wait for a very open mouth and then just pull her in closer. She should be almost on the nipple before she opens her mouth.

If in doubt, try standing while feeding. You have to hold her in close enough otherwise you will drop her, as you don't have a lap to hold her on. Once you have got the positioning right the intense agony should stop within a few feeds as your nipples begin to heal (oh I remember that pain well!). If this still doesn't work, try calling a breastfeeding counsellor who may be able to come out and watch you feed. It's amazing how a little tweak here and there can make such a profound difference.

Suebfc

> **Mumsnet tip**
> Rub breast milk around the nipple area, especially the sore bits, after a feed. Not sure why this works, but it does.

I am a breastfeeding counsellor and there's a lot we still don't know about what would prevent or cure sore nipples. All the symptoms – cracking, peeling and bleeding – are evidence of trauma and in the majority of cases it's a result of the baby's suckling grazing or breaking the skin with the tongue or hard palate. Mostly, this can be improved by altering the positioning. Sometimes the attachment gets better as the baby grows and opens his mouth wider.

However, I have known mothers who are unable to achieve pain-free feeding. Maybe these babies have an unusually shaped palate, or a tongue that's tied, or something else that makes feeding a challenge. Nipple shields can sometimes help but they can also lead to problems as they don't help the baby learn to latch on better – though it is possible to latch with a nipple shield, if the shield fits (and often it doesn't).

It's not true that fair-skinned women are more prone to sore nipples – the worst case I have seen this year belonged to a black mum from West Africa. The old method of dry healing is no longer thought to be helpful for cracked nipples – moist healing is the way to go.

Sometimes, soreness is due to thrush (though there may be a history of difficulty with latch as well) and this is often missed. Both mother and baby need treating, whether or not the baby has symptoms. The mother might not have any symptoms on her nipples either.

What makes me cross is that women are told that pain is normal and they should just put up with it. It isn't normal or inevitable, but we can't always put it right (though with the right skills, we almost always can).

TikTok

What the experts say

You may both settle well (to breastfeeding) in as little as a day or as long as two weeks.

Dr Yehudi Gordon (*Birth and Beyond*)

Mastitis – what helps?

Mastitis is horrible. I had it after both of my children were born. Both times I had a raging temperature and it made me very weak. The second time I had a bright red colour that passed from my head downwards. I had it on both sides and can remember the pain of feeding – it was like sharp blades – I cried at each feed. Eventually it passed and I continued to feed for four months. The best cure was a breast pump that helped to express the infection out. As for the pain – there's nothing I can suggest except endurance – I'd rather give birth any time than have mastitis!

Issa

I had three bouts of mastitis in as many weeks – a sky-high temperature and a lot of pain in the affected breast. I was told to keep feeding from that side because my son would help to suck the badness out and to keep massaging the lump down towards the nipple. Both activities were extremely painful for the first day but it did help after that.

Nao

I suffered from mastitis three times in four months. I discovered that it was best for me to feed my daughter from both breasts at each feed and that way the milk flow kept going sufficiently well to stop the blockages. I found that problems occurred when there was too big a time lapse between feeding on any one side.

Tany

> **Mumsnet tip**
> Cabbage leaves are good for engorged breasts. Put them in the fridge and lay them on the breast – it helps to reduce the swelling. Savoy cabbages are apparently the best variety!

The normal advice nowadays is to favour the affected breast – it helps stop further blockages and reduces the chance of the infection becoming an abscess. Feeding can be agony, though. People are sometimes wrongly told to stop feeding from the affected side and then worry that the mastitis has caused a loss of milk in one breast, when in fact it's stopping the feeding, rather than the mastitis, that causes the loss of milk. The milk should pick up again gradually once feeding is resumed.

Janz

I had mastitis twice but continued to feed and had no problem with milk production after the mastitis had cleared up. I know stopping feeding (or expressing) from the breast can slow or stop milk production, so it's crucial to carry on.

Chelle

Try combing the breast to get rid of the lumps (yes, using a hair comb!) from the armpit towards the nipple in the affected area – it works like a massage. If you can find time for a warm bath, it may help to do it in there, but be warned – you might find you get a let-down reflex and a Cleopatra-style bath! Moving your arm in large circles can also help.

I used to get a fair few blocked ducts but they were usually down to either bad positioning or carrying my daughter badly. (I once forgot the sling and ended up carrying her further than expected.) If either of these happened to coincide with a period when I was feeling particularly tired it seemed to make the whole thing worse, so it's always worth taking the chance to chill out as much as possible, going to bed with the baby if possible, sleeping when baby sleeps. During my worst bout my daughter wouldn't feed from the affected side and when I hand expressed (much gentler than a pump) I could see why – lots of pus rather than milk. Yuck! Antibiotics cleared it up really quickly, though.

SueW

> **Mumsnet tip**
> Where I live, in Germany, they advise putting cold quark or fromage frais straight out of the fridge onto the affected breast. It has the same effect as cabbage leaves and is perhaps rather messier... but I found it worked really well.

Combing works – but try an 'Afro' type comb, preferably with nice blunt teeth, and lubricate with a little warm olive oil. Comb towards the nipple and try and feed immediately afterwards.

Tissy

I used the combing method and also cabbage leaves inside the bra and took a homeopathic remedy called phytolacca, which was a slow acting remedy but I am sure it helped things along. There was a definite lump underneath the breast, but no massive engorgement and I couldn't believe how much it hurt.

Puffin

I found massaging the painful breast and a hot bath was useful. Be careful when getting out though, because the combination of the hot bath and the fever may make you light-headed. Then, through gritted teeth, get the baby to feed on that side to get the milk flowing. I used antibiotics when I had a bout and it cleared up in about five days, but it was very nasty.

Tinker

Mastitis is indeed agony. I had it with all of my children and found antibiotics were the only thing that cured it. To help the breast drain though, you can try feeding in different positions, if your baby will cooperate. One position which is a bit awkward for you but seems to encourage the milk to drain freely (presumably due to gravity) is to lie the baby on the floor or on a bed and lean over him/her to feed.

Baabaa

Try putting a hot, damp cloth on your breast for a minute or so just before you breastfeed. As the cloth quickly gets cold, keep a bucket of very hot water next to you so you can dip the cloth in it a few times. I found it did the trick for me. Once you have removed the cloth, get the baby to breastfeed on that side.

Pupuce

I had mastitis twice when my daughter was only a few weeks old and needed antibiotics on both occasions to clear it up. I found hot baths helped a lot – and not just massaging the affected breast but actually hand expressing. I also relied on one of those hot bean bottles (which you heat up in the microwave). It has the same effect as the warm flannel but keeps warm much longer).

Anibani

I was the mastitis queen! I decided to try bottle-feeding at around six months but every time I tried the odd bottle I would get mastitis. Eventually I did manage to stop feeding but only with a lot of help from my health visitor, breastfeeding counsellors and also a homeopath. We all came to the conclusion that the reason I was so prone to it was because I produced so much milk and my child was a frequent snacky feeder and never fully drained all my milk.

I was just very unlucky. I also think mastitis is more painful than giving birth and yet hardly anyone tells you about it.

Gaby

What the experts say

It is poor feeding technique rather than repeated infection that causes recurrence; improved feeding technique rather than medication that prevents or controls it.

Penelope Leach (*Your Baby and Child*)

Breastfeeding in public – would you, should you and what reactions have you had?

I've breastfed all three of my children wherever we've happened to be at the time and never had a problem. My eldest is 12 now, so I don't think public tolerance is a new thing, particularly. I think it's very difficult to tell whether you're feeding or not if you just stick the baby under your top.

Plushpants

> **Mumsnet fact**
> The Queen, Madonna, Mrs Thatcher and Pamela Anderson all breastfed. www.breastfeeding.org

I always took the 'if you don't like it, don't look' approach. I did once ask someone who suggested I use the loo to feed my daughter whether they would be happy eating their lunch in the toilet, which shut them up.

Azzie

I adapted pretty quickly to feeding in public. I regularly fed at church but was bemused when I heard one lady comment (not very indiscreetly) that I could be more discreet about it. I felt God probably had some hand in designing the nipple-seeker so maybe a few prayers for improved design might be better placed. I was also asked if I wanted to go to the mother and baby room at John Lewis in Bristol – I was in the bra department at the time – hardly a breast-free zone!

Personally, I don't want to be sent off to the feeding room because that's where these things should be done, especially as they all seem like Piccadilly Circus with lots of coming and going, not much room and a lingering smell of poo.

MalmoMum

When my son was tiny we went to a wedding during which I fed him several times. Many of the guests (particularly the not-too-sober males) approached us thinking he was having a cuddle and put their hand down to stroke his face, just missing my boob. I do have a couple of male friends who are breastfeed-phobics, and race out of the room at the click of a bra-cup descending – if they stayed and realized how little they were missing they might get over it.

Now I've switched to bottles I actually feel more embarrassed about giving my son a bottle in public than I ever did about whipping a boob out.

Dm2

Once, on the train, an old lady came over while I was breastfeeding. I was worried she was going to start telling me I was shameless and rude but she just said how nice it was that I was breastfeeding. She had breastfed all three of her children and was under the impression that everyone bottle-fed now.

Bexi

Mumsnet tip
If you're anxious not to give offence when feeding in a café or restaurant, try draping a serviette over your shoulder to cover the baby's head. I managed to give my 4-month-old 'tea' at the Ritz without any bother by doing this.

Over the years, I have noticed that when I ask for permission to breastfeed, it seems to create an uncomfortable atmosphere, so these days I just get on with it without asking and this seems to go down better. I think after the initial shock people get over it quickly and take the cue from you.

Nance

I don't ask, I just do it, although I try to be discreet about it and not flaunt my breasts in public. I was in a restaurant recently and was shocked by how obvious one woman was being about breastfeeding. She had very large breasts so they were probably harder to hide but I could see everything. Maybe that's what offends most people. It certainly raised my eyebrows!

Pupuce

I get more hacked off when I see bottles of formula popped into a baby's mouth than a pair of breasts. I was the first to use decent breastfeeding facilities if they were provided – but I really couldn't care less if a mother obviously breastfeeds in front of me.

I was intrigued in hospital when the one woman who was bottle-feeding in my ward told me that the only reason she wouldn't breastfeed was because she couldn't do it in front of her dad!

Lizzer

What the experts say
Don't be embarrassed about breastfeeding in public. Be as discreet as you need to be, but remember this is your baby's food and your baby deserves to eat now.

Sandra Hardin Gookin (*Parenting for Dummies*)

Some women are uncomfortable with their bodies and feel self-conscious or inhibited about nursing. This is no crime.

Deborah Herman (*The Complete Idiot's Guide to Motherhood*)

I have to say that I was and would still be embarrassed feeding in front of my dad. I know that nature intended us to breastfeed, etc. but I cannot remember the last time I saw any of my family's more intimate body parts and somehow I would feel very uncomfortable with him being there. Sad, but true.

Molly1

I get so fed up with men dictating where we should feed our babies. I've met so many 'soon to be dads' who get all shirty about women feeding their babies in public ('I wouldn't let my wife...') as if it is something disgusting. I think there is a big difference between 'nudity' and breastfeeding. If we go around hiding in corners, how is breastfeeding in public ever going to become fully acceptable?

Countrybumpkin

I never thought I would feel happy breastfeeding in public, but I once did it on a commuter train, with a businessman sitting across the table. I think he was a little embarrassed, but I certainly didn't get the feeling that he thought I should stop. Surely most people would rather not listen to a screaming baby and quite often, especially when they're tiny, that is the alternative. I do think that if you feel embarrassed about it, then other people will. If you just get on with it without a fuss, then most people don't even notice.

Emsiewill

> **Mumsnet fact**
> Humans are one of 4,237 species of mammals, all of whom breastfeed their young.   www.breastfeeding.org

I have to say that I didn't enjoy breastfeeding in public. I did it a few times and found it embarrassing. I particularly remember a trip to Ikea, where I fed in the café and had a family on the neighbouring table literally craning their heads to try and get a glimpse of what I was doing. I felt much more comfortable feeding at home in a quiet, private room.

Enid

I envy those who could breastfeed comfortably in public. I was so rubbish at it in general; there was so much nipple waving about, positioning, repositioning, squelching – none of that discretely shoving baby up and under the shirt. There was no way my public breastfeeding efforts could have been mistaken for just giving baby a cuddle. I was mortally embarrassed even if the general public didn't bat an eyelid. Just to defend those who might suggest you take baby to the changing room, toilet, or whatever, I am sure some of them think they are being helpful by offering you a place of privacy, as opposed to wanting you not to do it in front of them!

Jasper

I found it easier to breastfeed in front of total strangers than in front of some of my friends/family and in particular in front of an old boyfriend – with thoughts of 'then' and 'now' pictures going through his mind!

I'd love to say that I would positively choose on all occasions to feed in a busy public place as a mark of support for fellow breastfeeding mothers. I definitely believe this is the right thing to do, as long as your baby is happy being fed in a very busy environment. However, I admit I would seek out privacy if possible.

Frank1

Whilst I'm very pro-breastfeeding I do think that if it's done in public it should be done with a modicum of discretion. It's important to remember, and have respect for, the members of the public who find this sort of 'nudity' offensive and embarrassing. Equally, those members of the public should accept that it is a woman's right to breastfeed where she chooses and if she is doing it discreetly, where is the harm in that?

I think most women would prefer to feed without an audience, especially when the baby is tiny and still needs help with latching on. The biggest problem is not peoples' attitudes to breastfeeding in public, but rather the total lack of pleasant, hygienic and comfortable facilities (and I don't mean a few uncomfortable seats in a baby changing room or the Ladies loo).

ChanelNo5

What the experts say

I admit to being entirely shameless about it. I loathe seeing a baby on a train or on a bus, wailing miserably and rooting around in its mother's clothes, while she blushes and soothes and gets crosser and hotter by the minute. The pair of them ought to get on with it, and feed.

Libby Purves (*How Not to Be a Perfect Mother*)

I think many people do feel uncomfortable about breastfeeding in public, and it takes bravery to do it. But if it's acceptable for the baby to have a bottle in whatever place he is in, then it has to be acceptable to breastfeed.

Tiktok

The only problem I had with breastfeeding in public was remembering to put them back. My brother-in-law said coming to our house was like opening page three of the *Sun*. I did think it was amazing how pre-birth I would have been mortified by male friends even seeing me in my bra, but post-birth I sat on the sofa as bold as brass and got them out for all to see.

Hollee

How do you persuade a breastfed baby to take a bottle?

I tried everything with my first child. In the event, she never took a bottle at all, but her day nursery got her on to a cup at six months. I became anxious when I tried to get her to take the bottle – so it's probably worth getting a grandparent to try it when you are out of sight. My third child didn't have a bottle until just before I went back to work when he was ten months. Her nanny gave it to her and she took to it straight away, rapidly rejecting any idea of breastfeeding, which was a bit sad. I am now trying to wean her off it and she is not keen. You can't win!

Rosalind1

My daughter took an ounce of expressed milk at six weeks but when I tried her again at 11 weeks she screamed and refused. I tried for the next four months but in the end she went straight onto a feeder cup, though it didn't help as a substitute for the bedtime feed – a spout just isn't as comforting as a bottle teat. My advice if bottles don't work, is to use a cup and make sure there's something comforting, other than your breast, that your child associates with going to bed, like a teddy. I gave up with the bottle when I realized I was getting more stressed out by her refusing a bottle than by not being able to go out before 8 pm. It doesn't last forever. I do, however, regret listening to those people who said 'don't introduce a bottle too soon'. My next one will have expressed milk from a bottle much earlier and more regularly.

Biza

I was told not to introduce a bottle in case it hampered breastfeeding. Friends who didn't heed this advice breastfed and gave the odd bottle for the sake of a bit of independence. They now have babies who happily drink from a cup, whereas my son refuses anything other than the breast.

Esme

What the experts say
Some mother-baby pairs can cope with occasional bottles at three weeks, but you'd better wait until six weeks if you possibly can and twice that long if breastfeeding is a real priority for you.

Penelope Leach (*Your Baby and Child*)

I have heard lots of conflicting advice about when to introduce bottles – my midwife said not for at least eight weeks, even for expressed milk, whilst my health visitor says that if you intend to use bottles at all, you should introduce them before four weeks – all most confusing.

Starling

I believe that the advice to wait to introduce the bottle is wrong and can cause unnecessary strife. I have many friends who have introduced a bottle early (two to three weeks) and are now happily breastfeeding, but have a refreshing modicum of freedom. You have to keep it up, though. Our little girl took a bottle at two weeks, but we didn't persevere and at six months she wouldn't entertain the idea at all.

We've tried everything – various teats, cups (valves/no valves), different times of day, hungry/not hungry, dad trying – all to no avail. Eventually I tried withholding breastfeeding until the evening, which was horrible and didn't work – she took so much milk from me she was sick. I went back to work having been told that my child would take a drink once I wasn't there but she wouldn't – she dug her heels in and was very upset. We eventually had limited success with a beaker but beware of advice that says either babies will adapt once you go back to work or that you shouldn't give a bottle in the first few weeks!

Jennys

The reason health visitors say no to using bottles early on is that giving bottles in preference to breast can affect the supply of milk. Your body needs lots of stimulation to produce milk in the early weeks. But if you want to introduce bottles you can either breastfeed first then offer a bottle of formula or offer a bottle once a day using expressed milk for the first eight weeks or so until supply settles down. Using the pump to express stimulates the body anyway, so it's actually an ideal way of combining the benefits of keeping up your supply, giving your baby your own milk and getting the baby used to the bottle. It is useful too if you want to go out and have a few drinks!

Eulalia

I found my son took readily to a bottle, but only with a very slow flow teat (the sort you use for very young babies). I think this is because breastfed babies are used to sucking pretty hard, which means they tend to gag and choke when given faster flow teats. He is four months now, but still uses newborn teats.

What the experts say

I took a look at my own breast and nipple when my son nursed and decided that the bottles I was using looked nothing like me. I found a nurser nipple that looked and felt like a mother's nipple and he liked it.

Deborah Herman (*The Complete Idiot's Guide to Motherhood*)

Bottles are another confusing area for parents. The truth? There's not a whole lot of difference between them. Honestly, they're all about the same.

Sandra Hardin Gookin (*Parenting for Dummies*)

My son was very reluctant to take a bottle but I found the small soft-spouted beakers were good for getting him used to the taste of formula milk. He completely refused the first brand of milk I tried but was better with the next. Start off with ready-mixed cartons to begin with as a tin of rejected formula is a very expensive mistake. He is now feeding happily from a bottle, after some perseverance.

Kells

My daughter refused to drink any milk other than breast milk. We came to the conclusion that she just didn't like milk (she seemed to prefer juice) so we made sure she had plenty of yogurt and other dairy food to make up for the milk she wasn't drinking. When the breast was no longer on offer she gradually started to drink more milk and now has a large bottle first thing, and a few ounces before bed. She's a perfectly healthy child – my advice is to stay relaxed and offer as many alternatives as you can.

Azzie

My daughter would never take a bottle (or a dummy). It broke her dad's heart because he so wanted to give her a bottle of expressed milk. Before I went back to work I fought for two weeks with her but eventually gave up. She went straight to a cup and had expressed milk from it until my child-minder said she was just as happy with juice. I worried about the milk-free daytimes but hey, we have to find something to worry about, don't we?

Treaclebat

I had this problem with my daughter when she was four and a half months and it just turned into one long battle. What finally worked was sitting her in a chair facing me and giving her milk from a spoon at the same time as her food. This seemed to get her used to the taste. She eventually started to use a bottle but was never really keen.

Scooby2

> **Mumsnet tip**
> I found trying different shaped teats worked with my daughter. But I had a bag full of bottles and teats all shapes and sizes by the time we'd cracked it – so it's worth borrowing some if you can, rather than wasting money buying them.

My breastfed daughter refused the bottle at three months – both expressed milk and formula. She wouldn't entertain the teats in her mouth at all, even though she shoved everything else in there. I tried her with a cup (without a spout); it was very messy and slow, but at least I knew she'd take formula. So I bought a different kind of bottle, left my husband with her and hid upstairs (Hoover on as I hated the screams) at feeding time. For the next few days I got my husband to give my daughter her bottle once a day. Once she realized that there was no alternative she took the bottle and has done so ever since with less and less fuss. It's so good not to have her totally dependant on me for her feeds. Next time I'll begin bottle feeding earlier.

Kate71

My son never drank milk from a cup or bottle. Eventually I stopped breastfeeding at ten and a half months, on the assurance that he would then do so...but he never did, though he would drink juice from a beaker. He just never liked formula or cow's milk. We made sure he had plenty of cheese, yogurt, fromage frais, milk on cereals and milk pudding and didn't worry about it.

Scally

> **Mumsnet tip**
> Try a straw. My daughter, who never took to bottles, took to straws at an early age (about six months) and they're sometimes a bit easier to control than plain beakers.

I used a soft-spouted beaker when my baby was about 11 weeks. She wouldn't take a bottle after six weeks but managed the cup because it had such a gentle flow. I used to freeze my milk in an ice cube tray so anyone could pop a couple of cubes or some water into the cup when I was away. It worked well for us and I didn't use a bottle when I stopped breastfeeding at 12 months as she went to bed with a cup of water.

Lizzer

Someone I know had success offering their child chilled breast and formula milk – apparently her son seemed to treat it as a different drink, rather than a breast-substitute and took to it then.

I think the warnings about nipple confusion are wrong. We introduced our son to a bottle a day from about two weeks and I'm sure it's helped me breastfeed for longer because I've had freedom from breastfeeding right from the start. One warning, though – when he got to seven months he was down to just two feeds a day so for about four weeks I didn't give him a bottle at all. The next time I offered it to him he wouldn't take it. By this stage it didn't really matter as he would drink from a cup, but I could have been caught out.

It's such a shame that we aren't told all this in pregnancy, along with the 'breast is best' mantra. I know so many friends who've had enormous difficulties with getting babies on to a bottle and it's unnecessary.

Amber1

Bottle-feeding – how do you cope both practically and personally?

Having just transferred to bottle from breast I would say that a steam sterilizer for the microwave is a godsend: easy to use and really portable. It's also worth making up batches of bottles at a time and keeping them in the fridge – they will keep for up to 24 hours.

Bottle-feeding can be just as special as breastfeeding, if you make the atmosphere right – close holding, eye contact, hand-holding and stroking can all still be done on the bottle – the advantage is that dad can do it, too. My husband found that feeding our son a bottle really helped him to bond with him.

Zoe

It's worth buying several sizes of teats as some babies get on better with one rather than another. Get a bottle of gripe water, too. Don't buy too many tins of milk at once as some babies don't take to one brand and you may need to switch. If there are mini bottles available in hospital, try several.

Robinw

Feeding a baby with a bottle is easy and I think we should respect people's choices and not try and change their mind by preaching on about the 'lovely cuddly moments' you have when breastfeeding. It's patronizing to suggest that mums that bottle-feed don't experience the same closeness.

I had a microwave sterilizer, which was great, and I warmed up my bottles in the microwave, too. Going out never caused any problems as I had a bottle carrier that kept the water hot so I could add the powdered formula when it was time for a feed. I gave up sterilizing at six months and my son moved on to cow's milk from a cup at 12 months. I don't think he's suffered from being a bottle-fed baby from birth and if I have another child I will do exactly the same again.

EmmaM

> **Mumsnet fact**
> In March 1999 there were 170 visual references to bottle-feeding on television and just one to breastfeeding. There were 27 references to the difficulty of breastfeeding and one to the difficulty of bottle-feeding.
> *British Medical Journal* 2000

I had lots of reasons for not breastfeeding, the biggest being I just didn't want to! It's worth finding out if the hospital provides bottles of milk for non-breast-feeders. The one near me doesn't tell mums planning to bottle-feed that they need to bring in their own bottles and formula in a deliberate attempt to get them to breastfeed, which I think is outrageous.

Compared to stories of the early weeks of friends who breastfed I can honestly say I had a ball. I was out shopping and meeting up with friends two days after my daughter was born, which doesn't seem to be possible if you're struggling to breastfeed for the first time.

Hwr

I made sure my daughter got used to room-temperature bottles, rather than warm, which saved a lot of hassle. I bought a container to hold the measured-out powder, put boiled water into the bottles and kept them in the fridge for 24 hours. This made night feeds and going out very easy. I didn't need to use cool or warm bags as it was just water in the bottle. If it was during the day and I took the bottle of water straight from the fridge, I put it in the microwave to take the chill off it rather than actually warming it up (though I was always careful to shake it and check it first, just in case!).

Paula

I found breastfeeding difficult with both my children but was determined to give it a go. Before my daughter was born I asked my midwife if I should buy some formula milk just in case and she said 'no'. A week after coming home from hospital I had a day when my daughter was attached almost the whole time. I ended up in tears at 2 am because she was still hungry and crying. My husband rang the midwife and she told him to go and get some formula. Second time round I had the formula ready and if my son still seemed hungry after breast-feeding I'd give him a couple of ounces of formula, which seemed to do the trick.

I gave bottles at room temperature. I used to make up all the bottles I needed for the day in the morning (this is the only time in my entire life that I have been organized) and keep them in the fridge. I used the microwave to take the chill off. It's important, if you do this, to shake the bottles well to get rid of any hotspots.

Ailsa

> **Mumsnet tip**
> Prepare warm milk quickly by mixing eight scoops of milk powder with 120ml (4 fl oz) of cool boiled water and refrigerate. When the time comes for your baby's feed, simply add another 120 ml (4 fl oz) of just boiled water to the refrigerated bottle.

I breastfed both my two for the first few weeks and hated every minute of it (something I wasn't expecting). I persevered because I wanted to give them breast milk for all the right reasons (it is the most wonderful stuff) and I thought it might get easier, as a lot of women find. I never experienced a single happy, cuddly or relaxing time when breastfeeding, but as soon as I switched to formula,

I was a happy new mum (and dad and baby were happy, too). I envy those who do have happy experiences breastfeeding.

On my daughter's first night home she sucked at my breast and screamed for about five hours. In the end my husband went to out for a tin of formula – I had confidently not thought it necessary to purchase one! She wolfed down a few ounces and went off to sleep.

Jasper

Before I gave birth to my son I was so confident in my ability to breastfeed that I didn't buy any of the equipment needed to bottle-feed. Things started well but then I developed cracked nipples, even though I was told I was doing things right. The day I got out of hospital I sent my husband to buy a sterilizer, bottles – the lot. I spent a week crying at my inability to breastfeed and felt guilty that I wasn't giving my son the best start in life. I am a scientist and I know all the arguments for breastfeeding, which made it all the harder. Eventually I compromised by expressing using an electric pump, which was quick but made me sore, and fed my son expressed milk in bottles. In the end, my health visitor told me it was okay to stop since I'd probably passed enough maternal antibodies on during the first ten days.

Once I'd decided to bottle-feed I felt relieved that at least I had made a decision. I still feel guilty about it, though and it makes me angry when I hear people criticizing mothers who bottle-feed without knowing their circumstances.

Pigwig

What the experts say

...contrary to some breast feeding gurus' advice, your baby will not suffer physically or emotionally if you decide to change to formula milk.

Gina Ford (*The Contented Little Baby Book*)

I know that stating these facts can be painful or even enraging to some women who have not breastfed their children, but the continual denial of the superiority of breastfeeding and breastmilk, supposedly to spare women's feelings, is a patronising deception.

Gabrielle Palmer (*The Politics of Breastfeeding*)

I was always sure that I wanted to breastfeed, but my daughter wasn't! I struggled for six weeks and then gave in and switched to bottles. It was the hardest decision I've ever had to make, but I had lots of support and my life and my daughter's life became much happier. One of the best things about bottle-feeding was that my husband got really involved and he assures me it helped him bond with our daughter.

Amymum

The paediatricians we had dealings with in two neo natal units advised that if breastfeeding (or expressing to feed) is not possible, ideally only formula milk that contains long-chain polyunsaturated fats (LCPs) should be used as these are proven to aid brain development. My son was premature and I tried breast-feeding to give him what I considered to be a better start than he had already had. But when he didn't gain weight and I gave in to formula milk, at least I was able to reap some comfort from knowing he was having milk that contained LCPs.

Late30smom

In defence of breastfeeding, it's not easy for everyone but if you can get past the first few weeks it usually becomes very easy. The same cannot be said for bottle-feeding as it doesn't change – the faff of dealing with bottles is the same at six months as it is at day one.

Eulalia

Mixed feeding – can it work?

After three weeks of trying to breastfeed, my baby continued to lose weight and cry with hunger what seemed like all the time and feed continuously. I was at breaking point. My husband insisted on trying some formula. It transformed everything and I went on to breastfeed for 14 months. I could sleep for more than two hours at a time and knew that my baby would at least occasionally have a full belly.

My milk supply took a good six weeks to get established and though the occasional bottle of formula probably hurt supply, I don't think I would have made it through the early weeks without it. I tried expressing at four weeks but was lucky to get one and a half ounces after half an hour. After six weeks our baby was being totally breastfed. It seems that the breastfeeding lobby's stance – it's either 100 per cent or nothing – leads to a lot of women giving up, because it just seems too difficult. My advice would be to try and avoid giving formula but don't rule it out.

Ringer

Breastfeeding problems are usually confined to the first six weeks, which is why health visitors say not to introduce bottles, but everything can be done in degrees. If you use one bottle of formula a day and your supply seems okay then that should be fine. I think it's better to take the risk and give some bottles than to just give up breastfeeding completely. There's no turning back once you do that. Certainly it's ideal to have mixed feeding when a mum returns to work and I know people who have done that very successfully.

Eulalia

What the experts say
Not all babies switch happily between breast and bottle, and rather few can do so before they are two to three months old.
Penelope Leach (*Your Baby and Child*)

We're all told that breast is best, but life is sometimes just about finding out what works for us and breathing a sigh of relief. I certainly found that after a few weeks giving my son a bottle was a welcome option.
Penny Wilson (*Wipe: Survival Tactics for Parents with Attitude*)

On the advice of my doctor I started to mix breast and bottle at six weeks and it was the best of both worlds. Dad gets to bottle-feed, mum gets some sleep, baby gets her antibodies and no lugging bottles out in the day. Plus the baby seems to sleep longer after a bottle. This should be promoted more as the 'third-way' and yet midwives say you shouldn't do it as it interrupts the flow. My body adjusted quite easily by feeding at roughly the same times. I find it frustrating that so many women give up breastfeeding completely because of the problems it can entail, and yet they don't have to.

Lil

My health visitor painted a picture of 'it's all or nothing', in other words, don't mix bottle and breast. After three months I was mentally and physically shattered. My husband made me see sense and we agreed to give our son a bottle for night-time feeds. Within days I felt so much better – I began to get some decent sleep and my husband could help with feeding. I'm sure it's true that you need to get your milk 'flowing properly' over the first few weeks, but after that there shouldn't be a problem – my supply adjusted after just a couple of nights. I'll definitely be opting for the 'third way' next time around.

Motherofone

We all know the risks to your supply by introducing mixed feeding but I think there needs to be some recognition that for many women it's the only way they can manage breastfeeding. I consulted a breastfeeding website after my baby had his first bottle and was reduced to tears by their warnings about the damage even a small amount of formula would do. The message was that you were severely reducing the benefits of breastfeeding and formula should be avoided full stop.

Croppy

> **Mumsnet fact**
> By the time their baby reaches six weeks of age, more than one third of women have stopped breastfeeding.
>
> National Childbirth Trust

My son was exclusively breastfed for the first 12 weeks, after which I started mixed feeding. He is now mainly bottle-fed with just early morning and late night breastfeeds. When I was pregnant, I was adamant that he would be breastfed for at least six months but I didn't realize how difficult it could be. My son is a very relaxed, unenthusiastic feeder and even at 12 weeks could take over an hour for each feed. Despite this, he had no problems with weight gain, and seemed generally happy. I, on the other hand, was worn to a frazzle. I had expected to be feeding a lot during his first weeks, but at three months he was still wanting at least eight feeds a day. I had reservations about formula milk, but it has made both of us happier – he feeds more quickly and appears more content and I no longer feel surgically attached to him.

While we all know that breast is best, no one should feel guilty if, after giving it their best shot, they feel unable to sustain breastfeeding on its own long term.

Starling

What the experts say
Remember that your baby needs to feed little and often during the first week to help stimulate a good milk supply. Unless advised by the hospital, ignore any pressure to top him up with formula. This is old-fashioned advice and the fastest way to end up formula feeding.

Gina Ford (*The Contented Little Baby Book*)

The statistics show that many mothers stop breastfeeding in the first three days, which is understandable when they're emotional, exhausted and distressed if the baby is difficult to feed. Often a bottle of formula is suggested, and demoralized mothers think that means the end of breastfeeding, which of course it needn't be, but that's how it's interpreted. Formula is hardly ever medically necessary – more a lifeline to a distraught mother and baby – but too often it's given without enough discussion of the consequences.

Tiktok

I started mixed feeding on the advice of my hospital when my son was readmitted for jaundice and it was discovered he wasn't putting on sufficient weight. Mixed feeding has definitely seen his weight gain improve but my milk is now low, and my baby is refusing my breast in favour of a bottle. This is despite expressing and using a supplemental nursing system to try and boost my milk. I am devastated by this outcome. If you're thinking of mixing breast and formula, be careful because you may end up not having a choice about feeding by bottle in the end.

Lou33

My baby was one of the rare ones who refused the breast once the bottle appeared. I was talked into adding a supplementary bottle of formula from 12 weeks because she had severe reflux, wasn't keeping much milk down and wasn't putting on weight. From the moment I gave her the bottle she physically refused to breastfeed and would push the breast away with both hands. I expressed milk for a few weeks but eventually had to stop through stress and exhaustion. I felt really sad about how our breastfeeding stopped but at least she did then start putting on weight and is now very healthy. I'd second the advice to be careful if you're thinking of adding a bottle, you never know what the reaction's going to be – they might refuse, or they might just prefer it to you.

Joanne

Going back to work – can you still breastfeed?

I returned to work full-time after 14 weeks and managed to maintain some level of breastfeeding until 15 months.

I expressed twice a day for around eight months in the first aid room at work, where I kept an electric pump. This is a major hassle (in terms of bringing in sterilized equipment, keeping the milk cold and just being away from your desk for 20 or so minutes at a time). There were also times when meetings dragged on and on, and I couldn't get to the pump which left me with two large Zeppelins – awful. The fact that I work in an all-male environment and most of my visits to express were accompanied by loud mooing noises also made it a less than fun experience! Looking back at it, I can't quite believe I did it and I'm not sure I would do it again to that extent.

Psychologically, though, it helped with my returning to work. It was wonderful to come in from a day at the office and snuggle up for a feed. It also helped me to cope emotionally with a nanny as there was at least one thing I could do for my child that she couldn't!

Ringer

> **Mumsnet tip**
> If you go back to work part-time, as I did, try and be consistent about your feeding routine. By the third day at work my body would have just about adjusted to dropping the daytime feeds, but then I'd get lazy and breastfeed during my days at home. When it was time for work again I'd be back to square one and very uncomfortable. Not recommended!

I went back to work when my son was four months old. By then my milk supply was well settled and able to cope with differing levels of demand. I hired an electric breast pump and ignored my husband mooing softly at the other end of the sofa. I built up a week's frozen supply but gradually phased out day-time feeds as it wasn't convenient for me to express at work. I think it's crucial to introduce your baby to a bottle early, at about six weeks. I had no problem continuing to feed and experienced slight discomfort for a couple of days while my supply adjusted.

Clare2

I breastfed my second and third babies in the evenings and early mornings when I went back to work, and expressed a little at lunchtime, just to ease the milk supply. You can usually stop doing this after a few weeks. Or, if you find that expressing goes well for you, you could start doing more of it.

My two babies upped their night milk consumption after I went back to work, though I never minded because I felt guilty about depriving them of it during the day. Bear in mind that not everyone takes to expressing easily, especially with their first child so it's also worth remembering to take it easy if things don't go quite according to plan.

Javarose

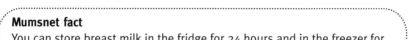

Mumsnet fact
You can store breast milk in the fridge for 24 hours and in the freezer for up to three months. Royal College of Midwives

To keep up with full-time breastfeeding you need to use lunch breaks to express some milk and store it in the fridge or build up a supply of milk over the weekend and freeze it. Make sure you have a good pump – an electric one is much less work – and do your expressing when you are relaxed.

Eulalia

I **went back to work part-time** when my son was three months old – he had one bottle of expressed milk while I was at work and I would express for the next day when I got home. I couldn't express at work (only tried once in the car park) but my milk supply survived with just expressing in the evening and although my boobs were huge and rock hard I seem to have good valves (my husband's terminology) and didn't suffer from leaks.

Chelle

I **went back to work** at six and four months respectively with my two babies and continued breastfeeding morning, evening and night (for 18 months in one case) afterwards. Your body soon adapts – although I did need to use those plastic breast shells on the long journey home and occasionally had very embarrassing wet circles on my front when I was on the train. I suggest wearing something washable with a scarf you can drape over the relevant bits! The breast shells make you look very pneumatic, but if you can't look big-busted when breast-feeding, when can you?

It was really nice to get home and have to sit down to feed and cuddle the baby straight away – no sorting out supper or putting away the washing until I'd sat down for 20 minutes.

Copper

Mumsnet fact
Breastfeeding a baby saves you an estimated £450 a year.
National Childbirth Trust

For the first month back at work I breastfed in the morning, expressed at lunchtime, expressed in the evening when I got home (I missed the evening feed because I couldn't get home in time) and breastfed again at 10.30 pm. My daughter got formula while I was at work, or the breast milk I had expressed the previous day. That worked okay, but at four months I was happy to give up and switch to formula – and she seemed happier to be bottle-fed too (she had got very nosy by that stage and wanted to look around!) We stopped the 10.30 pm feed at five months. We used to love that feed – my husband woke her up and changed her nappy and gave her a cuddle and then I fed her – but it reached a stage where it was getting very difficult to wake her and she was hardly taking any milk.

Sis

Mumsnet tip
Get babies used to a bottle fairly early – my first baby wouldn't take one at all because I left it too late. If you can't express much to begin with, don't panic and assume you've got no milk – you have, but the baby is much better at getting it out than you are!

My daughter is now seven months old, I have been back at work for nearly two months and, although it is very hard work, it can be done. I haven't kept up the daytime feeds as I felt that it was just too difficult expressing at work but still manage a night-time and morning feed. I'll keep these up until I feel that we are both ready to drop them.

Pamela1

I've recently returned to work and, to make it easier when I went back, I introduced a bottle of formula at lunchtime beforehand. I then introduced another bottle so my daughter now only gets fed breast milk from about 6 pm onwards and in the morning, otherwise it's formula. I am lucky that she has always fed four-hourly so it doesn't seem to be a problem. I will soon need to drop the morning feed even though I know my breasts will suffer a bit, but I have found they are usually fine after a couple of days. At weekends she might get the extra morning feed from me, because I am too lazy to get a bottle ready!

Sometimes she doesn't want to feed when she first gets up so has a bottle instead at around 9 am, other times she will wake about 5 am and I end up feeding her in bed with us – you just have to be flexible.

Crunchie

Biting while breastfeeding – why do they do it and what can you do?

My 11-month-old was biting so I tried pulling him in closer to me and it seems to have worked. Having said that, I do wonder if he's trying to tell me something. He still feeds when he wants to but apart from his main feeds morning and evening the feeds are smaller and more like a snack or for comfort. If we are out he will drink water or juice and not ask for a feed unless he gets tired – so perhaps he's telling me it's time to wean, which is a shame as I enjoy our feeding times.

Peanuts1

My son started to bite when he didn't want to carry on breastfeeding. I wanted to continue until he was at least a year but unfortunately he just didn't feel the same way and there wasn't anything I could do other than reluctantly respect his wishes. This is by no means the only reason for biting but it's one possibility worth considering.

Another reason some babies chew is that once you get down to a couple of feeds a day and the child is increasing food and drink intake, the milk supply can decrease very quickly, and some babies bite/chew because they're not getting any milk. There are various ways of increasing supply (such as additional expressing) which might be worth a go.

Bo

> **Mumsnet fact**
> Basketball superstar Michael Jordan's mother breastfed him until the age of 3 and credits it with turning him into the 'athlete he is'.
> www.breastfeeding.org

The natural tendency when you're bitten is to pull away from the pain. However, a good way to deal with it is to bring your baby in closer to you. That way, he gets a face full of breast and will let go.

Baabaa

My son has bitten me a few times and I also used a firm 'no' followed by putting him down when he does it. I let him drink water out of a bottle at night if he's thirsty and have discovered he likes chewing the teat on the bottle. I've now started saying, 'remember, no biting at the end' and words to that effect in a cheerful reassuring way and he's been really good. He was only biting at the end – one last chew to finish off.

Bruntwig

I'm convinced my son does it for attention. My daughter fed for 18 months and never bit me once. He only has four teeth and bites if I start to use the phone or look away. It can easily turn into a huge game (for him) and if I react at all he finds it hilarious. I try to be stern because I worry for my nipple, but he looks so cheeky when he's done it that it's hard not to laugh.

Hollee

I had this problem with biting when my daughter was about eight months and rather than yelling 'ouch!' (easier said than done) I yelled 'no!', took her off (little finger in the corner of her mouth), put her down and walked out of the room. She cried, but she didn't do it again! If she went to nip I would only have to issue a quiet but stern warning 'no' and she would get the idea.

What the experts say
However many teeth they have, most nursing babies don't bite the breast.
Penelope Leach (*Your Baby and Child*)

When those little teeth start coming in, babies may take the opportunity to use your breast as a teething ring. Unfortunately there's not much you can do.
Sandra Hardin Gookin (*Parenting for Dummies*)

Babies physically can't feed and bite at the same time, as the way they attach means their lips cover their teeth, so new teeth don't have to mean the end of breastfeeding. It's worth watching closely towards the end of a feed though, as this is the most common time to nip. If they start to come off a little, take them off the breast before they get a chance to bite. Your reaction to biting is hilarious for the baby and it can end up being a game for them. If they learn that you mean business and biting will not be tolerated even once, they will figure out that it isn't worth missing a feed for a bit of fun.

Mollipops

My son did it but it was a very short phase so it's worth hanging on in there!

Eulalia

Stopping breastfeeding – how do you make the transition?

I cut down gradually until I was only doing a night-time feed. When my breasts got painful I expressed just enough to stop them hurting and they eventually stopped producing so much. At night I gave a bottle with some formula and then topped up with breast milk, so gradually he took less from me and my supply dwindled. Daft as it sounds I was really upset when I stopped even though my son couldn't care less as long as he got his milk from somewhere.

Selja

I stopped feeding my daughter at 12 months and made it a very slow process. I went with what she wanted and she dropped down to two feeds a day, one in the early hours of the morning and one at night. She eventually got into the routine of settling herself with a cup of water at night from around ten months and then started sleeping for longer in the mornings and just decided she wanted her breakfast straight away rather than a feed. I stopped for a couple of days and then started again before finally realizing she was happy without it. I was really upset that it was all over but I was happy that she had chosen to stop herself. Unless you really want to finish then hang on until your child decides to do so themselves. Having the decision made for me made me think I'd encourage number two to carry on for longer, as I miss it so much.

Lizzer

My daughter was still feeding at midnight at ten months, but when she was about one year old, she suddenly went off breastfeeding. Fortunately, this more or less coincided with my own preference.

Javarose

> **Mumsnet tip**
> If middle of the night feeds are a problem, it's worth trying a cuddle and giving water from a cup until the child works out it's not worth waking up for.

I cut down the feeds very gradually, starting by giving half my milk and half formula (bottle or cup) at one feed. I suggest doing this for a week and then stopping breastfeeding at that feed altogether. See how that goes for a week, then do the same with another feed. It means you're only dropping half a feed a week so it's slow progress, but I didn't get engorged at all and after about six weeks I was free from breastfeeding.

LisaV

A number of things helped me to stop. I was expressing anyway, so very slowly I just cut down the amount of milk I expressed. I also took pure peppermint oil capsules and wore a tight sports bra over the top of my nursing bra to try and alleviate some of the discomfort. It took me about three weeks to dry up completely.

Molly1

My daughter was exclusively breastfed for 18 months as she was allergic to dairy and apparently allergic to bottles. She loved breast milk and the whole cuddling feeding thing – but having got it down to two feeds a day, I wanted to stop. I stopped mornings by getting up and entertaining her anytime from 5 am onwards to prevent her coming in our bed and wanting to feed – exhausting, but effective. Then my husband did bath and bedtime every night for three weeks. I was amazed that the habit broke, but it did. She still (aged 3) goes for the breast if she's tired, hungry or upset and she holds onto my nipple and cuddles up, which looks strange in public, but is a small price to pay, I think, for a bit of freedom from feeding.

I think there's so much written on starting breastfeeding and so little help on stopping it. Beware of those who say their children gave up of their own accord – it certainly works for some, but it did not work in my case, if anything, as my daughter grew older and more vocal, she was able to make it quite clear what she wanted.

Biza

What the experts say

When it comes to stopping you have the choice of gradual withdrawal or going cold turkey and stopping with a bang.

Dr Christopher Green (*Babies!*)

Going cold turkey has to be the worst advice ever given in the history of advice giving.

Sandra Hardin Gookin (*Parenting for Dummies*)

My sister breastfed her son until he was 22 months and had no problem stopping. Babies are only babies for a short time – there is no hurry for them to grow up. Most will wean themselves off and there are no traumatic scenes of denial. Breastfeeding is not bad for them just because they are eating solid food.

Eulalia

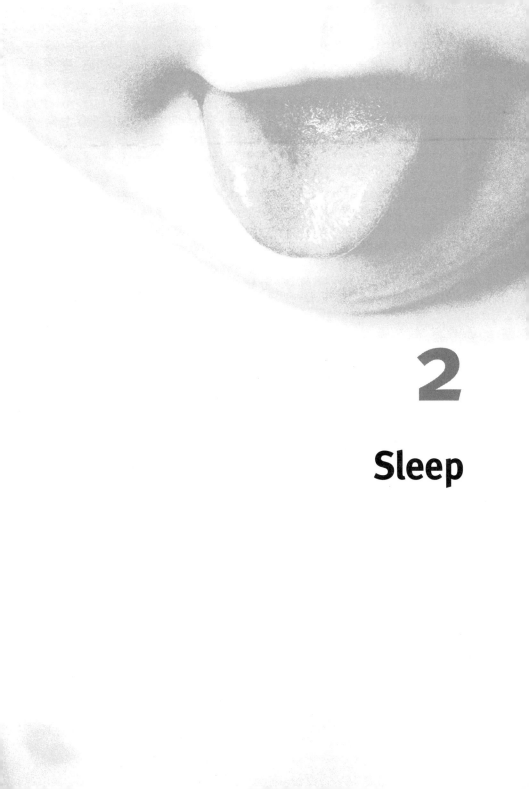

2

Sleep

Introduction

Sleep is *the* major preoccupation of parents, be they first timers or experienced and hardened veterans.

It starts as an innocent with a bump when friends, colleagues and even total strangers admonish you to enjoy your late nights and lie-ins because life will never be the same again. You smile benignly in the smug knowledge that, as babies, both you and your partner slept through the night from two weeks and, as adults, you could win a hatful of golds in the sleep Olympics. Sleep runs in this baby's genes – your baby will be different.

But the chances are you're doomed to join the ranks of the sleep-deprived. According to the University of Loughborough's Sleep Research Centre the brain pattern of someone in their twenties who has not slept for 36 hours will have much in common with that of a 60-year-old. Surveys show that the average mother gets only four hours' sleep a night during the first four months. For some it's worse. What if your newborn simply won't be parted from you and howls like a wolf every time you set her down? What can you do if your baby sleeps all day and wants to party all night? And if you rock them to sleep every night are you condemning yourself to thousands more nights of rocking? Even if you're one of the chosen few whose baby miraculously manages eight hours from the word go, don't think that your sleep dilemmas end there.

Many angelic sleepers decide that 5.30 am is an appropriate time to start the day. You might know it's still the middle of the night but how do you get the message through to a bright-eyed, bushy tailed nine-month-old? Should you resort to controlled crying? Is it a humane way to teach your baby the rules of the sleeping game or cruel and strictly for control freaks?

What about three-in-a-bed? Is it the natural, practical answer to broken nights or a foolish indulgence certain to store up sleeping problems for years to come?

Endless other conundrums await you. Should you let them use a dummy to sleep and if so, how can you get them to take it… and how can you get them to give it back? How many naps should they have? What if your good sleeper turns bad? How do you move them out of your bed and into a cot? There's no shortage of sleep experts only too happy to provide you with schedules, mantras and battle plans for achieving that elusive eight hours. But who knows which is the best advice? Gina Ford's strict-routines-from-the-word-go method or Penelope Leach's follow-the-baby's-lead approach? The answer is to see what the real experts have to say. Those who've been, and are still, living on the sleep front-line, who know best what works, what doesn't, how to cope, keep your sanity, save your relationship and get some shut-eye.

Settling a newborn – any tips?

We went for around three weeks without our newborn going near his crib as he would scream blue murder if he was put there. The only place where he did seem to settle was the car seat. I was extremely concerned that this was setting a bad precedent. However, like most things with newborns, it just gradually got better. It was just a case of being patient and persevering with trying to get him to sleep on his own. One thing I found helpful was to put a muslin square under my baby's head as he fell asleep in my arms, then when I transferred him he wasn't woken by the cold sheet. Also, from around five weeks, I encouraged him to have a good kick on his sheepskin. This tired him out and meant he slept longer and deeper.

Ringer

We realized that our son didn't like having empty space around him. So we swaddled him in his blanket and put other blankets around his body so he was supported on all sides when he was in his Moses basket. I think this added to his feeling of security. Anyway it worked and he slept soundly after that.

Debster

Even at four weeks my newborn would not go to sleep on his own, preferring my or anyone's arms or our bed. If we put him down in the Moses basket when he was asleep, he would only sleep for a maximum of 20 minutes and so some days got very little sleep. I was worried this might be the start of bad sleep habits but now he's seven weeks and is settling much better, especially when I put a worn T-shirt of mine in with him.

Katyw

What the experts say
There is more chance of establishing a good habit if you let them fall asleep in the comfort of their own cot without too much parental prancing about.
Dr Christopher Green (*Babies!*)

We found swaddling worked really well for us – our twins went into cots on day two. If you use cotton cellular blankets and wrap babies so it's only their weight holding the blankets in place, it's very safe. We followed the Penelope Leach method – you can find it in all her books.

Aliceb

I had a problem with my baby not settling except in my arms and it's very tiring. The spin cycle on the washing machine was effective so sometimes I would put several consecutive 'spins' on but swaddling was probably the most effective thing for getting her to sleep and it saved my sanity. My daughter was far more settled at night when we wrapped her – you just have to be careful to make sure that they don't overheat. We used a cotton cellular blanket but when it was really hot we used a sheet. We also bought one of those little gadgets that plays noises, so she slept to the sounds of a stream. During the day, I carried her around in a sling. She is much more settled now at five months but it was, and still is, a hard slog getting her to sleep.

Sass

We used to let our newborn sleep in his bouncy chair – he was quite happy there. We had one that lies down flat, so if he dropped off sitting up slightly, then we could lie him down later. It also had carrying handles too, so it was just as portable as a Moses basket.

Emmam

A swing worked for my son. You can buy the 'with knobs on' type that swings electronically or buy a swing that you wind up yourself and costs half the price. We started using it when he was six weeks. It stopped him crying and then sent him to sleep. He's four and half months now and I find it a godsend when I need to do something and keep him pacified at the same time.

Alli

There were a few things that our little boy liked to look at when he was very little. Changing light patterns, black and white swirly things and particularly face shapes. He liked going in his baby bouncer seat and anything that kept him in a more upright position. Some babies love close human contact and it may be worth investing in a baby carrier. There are those who suggest that if you do that then you'll be carrying your child around with you forever – but you don't see many six-month-old babies who are constantly in these things and at least you'll have your hands free to do things.

Molly1

> **Mumsnet fact**
> Settling a new baby to sleep at the beginning of the night takes, on average, 25 minutes.   *Mother and Baby*

My son has never been a good daytime sleeper and it drove me berserk when all the books advised me to 'catch up on sleep when he is sleeping'. Now he is 14 weeks he is a good night-time sleeper but he still doesn't sleep much in the day. He is responding well to some daytime sleep training, such as putting him down morning and afternoon for sleep. I take solace in the fact that a wakeful baby is learning all the time.

Zoe

Sleepy newborns? Ha ha ha! I was expecting something quite different from what I got. Looking back, I realize that my son was getting lots of five to ten minute catnaps in the day, especially during feeds. I didn't count these as they were so short and hardly gave me an opportunity to get a break or anything. However, they can interfere with a baby's ability to sleep longer. If your child is catnapping, see if you can try to encourage him to stay awake – even if this means interrupting the feed. Be quite ruthless (I was getting cold washcloths and rubbing them on his face, then blowing on the wet patch!). A good rule of thumb is that a newborn can't stay awake more than two hours at a time (without a catnap). So after around two hours of being awake, retreat to a quiet room with little stimulation.

I underestimated how unsettling new surroundings and being held by visitors can be for a baby. I had a very alert newborn. I realize now my son was highly sensitive to his surroundings and easily over-stimulated. So I tried to limit the number of people holding him and kept things especially quiet and boring in the lead-up to bedtime.

Amber1

> **Mumsnet tip**
> When putting the baby to bed, take the whole mattress out of the Moses basket, settle her on the mattress, wrapped in her blankets, on your knee and get her off to sleep. That way, it's easy to decant her into the basket without her waking up.

My newborn spent most of his early days on my chest, as he wouldn't sleep if I put him down. At this age they like the security of your body after spending nine months in a nice warm place. Things do get better, though, and I enjoyed the closeness.

Peanuts1

Try taking your baby to an osteopath if he won't settle. I know plenty of people who've found it has helped ease a newborn's discomfort.

Pupuce

All newborns do sleep a lot – it's just a matter of when and for how long at a time. My first got her days and nights mixed up – she would sleep nearly all day and then be awake almost all night!

> **Mumsnet fact**
> Newborns typically sleep for 16–18 hours a day, gradually decreasing to about 9–12 hours a day by the time they reach two.
> *Encyclopaedia Britannica*

It takes a bit of trial and error, really, to see what works. Rocking and wrapping are good comforting things to try. If your baby seems colicky or 'windy' you could try holding them a particular way – one hold that worked on our daughter was laying her down along my forearm, tummy down, head to one side and resting on my hand, then walking and rocking her while I patted her bottom. Patting at a heartbeat rhythm and pace is also soothing, as is a clock ticking in your baby's room. White noise is supposed to be soothing too, like a radio or TV off-station. A baby lullaby tape is also worth a try.

Mollipops

My baby didn't sleep for the first three weeks at night, unless she was on my chest and I was upright! The minute I tried to lie down she would wake up and yell again. However, strangely she slept okay during the day, in a big old pram. I also tried the swaddling thing and that seemed to work. It was only when she was about three to four weeks old that she had any pattern or routine to her sleeping habits.

Crunchie

What the experts say
Occasionally a baby will have his longest sleep period during the day and his longest period of waking at night... This night-day reversal is less a problem than an indication that the child is inherently a good sleeper.
Dr Richard Ferber (*Solve Your Child's Sleep Problems*)

Try a lambskin. My two slept on them for years, also it was easy to take it everywhere, I could just put it on the floor and my son would settle straight away. He kept it in his bed until he was 5. I also used one for a new baby I looked after and he settled straight away.

Alibubbles

My son wouldn't sleep if he was horizontal (even whilst being cuddled). We found he preferred to be upright and so 'sitting' him in a bouncy chair and rocking it gently worked. We think it was slight reflux causing him discomfort. He's four months now and still prefers to nap at an angle, so we've tilted the cot.

Dm2

My son never slept as a newborn and my husband and I were getting desperate, then we tried the method suggested by Gina Ford in *The Contented Little Baby Book*. She recommends swaddling the baby and putting it to sleep in total darkness, during the day. We now have a five-month-old that sleeps from 7 pm to 7 am. If all else fails, try using a sling as the baby will probably sleep in there, close to your body, and you can get on with jobs around the house.

Art

It's worth putting a T-shirt you've been wearing all day that has your milk on it in the Moses basket so your baby feels close to you. We were worried when our three-week-old daughter would only sleep on her daddy's chest, but they can only do this for a few weeks, and the memories are so precious. There's plenty of time for routines later – though Gina Ford devotees may not agree. Just do whatever gets you the maximum sleep. I wouldn't worry early on if they want to sleep with you – as long as you can still sleep. They are little for such a short time.

Cc

> **Mumsnet tip**
> Never tiptoe around sleeping babies. Put the radio on, talk normally and keep them used to lots of noise (after all the womb is a noisy environment). Our two will sleep through anything now.

When my daughter was little she was either sleeping, feeding or screaming – none of the peaceful surveying the world the baby books tell you about. I found it very depressing, as I worried that things would never change and that I must be doing it all wrong. I remember sitting at my NCT post-natal group rocking and shushing my baby, desperate for her to be calm like all the other babies. But she changed and at ten weeks slept though the night. She was a long baby, so I had to put her in a cot at ten weeks and it seemed to work wonders. She started to be happier during the day, too.

Elliesmum

Babies change from week to week and so you can't know what your baby will like in advance. I bought an extremely expensive baby rocking chair for my daughter, which she never settled happily in – every time I tried she just howled but her two brothers both happily played and slept in it.

It's hard to know what to do when your attention is constantly being demanded. In general, I'd pander to their desire for your company, while always seeking other distractions of course. It's only for a few months.

Javarose

When your first baby is born you think that everything they do is setting them up for bad habits (like sleeping in your bed, needing lots of cuddles). But a few months down the line they become totally different creatures. At the moment my son gets cross if I put him in bed with me on a Sunday morning and wriggles free. But when he was born and I was off work, he loved it.

Lil

Broken nights at under six months – what causes this and what can you do about it?

If your baby suddenly starts waking having been a good sleeper, don't despair: it could be teething or a growth spurt. The problem is that this could continue, on and off, for months. Until they're happily on three meals a day and you can't be sure they're not waking from hunger you might just have to live with it (after that you could consider sleep training). Make sure you're not doing anything to reinforce the waking, like turning the light on or talking to your baby.

Jraven

My second child frequently woke up in the night. I'm convinced now that I wasn't producing enough milk in the evenings and that she was still hungry. I was on the verge of giving her a bottle in the evenings but was persuaded otherwise by a health visitor who convinced me of the benefits of pure breast for the first four months. Looking back I feel it would probably have been more beneficial for my daughter to have felt nice and full. If I'm in a similar position with my next child, I'll definitely give them a top-up feed at night.

Ra

According to Gina Ford a seven-week-old baby can go for a long stretch at night – and you can encourage him to do that between 11 pm and 7 am rather than 7 pm and 3 or 4 am by waking them for a feed at night. If you don't wake your baby at 10.30 pm there is a risk that they may take their long sleep earlier in the evening and continue to wake up in the early hours for longer. Gina Ford seems to think most babies can sleep from 10 pm to 7 am from about 12 weeks, some much earlier. Later you can drop the ten o'clock feed. We dropped it at around five months, but could probably have done so earlier if we had wanted to.

Sjs

> **Mumsnet tip**
> Invest in a baby sleeping bag. They can't be kicked off, so you won't have to worry that your child might get cold, they can't be pulled over a baby's head and they stop their little legs getting stuck between the cot bars!

My daughter woke every two hours or so when she was four to five months. Breastfed babies digest their milk a lot quicker than formula-fed babies, so I increased my daughter's feed intake and this seemed to do the trick. If they're on solids it's worth upping the quantities until they will not eat anymore. This sleepless period seems to go on forever but it does ease.

Subowater

I don't think introducing solids has any effect on sleep patterns. When a baby starts solids, especially as young as four months, all she is doing is getting a taste of something other than milk. When a baby is this little and has only been trying other food for a week it's too early to expect it to make a difference. I had my babies in bed with me from birth until around one. That might seem anathema to some folks but it worked for us and it meant we really were hardly ever disturbed at night as I breastfed virtually in my sleep. If you like the sound of a good night's sleep and you're breastfeeding, give it a try. People scare you by telling you that they'll never move out of your bed, but they do.

Jojo

Under six months isn't particularly old for a baby to be having night feeds and I'm sure that sometimes they are hungry, whatever the mantras about them sleeping through from six, eight or ten weeks. Recently, *I* woke up at 4 am, starving hungry, and had to go and eat a bowl of cereal!

Solids are lower in calories than milk, so babies may digest their meal quickly then wake up at night for something else to keep them going until morning. It's worth trying to squeeze another milk feed in during the day to see if that helps.

Baabaa

> **Mumsnet fact**
> Seventeen per cent of new fathers regularly get out of bed at night to help soothe their baby. Twenty per cent never get up.
>
> *Mother and Baby*

I know they tell you to start with solids at lunchtime but you can soon progress onto giving an evening snack as well. I did that with my daughter at four months and it helped with sleep to an extent. Another thing if you are breastfeeding is to tuck them in bed with you and get as much sleep as you can. I did this with my daughter for ages and it helped a lot. At least I felt rested the next day.

Lizzer

Make sure any new foods that your baby eats during the day are introduced gradually. I had a major problem with my youngest, who was a fine sleeper until she got to four months and then started waking frequently. We found out two years later that she was mildly allergic to dairy products. The waking up had coincided with a switch from breast to bottle but as she appeared to have no problems during the day and it wasn't obviously upsetting her we didn't make the connection. After we tried all the usual tricks and none of them worked we just put it down to her being a bad sleeper. Once she switched from dairy products she got a lot better. She didn't actually start sleeping properly again until she went on a dairy-free diet at two and a half.

Scooby2

My midwife suggested giving my son water when he was waking frequently, the theory being he wouldn't feel it worth it to wake when there was only water on offer. It took until he was six months before he slept through the night. I also tried giving a feed as I went to bed (at 11-ish) so that he wouldn't wake until the early hours but he was such a greedy pup that he would have that feed and then still wake up at 2 am for the next.

Selja

In the early months, assuming you're not working, take advantage of any time your baby is asleep to catch up on an hour's sleep yourself. Try to forget about the housework – it's amazing how much better you can feel after just an hour's snooze.

Suzi

What the experts say
Go to sleep with his head resting in your lap. As soon as he's asleep you can take him to his cot.

Dr Miriam Stoppard (*Complete Baby and Childcare*)

....

If your baby is put to sleep every night by being rocked, bounced and cuddled tight, caring and charitable though this may be, it could well lead to big trouble when it comes to the 3 am eye-opener.

Dr Christopher Green (*Babies!*)

I have found that a regular and pleasant bedtime routine is very helpful – upstairs to bath, story and bed. When they were younger, I started off sitting on the edge of the bed and moved a little further away each night. I think it's important that they learn to go to sleep without you holding them (it's that old sleep-association chestnut), because then they don't wake up and wonder what has changed. It's very difficult, though. My youngest, I have to admit, just slept in our bed so I didn't have to move her.

Violet

My four-month-old has never slept for more than four hours without a feed and for the last six weeks he has been waking every two and a half hours. He settles with a feed most of the time. I started giving him solid food from 16 weeks, which he loves but his sleep/waking pattern is unaffected. Since my health visitor and GP decided I was on the verge of depression I decided to get tough so I refused to breastfeed him after his bath until he had drunk some formula from a bottle (it took about 45 minutes, during which I felt like the most evil mother in the world). I then persuaded my husband to take the week off work and we are now giving him nice cuddly breastfeeds during the day in nice light places and only offering bottles of formula at night. On the second night he slept 7 pm until midnight then through to 5 am. Heaven! He only drank two ounces of formula at each feed so I guess the waking was habit rather than hunger after all.

Dm2

My three-month-old was sleeping six or seven hours a night but suddenly stopped and for the past six weeks or so has fed two-hourly through the night, though he's fine during the day. I've brought him into our bed for the middle of the night stuff and I'm just going to tough it out until he's on three meals a day and I know he's not hungry, then I'll do sleep training because I know from experience that it works. It seems like an uphill struggle at the moment, but it's such a short period of time in the grand scheme of things. One thing I've found that helps is that every time he wakes in the night I try to remember those anxious nights when you're convinced they've died and, instead of cursing (first instinct), I try and be thankful he's alive. It probably only works for mad hormonal folks like me and doesn't work every time, but it does help.

Biza

Three in a bed – is it a good idea and how do you do it?

Our daughter slept with us from birth. It was a conscious decision and was met with some resistance from friends and relatives. During the day she slept in a Moses basket so she certainly didn't have a problem settling herself and didn't seem to be dependent on having me close by. When she woke in the night she soon learnt to latch on by herself so I was relatively undisturbed but I found that she tended to drift off very quickly and didn't get enough milk so she woke again soon after, so I started to sit up properly and feed her but it was still a lot less disruptive than getting up and going to another room.

At around six months she started to sleep sideways and generally take up more than her fair share of the bed so we put her in her cot and she was pretty happy from the start. There have been plenty of sleepless nights since then for one reason or another, but I'm sure they would have happened anyhow. On a practical note, we have a very wide bed and we pushed our pillows to each edge so that she could sleep right up against the headboard well clear of any suffocation risk, plus she had her own blanket and wasn't covered by the duvet.

Emmagee

My 14-week-old daughter won't sleep in her cot. From birth she didn't want to sleep on her own and I ended up putting her in the bed with me in the hospital. When we got home, we established a night-time routine of bath, book, breast and bed, but every night it was the same battle to get her to sleep in her cot. I persevered for nearly four weeks and felt as though I was getting nowhere. When she did go in she only slept for a maximum of two hours before she woke and inevitably she ended up in bed with us. We liked having her there and she obviously wanted to be near me. I felt that denying her that could have a negative effect so I decided to put her straight into our bed after her feed. At least now I can watch a TV programme all the way through and can eat my dinner hot instead of cold!

Chatterbox

I started to let my son sleep in my bed at around five months. Before that, I had a carrycot right next to the bed on a table and just lifted him out when he woke for a feed. I breastfed him lying down and found that he was big enough to latch on by himself and I'd just drift off to sleep. At around the same time he outgrew the carrycot and so I just put him straight into my bed at bedtime – he's been there ever since.

I think a lot of parents bed-share but don't admit it or use it as a last resort. It is, however, a modern phenomenon to put babies into cots or rooms on their own – I felt that having my baby with me was less stressful for both of us.

On the downside, now he's bigger, he does tend to thrash about and I do get woken two or three times a night but I could well have been woken this often any-way by cries from another room. At least I don't have to get out of bed and can drift back off to sleep straight away.

Also it can be difficult if you go out a lot as your child will associate sleep with going to bed with you. In retrospect I should have started putting him to bed in his cot and then taking him in with me when he woke In the night. This way he could have got used to having his own bed but still known that I wasn't far away. If you take a child into your bed, he will probably want to stay there for two or three years, so be prepared – this is not a short-term solution.

Eulalia

What the experts say
Keep in mind that it's a virtually irreversible decision. So don't simply give in to your desperation for an uninterrupted night's sleep by taking your baby into bed with you on a regular basis.

Signe Larson and Kevin Osborn
(*The Complete Idiot's Guide to Bringing up Baby*)

[On three in a bed]
They will eventually want their own space and you can let them make that deci-sion on their own.

Karen Sullivan (*Commonsense Healthcare for Children*)

For the first three months I pretty much let my son sleep in our bed. I found a position where he was absolutely safe – away from any duvet or pillows and with just a cellular blanket over him. When he needed feeding he was right by my side, so I didn't have to get out of bed. He also seemed to sleep much better because he was lying next to me. It felt like the right thing from the start. I would always start him off in his Moses basket and gradually, as he got older, I started moving him back into it after a feed. Eventually he started sleeping the full night in the Moses basket (still waking up for feeds, though).

Bon

> **Mumsnet tip**
> My son wouldn't sleep in his own bed and always ended up in ours. In desperation I turned his bed round so that it was facing the same way as ours and since then he's slept in it without any problems at all. It's worth a try!

We've had our son in bed with us since he was tiny but it's been a mixed blessing. At times we have found the lack of privacy a bit annoying. It started as a convenience thing – we couldn't fit a Moses basket or a cot beside the bed – and

I found the night feeds much less taxing when he was in bed with us. As I went back to work when he was four months old, having him on hand for lots of night-time cuddles after spending the whole day away from him was invaluable.

When he was small we scooped the duvet away from him to prevent him getting covered by it. When he was on his own we stacked up pillows at the edge of the bed to stop him toppling out. Once he could crawl we put him down in his cot and he only came in with us later in the night. In the summer he had a vest and a muslin and in the winter a babygrow with feet.

When he was about six months old I stopped worrying so much about not letting a scrap of duvet near him but always took care not to cover his upper body or face. He recently began sleeping through on his own in his cot, and we quite missed him, but I'd never go and get him unless he woke and cried for more than a minute or two. The idea is that he gradually learns to spend all night in his own room as the norm. Our bed will always be there for him if he wants it. If you do opt for this route you might find yourself on the defensive. My mother was horrified.

Clare2

My son goes to bed in his cot and normally wakes up sometime between 2 am and 4 am when he comes in with us. With husband and son both fidgeting, my sleep is sometimes wakeful but bed-sharing allows some much-needed closeness for my son and husband (who works long hours). Another benefit is that when we go on holiday or sleep away we have no problems. He's slept with us almost from day one and I'm sure when number two comes along we will just buy a bigger bed for all four of us. I love the closeness.

Peanuts1

What the experts say

Even if you and your child seem happy about his sharing your bed at night, and even if he seems to sleep well there, in the long run this habit will probably not be good for either of you.

Dr Richard Ferber (*Solve Your Child's Sleep Problems*)

....

The major snag is that once your baby has slept this way for a few months, you are very unlikely to be able to persuade him, without a long and miserable fight, that a separate cot in a separate room is nicer.

Penelope Leach (*Your Baby and Child*)

....

Not one good argument has emerged for the cot in a hundred years.

Deborah Jackson (*Three in a Bed*)

I've bed-shared with all of my three. It didn't start intentionally and I felt guilty to begin with. It's not a formal arrangement and a lot of musical beds goes on but at least we get some sleep. My son stopped getting in our bed at three and a half and now only ever gets in when he's ill. I know it's not the same as permanent bed-sharing but I can vouch for the fact that it won't make them clingier and you'll probably get more sleep. There is nothing nicer than snuggling up to a cuddly baby and they are only little for such a short time, so why not get those cuddles in while you can? They won't want to get in your bed when they're 14, will they?

Emmy

I was considering sharing a bed until I found out I was having twins and thought there just wouldn't be enough room for all of us.

In principle, I think it's a lovely idea but two years down the line – with two babies who've slept in a cot in their own room from their second night at home and hardly ever had a broken night – I'm not sure it's the best solution. Everyone I've met seems to say that neither you nor your child get an unbroken night if you bed-share. Sleep means everything to me. If I get it, I'm a much more fun mother in the day and if my twins don't get it, they're much harder work.

I guess it comes down to whether they're good sleepers or not. If they look like they are going to be then I'd stick with the cot. But give them a chance to be good sleepers. If you teach them early on to sleep in your bed, then nothing else will do afterwards and it seems to me you're consigning yourself to broken nights for a long time.

Berta

A baby that won't sleep in its cot is a problem for the parent, not the baby. If society regarded babies sleeping with parents as normal, then the question 'how can I get my baby to sleep in her cot?' wouldn't arise in the first place.

Baabaa

My son slept in my bed with me from the moment he was born. I took him out of the hospital cot and put him next to me. It seemed entirely natural. He'd been in my tummy for nine months and separation seemed wrong. He's now 5 years old and often gets out of his bed in the middle of the night and snuggles up with us. I've confronted a good deal of confusion from other parents who've thought my methods unconventional. But do what's right for you because as much as they've scoffed, friends also say they've never seen such a strong bond between mother and child.

Bed-sharing meant I wasn't tense, wondering if he was okay in the night. The only problem is that they have a tendency to lie horizontally in the bed once they get a bit bigger, which can cramp you. By that point it could well be time to put a small bed next to yours and slowly move it a little distance from your bed towards independence. I'm all for three-in-a-bed. As I didn't have to get in and out of bed for breastfeeds, I found I was less exhausted.

Ro

I used to take my first baby into bed when he woke in the night for a feed and then keep him there. I loved having him in bed with me for cuddles and it definitely meant we got more sleep. I was a bit anxious about the duvet, pillows, husband and other people's reaction. My mother-in-law was horrified and I even got a letter from my husband's elderly aunt! I'm glad I didn't take any notice.

The bedding was never a problem, I just made sure there was a big gap between our pillows and that the duvet was tucked in the end of the bed. When my second baby was born she came straight into bed with us too. By that stage our eldest was in his own bed – he had stopped coming into our bed when he began sleeping through the night.

It felt right to have my little girl in bed with me. It was our time. She breastfed when she wanted and even slept through the night when tiny. She now sleeps in her cot in our room because she was waking up a lot and I was feeling shattered. She was refusing breakfast as she'd had her fill in the night. It has taken about a week for her to really settle in her cot. She wasn't hugely miserable or I wouldn't have done it. I thought I would really miss her but we both sleep better now and still have our morning feed and cuddle together.

Qd

What the experts say:
The trouble is that many parents find it hard to sleep soundly when their baby is close by.

Dr Christopher Green (*Babies!*)

Co-sleeping, parents and children sharing a bed at night, does work well – but chiefly, it seems, in other societies. In a society like ours, which stresses the development of independence and the importance of privacy, co-sleeping is associated with a wide range of problems.

Eisenberg, Murkoff and Hathaway
(*What to expect the First Year*)

For 95 per cent of evolution, babies have slept with their mothers. Independent sleep is a relatively recent idea.

Penny Hames (*NCT: Help Your Baby to Sleep*)

Both my children slept in bed with me on and off for the first ten months of their lives and then transferred to a cot with no problems at all. Usually, I'd start them off in a cot at bedtime and bring them in to bed for a feed. Both of them wouldn't (and still don't) keep their covers on so I have always dressed them in a sleepsuit (and vest in winter) plus a sort of fleecy all-in-one to compensate for the lack of blankets.

The downside of bed-sharing is that you probably get less sleep as you are aware of their every noise and movement. Nevertheless, I reckon if you're happy with having your child in bed with you, ignore the critics and just remember that they are only tiny for a short time.

Imps

Sleep training and controlled crying – should you try it, does it work and when can you start?

It seems that people expect little babies to be able to sleep through the night on their own and if this isn't the case, they will do some pretty terrible things (like letting them cry) to 'train' them to sleep. They then wonder why their children behave badly or why their relationship suffers later on.

My advice is to go with the flow as much as possible when they are young babies. Create a nice night-time environment for the child, where he feels relaxed, warm and comfortable, and let him learn to sleep in his own good time. The best place for this for the first six months is in your bed or in your room, but that doesn't suit everyone.

Babies have different sleep patterns to us for many reasons and so it is not healthy for them to be forced to sleep through the night until they are naturally ready to do this. Making them cry it out causes them an unbelievable amount of stress as it causes hormones to be released to their brains indicating there is something wrong. Until this need is met, the baby is programmed to go on crying and become more and more stressed. It is not being naughty.

What the experts say
Since 1974 I have been promoting my controlled crying technique for helping young children learn to sleep, with considerable success. The aim is to let them cry for a short period of time, but not long enough for them to get upset or hysterical.

Dr Christopher Green (*Babies!*)

The child cannot wake himself up on purpose. There is therefore no possible logic in regarding night waking as a bad habit which can be broken by leaving the child to cry.

Penelope Leach (*Babyhood*)

It is cruel and barbaric to let a baby cry. People do it due to external pressures or because they fear the consequences of not doing it, not because it makes them feel good. It is not good for the child or your relationship with her. Part of being a parent is making sacrifices for your children and you can't expect your life not to change. Your relationship with your children will be so much stronger for going to your baby when she cries, feeding her when she's hungry and making her feel secure and wanted.

It is hard being a parent but mothers have an in-built ability to cope with a reduction in the hours they sleep and the depth of it without it affecting them too much.

Josie

Controlled crying is not for me. I will try every other method I can think of instead of using this one. I could not bear to leave my son crying and crying, getting hot and even more upset and totally ignore him. Anyway I cannot see anything wrong in cuddling your baby to sleep, it is lovely for both of us.

Peanuts1

Controlled crying is by no means for everyone. I've found it useful at some points and not at all at others. I've got friends who tried it and wound up with situations where their children got more and more worked up, and so did they. They weren't 'softies' who let their kids get away with whatever they wanted, it just didn't work. Babies' cries are their only way of communicating and I don't think it's necessarily positive to try and 'control' that communication, even if it isn't always what we want to hear.

Scummymummy

I agree that controlled crying is only useful for *some* parents – let's face it, it's not really for the child, is it? He's just upset and wants comfort. Sometimes I think people read too much into children's actions, they say 'he's doing it on purpose'. Well, he probably is but his purpose isn't to make you miss the last five minutes of EastEnders, he's just upset/scared/in pain and can't tell you any other way. What is controlled crying teaching them? I think it makes them work out that mum or dad isn't going to come when they call, so it's certainly easier for the parents, then, isn't it? Having a child who doesn't cry all the time and who learns to be obedient. What's that Victorian phrase I'm looking for? 'Seen but not heard.'

Lizzer

We've tried controlled crying and it categorically did not work for us! Seeing my daughter reduced to a quivering, sobbing, vomiting heap was good for neither of us. Although she is very sociable (she's 5 now) she is still paranoid about being left alone and those never-to-be-forgotten nights of controlled crying pass though my mind as possibly being the cause.

From what I've read about controlled crying, going in to see your child only at regular intervals is mainly for the parents' benefit. It doesn't really help the child because a baby has no sense of time and five minutes may just as well be five hours to them. Success with controlled crying perhaps depends more on the child's personality than the technique itself.

What the experts say

Many parents – millions, probably – have found that they can train their baby to sleep through the night from the age of six months using simple behavioural methods (controlled crying).

Priscia Middlemiss (*How to Get a Whole Night's Sleep*)

No child will benefit from being left to cry. She may eventually fall asleep out of misery and exhaustion and will believe that she is unworthy of your attention.

Karen Sullivan (*Commonsense Healthcare for Children*)

I also feel that controlled crying can undermine a parent's confidence if it doesn't work. The books seem to offer a 100 per cent sure-fire way of getting your baby to sleep. If it fails they seem to blame the parent for not implementing it properly. That's my take, as a 'failure' at controlled crying, anyway! I don't deny that it works for some babies but it's unfair to parents to lead them to believe it always works.

There are plenty of other ways to get a baby off to sleep, such as bed-sharing, rocking, feeding, a dummy, playing soothing music, or good old pacing the floor.

Baabaa

I'd say that rocking, dummies (and to a certain extent, feeding) are exactly the reasons why there are so many people whose babies wake at night. They say, 'my baby can't sleep because his dummy fell out', 'my baby can't sleep if I don't rock him to sleep'. This is how bad habits start. Doing it once or twice is fine but if you get into such habits you'll soon be wondering how to cure them...controlled crying maybe?

Pupuce

Mumsnet fact
Infants who cannot soothe themselves to sleep by age one are more likely to wake during the night and require help falling back to sleep by the age of three.

Journal of the American Academy of Child and Adolescent Psychiatry

I am in the process of using Dr Richard Ferber's book, *How to Solve Your Child's Sleep Problems* on my six-month-old, who was waking once an hour for food in the night. I think the sleep training routines he suggests are working. I do now believe children have to learn how to fall asleep without a breast/bottle/being rocked, as when they wake in the night they do not know how to get back to sleep without the particular thing they associate with getting to sleep. What I like about Ferber's approach is that you still go in to reassure them as often as you like. If you just leave them totally then, understandably, they get quite distressed as I think they wonder if you are ever coming back.

Using the routine suggested in the book – going in every so often to reassure her – we have seen a marked improvement. She's only been up once a night for three nights now and seems just as happy during the day (and loves us just the same!) Actually, it was easier than I thought it would be because I still respond to my baby when she cries. I would say give it a go. If it doesn't feel right then give it a very moderate go – go in more often than Ferber suggests. There are no hard and fast rules.

Janus

We bought the Ferber book when our daughter was six months old. Our daughter used to be very difficult to get to sleep and then she would constantly wake up. We followed the programme of leaving her to cry and going in at the assigned intervals. The first night she cried for about 25 minutes and the second night it was about 15; after that she slept through and this was a child who before would probably have only slept about three to four hours a night at the most. I think the most important thing is to make a plan of how to deal with it and then stick with it.

Amandag

I think that everyone makes their own decision. My health visitor advised the controlled crying technique, which involves leaving the baby to cry for three minutes before going back into the room to calm them, and then leaving the room for two minutes longer each time. He never cried for more than ten minutes before falling asleep. It took me three nights (at age six months) to get my son to go to sleep without being cuddled. All I can say is it has made me feel human again. I simply cannot cope without a decent amount of sleep. If he is ill and sleeps in bed with us we have to go back to the controlled crying routine again. If that makes me cruel and barbaric, then so be it.

Paula1

> **Mumsnet fact**
> One sleepless night has the same effect on co-ordination, reaction time and judgement as consuming up to the weekly limit of alcohol recommended in Britain – 14 units for women, 21 for men – at one sitting.
> *British Journal of Environmental Medicine*

Ferber's book has worked well for us. I was absolutely desperate – and, to be honest, so was my son – before we tried controlled crying. He was awake every night for between an hour and two hours from 2 am to 4 am. It was impossible to get him to go to sleep. He was happy to sit on my lap but he wouldn't sleep in our bed and he wouldn't sleep with me in the spare room. If I put him back in his cot he would howl. He wasn't hungry or thirsty – he would gag if I tried to give him milk or water – and he wasn't wet either.

Controlled crying was hard work. I turned the light on in our bedroom and watched the clock and went in every five minutes. The first night he cried and whinged on and off for an hour and a half, which was about the same time he would have been awake for anyway. The second night we repeated the procedure for about 40 minutes and the third night I only had to go in once. We have not had any serious night-time wakings since then.

For me, it really was not a case of him being seen and not heard or interrupting my television viewing time. It was a genuine desire to ensure that we both got a decent night's sleep.

I really don't think that most parents who follow a controlled crying programme are doing it to make their lives easier. It is one of the most testing things I have ever done.

Molly1

I too could barely bring myself round to controlled crying but exhaustion drove me to it. What worked for me was going in initially as soon as my child cried, then leaving her for one minute, then two minutes, four minutes – increasing by two minutes at a time. The longest I left her was ten minutes, after which she did settle down. The next night five minutes was all that it took.

Jg

There is a benefit for parents when controlled crying works – we really enjoyed the first decent night's sleep we'd had in over four months – but there's also a benefit for the child. Sleep meant we stopped wandering around like zombies during the daytime and that we were more patient and less tetchy with our son. He seemed to enjoy himself more during the daytime too, as he also was not exhausted from lack of sleep.

What the experts say
Allowing some crying while you help your child learn to improve his sleep will never lead to psychological harm.
Dr Richard Ferber (*Solve Your Child's Sleep Problems*)

A baby that's left to cry quickly learns that adults don't respond to his cries for help and love. He will stop asking for attention and may become solitary and withdrawn.
Dr Miriam Stoppard (*Complete Baby and Childcare*)

We were amazed that controlled crying worked within three days. It was definitely worth it for our family, but I think that you have to be approaching breaking point before trying it. My husband and I sat and cuddled each other for comfort for the first night when we had no idea how long the crying would last – it was really, really awful sitting and listening to him cry and not going to comfort him straight away.

Sis

The hardest but most valuable thing we did was to sleep-train our son. At nine months he would still be waking up every three to four hours during the night and it would then take us up to an hour to try and get him to go to sleep again. I was so depressed and tired that I rang my health visitor in tears. Her advice was brilliant. We put him to bed and left him to cry it out, checking on him only when we couldn't stand the crying anymore, but never taking him out of his cot. The first night was terrible, he cried for over an hour. It was very upsetting for all of us. But the next night he cried for less and the next night even less. On the fifth night he rebelled and cried for over an hour again but by the end of the week he slept all night through (and I mean from 8 pm until 6 am). In the space of a month, getting up in the night became a rarity. My son is a lot happier now he is getting plenty of good quality rest and so are we. You have to have an iron-will to do this though, and you may find it reassuring to discuss it first with your health visitor.

Emmam

> **Mumsnet tip**
> If you decide to do controlled crying treat yourself to a magazine or book, and in the five minute intervals sit somewhere outside your bedroom and read. Reading helps to take your mind off the horror of listening to them cry and passes the time.

It may sound awful but when you've had a bad sleeper you will try anything. We first tried controlled crying – having always been woken every two to three hours for a feed – when she was about six months old. She wasn't left to cry for hours – we went in at regular intervals to reassure and say goodnight. The first night it took 45 minutes, and I admit that most of the time I was sitting outside her room with a watch, crying myself. The second night it took 30 minutes and the third night she went down quite happily. I continued to do night feeds for quite some time, but reduced the feed time (as Ferber suggests) by a couple of minutes a night. I've never particularly enjoyed the process of sleep training and we have had to repeat it after she's got out of sync through illness and so on, but I can say that it works. It made me a better mother, much less snappy and cross, and it made my daughter happier in the day because she wasn't exhausted. Sleep deprivation is a form of torture and quite different to a bit of general parental tiredness, which I admit is to be expected.

Biza

I'm not particularly pro or anti controlled crying. We have never followed a proper controlled crying programme with things like sleep charts. However, on the odd night or two, if I feel my son is getting into a bad sleep habit, after checking that he is not in pain or thirsty (and often giving him a cuddle in our bed as well for good luck!), I firmly say 'night night' put him back in his cot and leave him, even if he breaks into a sob. I'll check up on him, but he will almost inevitably fall asleep after ten minutes.

Mumsnet fact
At nine months, one baby in five finds it hard to get off to sleep. Nearly half of all two-year-olds do.

Priscia Middlemiss (*How To Get a Whole Night's Sleep*)

Doesn't your approach to controlled crying and sleeping through depend on your own sleep patterns? I've never used it much because I can usually drift off to sleep in two minutes flat, even when woken up repeatedly in the middle of the night. If I had my husband's sleep patterns – once he wakes up, he's often awake and stressed for hours – I would have had to utilize every means available from the word go to guarantee my son slept through.

Frank1

My ten-month-old was as happy as Larry to fall asleep with us rocking him – if he came into our bed he thought it was party time. Our son had just got into bad habits – he wanted us to put him to sleep because, of course, it's nicer to be rocked to sleep than to lie on your own. But ultimately, we were all suffering – including him. He was knackered.

I would say that you have to treat each child as an individual. Some children are more needy of affection and reassurance day and night. Others seem to be more independent and hardy. A mother and father know their child well in most cases and are best able to judge whether their child will benefit from a bit of sleep training or controlled crying.

Green

Daytime sleep – how can you get them to nap in the day?

I found that consistency of sleeping times was the key. It did take a while, though. I used to let my son play in his cot before I introduced it as a place to sleep, so that the surroundings would be familiar. At first, I found that he would go to sleep much more happily in the morning than at lunchtime and also that he wouldn't sleep if he was hungry when put down – obvious, I know. I encouraged him to sleep again if he woke. I used be there at the first murmur in an effort to stop him waking properly. I also used a dummy to help calm him down and if he did fall asleep with it, I plucked it out. Sometimes a quick suck on the dummy (if he seemed to be waking too early) was enough to get him back to sleep – either that or stroking his face or cuddling him without picking him up. I also used to change his nappy and close the curtains before starting all this to signal it was bedtime.

What the experts say
You don't need to worry that a baby isn't getting enough sleep to meet his needs.

Dr Spock and Stephen Parker (*Dr Spock's Baby and Child Care*)

No baby under three months should be allowed to stay awake for more than two hours at a time, as they can become very overtired.

Gina Ford (*The Contented Little Baby Book*)

I have to say that because I hated the crying I often found it easier to hold him quietly in a chair by the cot until he either fell asleep or was so nearly there I thought he'd sleep when I put him down.

Alison222

If you want your baby to sleep longer in the day, try taking them out for a really long walk at the time that you want them to go to sleep. Do this for a couple of days and see if that will settle them into a routine, but try not to get too stressed about it. Not all babies are very receptive to following timetables.

Molly1

I wake my son up at about 7 am then make sure he is awake and active for two hours before allowing him a nap in his room of no longer than 40 minutes. He then goes down for his lunchtime nap at around 12.15 to 12.30 pm and sleeps for around one and a half to two hours. For a time, I found he was waking after around 45 minutes and I think this was a time of REM (rapid eye movement) sleep when babies are likely to be roused by light or sudden noises. Keeping the room really dark and trying to be quiet during this time encourages him to go back to sleep. If he does wake I try to ignore him for ten minutes – sometimes he goes back to sleep – or I try stroking his head, putting the mobile on again and leaving the room rapidly.

Jacksonville

My son only slept for short periods from three weeks old and he always woke grumpy from naps. My mother-in-law encouraged me to get him to go to sleep by himself for naps and bedtimes at five months and by six months he had regular one and a half hour naps morning and afternoon.

Jamie

> **Mumsnet tip**
> If you are confident that your baby is fed, warm and has a clean nappy, try not to go in for a few minutes after she makes some noise. I found when I gave mine a bit of time, he would often settle back down to sleep. Give them a few minutes of whinging or whimpering to see if they can resettle themselves.

My son wasn't a very good sleeper during the day until he got older. He sleeps in our bed or his cot now but I always soothe him to sleep with either a dummy and cuddle or a breastfeed. He nearly always falls to sleep in the car or his pram. One thing to try is to sleep with one of your baby's blankets then put it in their cot so they have your smell close to them.

Peanuts1

I found that a bit of routine helped my daughter and tried to set up a feed, bath, sleep routine for her from around three months. I bathed my daughter twice a day so that it was quite easy to get her down for her morning and night-time sleep.

I also went to baby massage classes, which helped to calm her down. You don't need to do a class, though, just get some almond oil or equivalent and run your hands up and down the legs, belly and arms. She loved it and after a class she would sleep for anything up to two hours when before she would only usually sleep for about 30 minutes.

Janus

My son, now eight months, has not had a proper daytime sleep since he was about four months. He does, however, sleep very well at night. I am somewhat surprised that daytime naps are such a big issue – if a baby doesn't sleep during the day, then that indicates that he or she doesn't need to sleep during the day.

Sweetie

I don't think it indicates that at all. At the age of nine months, my son's daytime naps had worked their way down to two 20-minute naps a day. He went ten hours straight at night, but in total that's not all that much sleep for a baby of his age. At that stage I was following his lead – waiting until he seemed sleepy and then putting him to bed. However, as his naps got shorter and shorter (and less frequent) so I realized that he was not very good at regulating his naps by himself.

I stopped following his cues and started putting him down at a regular time twice a day. He used to wake after 20 minutes but then I controlled crying. It took one day – he cried for two hours. The next day when I put him down at naptime he slept for one and a half hours – the first time he had done that in months. We continued with this routine for months, and gradually he slept more and more. He now sleeps for two to two and a half hours at lunchtime, and we have also extended his overnight sleep from ten to 12 hours. So his total sleep at nine months was about 11 hours. His total sleep now at 15 months is 14 to 15 hours.

He still has good and bad days, but since we took his daytime sleep in hand, he seems calmer, more patient, plays better by himself and is generally less demanding. Also, he used to wake up crying. Now he wakes up and babbles and chatters to himself for ten to 15 minutes before I go in. I realize now that this is a very good sign that he has had enough sleep. If he wakes crying, I try very hard to get him back to sleep for another half hour or so as I find it makes a real difference to his mood once he is up.

Amber1

What the experts say
To ensure good night-time sleep for your baby it is essential that you structure his daytime sleep. Too much daytime sleep can result in night-time wakings. Too little daytime sleep can result in an overtired, irritable baby who has difficulty settling himself to sleep, and who falls asleep only when he is totally exhausted.

Gina Ford (*The Contented Little Baby Book*)

Parents cannot force a baby to sleep. Attempts to do so result in an impasse for all concerned and often lead to the parents seeing their baby as cross and over-demanding when all he is really demanding is the simple human right to be awake.

Penelope Leach (*Babyhood*)

My son slept very little during the day as a small baby, which was exhausting for me. (I was amazed when my daughter arrived, and slept all day – at last I could see why people liked small babies!) With babies things change so fast – my husband's advice to a new father recently was: 'If things are going well, enjoy it – it won't last. If things seem terrible, don't worry – it won't last.'

Azzie

Early mornings – what can you do if your baby thinks the day starts at 5 am?

At around seven months my twins started suddenly waking at 5 am (6 am at the latest) after having slept happily until 7.30 am for a couple of months. All I can say is that it passed. It did help that we went on holiday to the US (the time difference meant that when we came back they were on a much later wake-up time and we were able to keep that up). Now they're 2 and sleep from 7.30 pm until 7.30 to 8 am almost without fail and have done for nearly a year. Once a good sleeper, always a good sleeper, I think.

Berta

It seems a fairly common problem but they do get out of the habit. Our son started getting up at 5.30 am and I just used to go in and tell him it was too early, lie him down again and walk out. Okay, so he then proceeded to scream the house down but I persevered and he came to realize that when I came in bleary-eyed and put his musical mobile back on there was no way he was coming out of his cot. When it was a more acceptable time to get up (6.30 am!) I'd make a real fuss of saying good morning, how are you, lovely day and drawing the curtains back. He now sleeps pretty much until 6.30 am most days.

Emmam

> **Mumsnet fact**
> Studies show that leaving a child to cry (systematic ignoring) reduces night waking by up to 30 per cent in two to three weeks.
> Karen Sullivan (*Commonsense Healthcare for Children*)

Recently, our son started waking up earlier than normal. We put it down to the fact that he was cold. He is very active when asleep and usually manages to kick off all his bedding within a few hours of going to sleep. We found a sleeping bag was helpful.

Sis

We have had great success with blackout blinds. Our little boy was regularly waking at 5 am and not going back to sleep but by eliminating all the light in his room (and I really do mean all – not even a chink coming through) we have solved the problem. It took him a few days to break the habit after we put up the blind – he woke at five and moaned and mumbled for a good half an hour the first couple of days – but now he is regularly sleeping through to 7 am. The room has to be extremely dark, though. We had blinds up before the breakthrough but they were not effective enough – too much light was creeping around them. The room would now pass a World War Two 'warden check'. I believe some children are very sensitive to daylight. Possibly they are light sleepers anyway and when they go through a lighter period of sleep, as is very common at 5 am, they open their eyes and see the daylight and find it impossible to go back to sleep. Even some adults find it difficult to sleep late in summer because of the early morning light.

What the experts say
Virtually all children with no major medical or neurological disorder have the ability to sleep well. They can go to bed at an appropriate time, fall asleep within minutes and stay asleep until a reasonable hour in the morning.

Dr Richard Ferber (*Solve Your Child's Sleep Problems*)

In my limited experience I have found my son will get into a bad habit within two days. If he is having trouble settling and I sit with him for just two days to get him to sleep, then he will expect it again on the third day. If a child eats well and has a good feed before going to sleep, it's very unlikely that hunger will wake them and it's worth giving controlled crying a go. I have found that it takes three days controlled crying to crack a sleep problem. It makes sense to do it when you don't have to work the next day. Also, make sure that they are stuffed full of food before going to bed, so you know it can't possibly be hunger waking them. I sometimes offer my son a biscuit along with his night-time milk drink if I'm not confident he has eaten enough supper.

Molly1

Our second child woke up at precisely 5.10 am from the age of three months. Very, very occasionally she went through until 5:30 am. We had blackout blinds and (later on) tried controlled crying. Sometimes you can follow all the suggestions and the baby just doesn't comply. Getting older appears to be the only thing that will work with some children. Had she been my first I would have been convinced I was doing it all wrong.

She eventually dropped the 5 am start at about 12 months (when she started walking). The problem I found with early waking is that it does make them (and you) irritable. She is much happier when she has had a full night's sleep (and so are we). If none of the other methods work out, just take a deep breath and keep telling yourself it doesn't last forever.

Scooby2

Waking at 5 am is common and usually a phase, but not always a short one. Trying to re-settle the child with a bottle of water is worth a go. He or she probably won't like it and if you're breastfeeding it's easier if someone else can do it otherwise the baby might smell you and think they could get something nicer. If that doesn't work I think controlled crying (if your baby's over six months) is definitely an option.

Pupuce

Mumsnet tip
Put a mirror over your baby's cot – those pull-out shaving ones work well. We found it kept our six-month-old amused in the mornings and gave us crucial extra lie-in time.

My seven-month-old daughter used to sleep from 7.30 pm until about 6.30 to 6.45 am but when the clocks changed and she had a cold (at the same time) she not only started waking up at about 5 am but also waking up in between. I relented and gave her a breastfeed (sometimes at 3am, sometimes later) because it's hard during the week when you know you have to get up for work, but at the weekend I did controlled crying to see what would happen. She woke twice but both times she was asleep again within 20 minutes.

Within days my daughter was sleeping through from 7 pm to 6.15 am – now she only wakes up in the morning due to her 40-a-day smokers' cough!

Pamela1

My seven-month-old boy started waking up at 5 am (6 am at the latest). My husband and I both work and so we were getting very tired and really close to the end of our respective tethers. We had a blackout blind fitted and taped up the edges to cut out all the light. We fed him in the evenings, so that he wouldn't get hungry too early – but all to no avail.

This is what we did: although we didn't buy a sleeping bag, we tucked his blanket under the mattress, so that it didn't fall off him; we didn't go into him more than once in the night (one visit for reassurance and then we let him cry himself back to sleep – difficult and tiring, but worth it); finally, we didn't go in to him in the morning until we were ready. I think consistency really is the key. Once we decided on a plan and stuck to it, it only took us about two weeks to get him into a better routine. The great thing is that my baby seems happier after a proper night's sleep, too.

Now he sleeps from 8 pm to 6 am. I sometimes hear him wake up at about 4 am (the time he used to wake up crying), but he just rolls over and goes back to sleep.

Linus

Moving around the cot – should you worry and what can you do about it?

My second baby has been moving around the cot since she was about two weeks old. I found it very disturbing as I often went in to find her with her arms and legs sticking out of the cot. Now I am surprised if I go in to her in the morning and all her limbs are inside the cot! I figure if she needs me to come and help her out, she will let me know. She seems quite happy as she is.

Micg

My six-month-old went on the move, particularly when she started rolling over. A couple of things that helped us were not using covers – she sleeps in a fleecy suit or a baby sleeping bag. Also, don't be anxious – if she's really in trouble, she'll let you know. Mine often gets her feet caught in the bars but I'm such a sound sleeper that my husband usually deals with it!

Fp

A baby sleeping bag worked really well for us. My daughter used to bang her head against the cot and various limbs would protrude through and get trapped in the bars, which would often cause her to wake but the sleeping bag has helped stop all that. I also found that she slept better in her own room (we moved her at about four months).

Berta

My four and a half-month-old started scooting around her cot rather dramatically during the night. Sometimes she hit her head on the sides and sometimes turned 180 degrees, making me nervous that she would become entangled in her sheet and blanket. She slept in my room and I found I woke regularly, either as a result of her calls for help or as a result of my anxiety. I've been using a sleeping bag for the last week and my daughter seems quite happy in it. However, the real success has been to transfer her from her big wooden cot to a travel cot. The travel cot has cloth sides and she can't get her arms and legs trapped.

Jayc

We used to swaddle ours when they were tiny and when they were bigger we'd tuck them in firmly on both sides to stop the blanket riding up – they seemed to like being constrained a little. I think travel cots are great to use, except that all that bending down to floor level plays havoc with your back. One other big advantage we found with travel cots was that dummies can't fall out of them.

Alex2

What the experts say
Swaddling can be an excellent alternative to a sheet and blankets for very young babies, giving warmth, tactile comfort and a much greater sense of security.

Rosalyn Thiro (*Baby and You*)

Our son started wriggling around in his cot as soon as he was strong enough to. When he was younger, to stop his little arms and legs getting stuck, we used a cot bumper at what tended to be his head end and then I attached cardboard strips to the rest of the cot. I am not sure if this would be 'health visitor approved' but it worked for us. Obviously you have to be careful when attaching the cardboard that you don't use anything sharp but that's just common sense. We tried a sleeping bag, but he loathed it and we had some of our worst night's sleep when he was in it, so now he wears an 'over the top' fleece suit if it is very cold or a jumper over his sleep suit if it is a bit warmer.

Molly1

My son started moving round the cot at four-and-a-half months and had a habit of pulling his blanket over his face during sleep then waking up terribly upset. I started tucking him in when I put him down for the night. When he was about five-and-a-half months I moved him in to a sleeping bag – if your baby is younger you could try swaddling.

Alli

Mumsnet tip
Invest in a baby sleeping bag if you're worried about your child rolling over at night. They cannot be kicked off, nor can the baby pull them up over their heads.

A sleeping bag is a fantastic item to buy if you want a good night's sleep. My son wore one when he was just one week old.

Domi

My son started rolling and getting stuck on his tummy, which he hated. At first I went in and turned him back but after a few nights it was only getting worse. He was turning over 20 times a night and was often on his tummy again before I'd even left the room. Eventually when he was seven months I left him to it (going in at intervals to show him I was there, as with controlled crying, but not rolling him back) and after 45 minutes of crying he slept through again and we've never looked back.

Amber1

3

Food

Introduction

Well you've survived those first three or four relentless months of parenthood and though you'd scarcely admit it to yourself the feed/wind/snooze routine is beginning to get just a little bit tedious. So praise the Lord for the dawning of a new challenge – one that will enable your baby to take their first big step towards independence.

Weaning is one thing your baby's bound to be good at – after all, just look at mum and dad – they can devour a fridge-full without coming up for air. But what do you give your precious one? For most of us baby food is unchartered territory. A hazy recollection of the succour gained from a Farley's Rusk aside, we're clueless. Weaning is a whole new ball game.

Still, if you're anything like we were you'll be adamant that your newborn will have nothing but the best. You might happily munch your way through an additive-packed microwave-friendly chicken tikka masala of an evening but your baby will have nothing but the best – organic home-cooked creations are on the menu. Out comes Annabel Karmel's best-selling baby-food bible and the never-before-used blenders. Let the pureeing begin.

It's only when the first spoonful is met with a look of utter disgust and is propelled back in your direction with admirable force that it begins to dawn on you that this weaning business may not be quite the walk in the park you imagined.

Could you have started too early? Should you try and force it down or give up entirely and start again later? Or maybe you've started too late and missed the magic window of opportunity to teach your child to enjoy new flavours. After all, as your own mother's fond of reminding you, you were weaned at two-and-a-half months and what harm did it do you?

Maybe it's your cooking and jars are the answer – they sell by the million so how bad can they be? But what will the world and, more to the point, your in laws think of you – there you are at home all day and you can't even puree a carrot for your baby?

Even if you've got the early stages of weaning all wrapped up, your food worries don't end there. What about nine-monthers who really will only eat Weetabix – does it matter if they have it three times a day and if it does, what can you do? Once you've empowered them with a spoon how on earth do you avoid bookshelves being splattered with scrambled egg and fromage frais? And what about going veggie – is it fair to foist your moral code on your child and is it detrimental to their health?

Of course, no two babies are the same but by seeing how others coped, we hope you can pick up a few tips, have a few specific queries answered and take comfort in the fact that very few get out of the kitchen without a few hiccups. After all there's really no use crying over spilt milk.

Weaning – when and how do you start?

I was advised not to start my baby on solids until she was four months at the very earliest because a baby's digestive system is very sensitive and weaning too early may cause problems later. I started giving my daughter very small tasters of organic baby rice and pureed fruits when she was almost five months old, which she enjoyed. I took it slowly and there were some days when she didn't want it, which was fine. It's important to go at the baby's pace – she varied from day to day.

Lou

There are lots of very sound reasons why solids should not be given before 17 weeks, mostly to do with long-term health and development. However this guideline has been changed a lot in the last 30 years. My parents' generation was encouraged to start weaning babies at a far younger age.

Clare2

> **Mumsnet fact**
> Introducing solids too early can lead to heart disease and diabetes.
> Ninewells Hospital Study

My last baby started to get ravenous at around ten weeks. He was having milk all day and still crying with hunger. On the allergies front, rice is the food that, statistically, you are least likely to develop allergies to. I don't think it does any harm to give a baby a bit of baby rice mixed with his normal milk at this age. It will fill his tummy up. I made the mistake of letting him have too much rice, so he drank less milk and gained weight less rapidly. So I reduced the amount of rice and he made up the weight again within ten days.

Javarose

I started feeding baby rice to my eldest at just over three months as he was so hungry all the time. He only had a little and never took less milk because of it and it made him much happier. He's never looked back. I know the latest guidelines say not to start until the baby is four months... but these are guidelines after all and all babies are individuals.

Hmonty

What the experts say
Every baby is different and some larger babies may just not be getting enough to satisfy them. Your baby will let you know when she needs to start solids.
Annabel Karmel (*Annabel Karmel's New Complete Baby and Toddler Meal Planner*)

You should be aware of the signs that your baby gives you, and follow her lead for the introduction of solids.

Dr Miriam Stoppard (*Complete Baby and Childcare*)

If the moment the food on your finger touches his tongue, the tongue and the food are both poked out, the tongue thrust reflex is still active. This reflex protects very young babies from choking by clearing foreign bodies, including food, out of their mouth, so if the reflex is still there,
he is not ready.

Penelope Leach (*Your Baby and Child*)

I think ten weeks for solids is way too early. The guidelines have been four to six months for ten years now. In addition, there's research to show early solids is linked to wheezing and other ill effects – check it out in the *British Medical Journal*. Formula-fed babies may need solids earlier, as formula doesn't change with the baby's growing needs, but not ten weeks.

Generally, healthy breastfed babies can be relied upon to let you know when they need something additional to milk, usually around six months. If they need more they'll be grabbing the stuff off your plate and showing an interest in what you have to offer. If they don't need it, they won't bother. Why give a baby something their digestion isn't ready for?

Tiktok

The current advice for introducing solids to a young baby is now six months. The World Health Organisation states that breast or formula milk is the only food required for the first six months. Introducing foods earlier means the baby runs the risk of developing food allergies and intolerances.

Breast and formula milk are far richer in calories than any solids, so in order to satisfy a baby at four months it's better to offer the breast or formula feeds more frequently. Some babies even lose weight when introduced to solids because their total calorie intake is less than with milk alone. Later weaning also means you can avoid some of that messy 'gloopy' stage!

Baabaa

Mumsnet tip
For an easy weaning meal, parcel up meat and veg in tin foil and bake in the oven with a jacket potato. When cooked, blend together with a processor and *voilà!* – meat, potatoes and two veg with no hassle!

One of my children didn't start solids until she was seven months and she certainly didn't starve. If your baby is okay on milk then don't make it a battle or everyone gets upset. Just keep trying different foods every few days and if they're not interested, leave it for a while longer.

Binza

My daughter indicated that she was getting ready for solids at five months by waking in the night regularly – when she had been sleeping through for months – and watching the progress of food to our mouths. Also, when I tried adding an extra milk feed she wasn't having any of it.

Bexm

My daughter was bottle-fed and didn't start solids until she was six months old. She was always content with her milk. My son was a different kettle of fish. He was started on runny cereal at 14 weeks as he was hungry all the time and the milk was not enough to satisfy him.

Tigger

> **Mumsnet fact**
> Seventy per cent of UK parents with children under 5 feel unable to say they know enough about nutrition to feed their children healthily.
> Mintel International

My little boy had an amazing appetite from the moment he had his first bottle but I left the solids until he was four months old and just upped the amount of milk he was having. It actually worked out that when he started to want more than the nine ounces of his bottle, he was exactly four months old.

Mazza

My son started solids at about four months and he would not stick to a teaspoon at a time at all. He went straight to about six teaspoons once a day. By the end of a week it was twice a day and three times followed fairly quickly. I have always found that sleeping through the night quickly follows the introduction of solids. There comes a point when milk doesn't provide enough food. I was advised to continue the milk feeds as usual and then top up with solids afterwards if the baby wanted them. That way they are still getting enough milk and only taking the solids they need.

Ginette

My baby was about nine months old before he really started having proper meals. I think the baby food industry pushes the idea of 'right' meals at the 'right' age too much. Some babies don't need any solids at all until they are six months and so they are bound to take longer to get up to speed with three meals a day than others who wean earlier. I've yet to hear about a baby starving because it won't eat.

I've been through about a year's worth of picky eating. In the end, we started all over again and went right back to baby rice and mixed it with expressed breast milk. That way she connected the taste of breast milk with the spoon as well. We then tried pear also with expressed milk and rusks too, which are a good filler. Some babies take months to really get into solids. It's important to try not to worry otherwise they will pick up on your anxiety and will start to connect the idea of eating solids with you being upset.

Eulalia

What the experts say
I have found that babies who are allowed excessive quantities of milk between four and six months and are not encouraged to enjoy solids usually end up very fussy eaters.

Gina Ford (*The New Contented Little Baby Book*)

My little boy changes his mind frequently about what he'll eat and has done ever since I first started feeding him. The only thing he has never refused is pureed fruit. When he has been 'off' certain things I have completely stopped trying to shove it down him for a week and then started again and often he will take it another time quite happily. I don't believe that at this stage in their lives they get into bad eating habits.

Molly1

Mumsnet tip
Store spare expressed breast milk in ice-cube trays to be mixed with early food at the start of weaning. It makes the transition easier.

It's certainly quite an exciting time when you start to wean – I felt we were really embarking on the next stage and I loved watching my daughter enjoying eating – even when she screwed up her face in disgust at some of my offerings.

Right from the start, my daughter loved banana porridge from a packet. I mixed it to a runny consistency with my own milk to start with and later, when I had less milk, formula. The health visitor told me that breastfed babies tend to go for sweeter tasting food in general, so it was one of the first things I tried as it has natural fruit sugars but is still milky, unlike pureed fruit (which my daughter hated for ages). The experts try to panic you by saying that you mustn't only get them used to sweet tasting food, but at this stage just getting her to enjoy solids was the first hurdle. She started really enjoying different savoury tastes after a month or so on this porridge and has no lingering sweet tooth.

Lizzer

My seven-month-old has just got into the idea of food, and boy has he got it. Before this he would clamp his mouth shut and turn his head away. I was really worried, but there's really no need. At this stage it's just about learning about the process of eating, not about nutrition. The one thing that seemed to help crack it was letting him have pieces of toast and rice cakes. But if you do this you should really keep an eye on them, as they don't have a clue what to do with the bits in their mouths.

Emmagee

> **Mumsnet tip**
> If you're having trouble with solids try putting the food on your finger and letting the baby suck it off. Some babies don't like the taste and texture of the spoon – it can be a bit of a shock after breast or bottle-feeding.

We found the spoon we used made a difference. We now use the little soft rubbery ones. The texture is much softer than the hard plastic varieties, so he doesn't mind it going into his mouth as much.

Mares

Mashed bananas always got mine going. Both my sons started off on these and they still get through a big bunch each week. Apart from being very yummy, they are so slippery, they slide down the throat before the recipient has cottoned on to what's happening. Just a tiny spoonful at first, though. I have cleaned up an awful lot of banana sick in my time.

Frank1

What the experts say

An infant does not naturally get adequate vitamins during the first year of life.

Dr Earl Mindell (*Parents' Nutrition Bible*)

For most children, eating fresh food in sufficient quantity and drinking formula milk until the age of a year, vitamin supplements are probably unnecessary.

Annabel Karmel (*Annabel Karmel's New Complete Baby and Toddler Meal Planner*)

I bought a small blender – the little blade was ideal, especially for meats in the early days. I got fed up endlessly shoving things through sieves. Get some ice-cube trays to freeze batches of frozen fruits and vegetables so that you have various 'meals' available and can try different mixes. Some babies don't like baby rice, so don't panic if yours isn't interested.

Maisy1

I do things in bulk – cook lots of carrots, parsnips, turnip and other veg then puree it with a hand blender and put it into ice-cube trays. That way you have lots of 'meals' from not very much effort and you only need to do it every few weeks. The best ice-cube tray was made from rubber and could bend – rigid ones snap when trying to extract frozen solids.

Harrysmum

I started off sieving stuff then realized it was taking me ages – and I had very little to show for it at the end. So I started to puree softer fruit and veg so that it didn't matter if a few small lumps were left over from blending. Good ones to use are butternut squash, parsnips and mango. I still did carrots and harder stuff, just not as often or in such big quantities.

Pamela1

I never bothered with sieving anything and just used to mash thoroughly. A friend of mine says one thing she'll never do again is try to sieve banana through a tea strainer!

Baabaa

I batch-cooked and froze foods in ice-cube trays then transferred the cubes to freezer bags. Then as the portions I needed started to get bigger, I froze the food in used margarine or butter containers. They are really easy to pop frozen food out of and you can make the portions as big or as small as you need.

Dixie

> **Mumsnet tip**
> An easy way to add protein to 'weaning' meals is to make up a batch of cheese sauce and freeze it in ice-cube trays. Simply add one to any combination of the veggies you have already frozen in batches.

I've collected loads of those black 35 mm film containers, sterilized them and then put the food into them for freezing. It's great for weaning in the early stages and when you go out. Just take one or two film cases with you.

Kkkkkatie

I tried to prepare my daughter's food following Annabel Karmel's infamous advice. The only thing my daughter would eat was jar food. I bought pureed banana and peach in jars and she ate it, after refusing to eat my hand-pureed banana. Isn't that weird? I must admit I find it all quite daunting – what to give to her, what she's allowed, what breakfast is gluten-free, and so on. I'm almost overwhelmed by all the information and find myself constantly referring to books in an effort to produce something appetizing and healthy.

Janus

Jars or home-made – which is best?

I am all for doing my own thing. I can't afford to buy jars. In fact I have yet to buy one. Some of them are full of modified starch so you aren't even paying for better food. The world seems to have gone convenience mad. I know a lot of women are working now but how long does it take to blend some fruit?

Eulalia

I was amazed at the number of times people asked us what brand baby food we were using when our son was little. We did use jars for holidays and meals out when he was very young, but that was all. I remember being incredulous at a friend complaining that she couldn't give her five-month-old a pureed banana as the hotel refused to puree it for her (why on earth she couldn't mash it with a fork was beyond me...).

Ringer

I suppose you can divide the jar-buyers into several camps – those that can't be bothered to make anything themselves; those that believe they are giving their child a balanced, healthy (and often, organic) meal; and those who use jars for convenience for times like childcare or holidays.

What the experts say

Fresh foods just do taste, smell and look better than jars of pre-prepared baby foods. Nor is there any doubt that prepared correctly, they are better for your baby.

Annabel Karmel (*Annabel Karmel's New Complete Baby and Toddler Meal Planner*)

Bought baby foods are convenient and often easier to use if going out for the day or until your baby's meals coincide with the rest of the family.

Sara Lewis (*Feeding Your Baby*)

I used to always send my son off to his childminder with a jar in his bag. Gradually I came to realize I could prepare something just as good, if not better and cheaper, myself. So I became the Tupperware Queen. When I haven't been able to use leftovers from the night before, or had something ready-frozen, I will stick a tin of Bob the Builder pasta shapes in his day-bag. Same convenience – different packaging.

If I could go back, knowing what I know now, I would still use jars for the odd time for convenience, but I would make much much more of my own stuff.

Emmam

It's little wonder that many parents feed their babies purely from jars. Remember that some families eat nothing but convenience foods so they're not going to suddenly start steaming and pureeing when baby comes along. Make home economics a compulsory school subject, that's what I say!

Beelzebub

I feel guilty about giving my children jars because I'm a stay-at-home mother and think everyone must wonder why I don't cook meals as I should have time to. The truth is, although I've tried many recipes, my children just won't touch anything I cook. I'm trying not to take it personally. I can make any amount of fruit puree but if I try say, a leek pie or chicken and tomato, she will literally wail, shake her head and, if any gets in, vomit! I literally end up in tears after spending 45 minutes or more cooking something that is obviously hated passionately. After my cooking was rejected for the umpteenth time, I gave up and moved to jars.

I use organic jars so at least there's no added salt and preservatives, so I ease my conscience that way. However, I know how time-consuming a baby is and if you have a fussy eater, other children, are working or just worn out, I think jar foods can just make things easier on everyone and that's not a bad thing, surely? No one knows what other demands a person has at home and I think people should give jar-feeders a bit of a break.

Janus

> **Mumsnet tip**
> Get your child used to eating jar food cold. Mine didn't seem to mind and it saves all that faffing around trying to find somewhere to warm the food up when you're out and about.

My son has had plenty of jars in his time and is none the worse for it. Being a mother is exhausting, whether you're with them 24/7 or away from them some of the time. I found mixing a favourite jar food with something like frozen spinach or my own concoctions was a good way to phase in food that had previously been spat out.

Clare2

I used the jars and mixed them with other food. So a piece of fish would complement a jar of mixed vegetables or a bit of home-made Spaghetti Bolognese mixed in with Spaghetti Bolognese from a jar would blend the different tastes. This helped me get over the everything-mum-cooks-is-vile stage. He hasn't had a jar for months now, but they were really handy for a while.

Snowy

> **Mumsnet tip**
> Baby jars from the regular baby food brands are great for freezing your own food in. They are the perfect size and don't crack in the freezer.

Both of my kids have always had a mixture of home-cooked (mashed-up adult food without the salt) and jars. When my daughter was nine months old we took her abroad for the first time. I was really worried about how she would cope with the hotel food, so thank goodness for jars; no preparation involved, no trying to find child-friendly restaurants or cafés, all we had to do was find somewhere to sit (usually on the beach), get the jar out, and as they say, Bob's your uncle! Luckily, she didn't mind eating the jars cold: you name it, she ate it.

Navaho

I have now got over my feelings of guilt and feed my son a mixture of jars and whatever we are having (my husband usually feeds him the jars when I work, he being an even worse cook than me).

Fish

What the experts say
They [jars] are frequently thickened with fillers that have no nutritional value at all and provide empty calories, and many of them contain sugar in one form or another.

Suzannah Olivier (*What Should I Feed My Baby?*)

Why do we feel guilty about giving jars? It's not as though they are filled with poison. Obviously, it would be a shame if your child got nothing other than jars because it would be boring, but it wouldn't kill him and he would probably be perfectly well nourished. I think they're a life saver. Sometimes I just do not have time to prepare food for my little boy. However, I am amazed that I feel reluctant to tell people that I use jars. It is a bit like breast versus bottle. It's as though you are saying that you just don't cut the mustard in the mum department if you use jars. I'm sure they are probably over-priced for what they are but I know that my little boy gets a greater variety of food than he would if I was cooking.

Molly1

My 12-month-old is addicted to jars. Not only do I worry that he is not eating good home-cooked food with lots of variety but also find the expense of the jars at nearly £1 a jar annoying. I tried one of Annabel Karmel's recipes – a fish pie that tasted great – but he turned his nose up at it so I resorted to opening a jar and sneaking the odd mouthful of fish pie in at the same time.

Esme

> **Mumsnet tip**
> If your toddler steadfastly refuses to eat your own cooking but is happy
> with jars, try washing and saving old jars and feeding your own creations
> from them. It worked for me.

My trick to stop using jars was not to buy them. Harsh, but it worked. I have an
emergency supply for when we are on a journey or away from home.

Maisy1

I got my son off jars when he was about seven months old by having him eat with
us – as far as it was practical. At first, we had to temper our own diet to cater for
the foods that a seven-month-old should have (although there aren't too many).
We started by zapping his portion through the food processor and dishing it up
from there; gradually we moved on to mashing and later just cutting up. I think that
as he could see us tucking in and enjoying what we were eating, then so did he.

Helento

With my first baby I spent hours cooking and freezing – I nearly lost a finger in a
hand blender! With number two I have only used jars: he likes the food and I'm
less stressed. Now at six months I am starting to whizz up some of our food for
him. I can recommend baked beans mixed up with cheese – scrummy!

Nw

What can you do with fussy eaters?

My seven-month-old refuses to eat anything that is savoury. I introduced a sweet puree at four months – a mixture of fruit puree and baby rice. After a couple of days I tried pureed vegetables, which was not a success. She dislikes them so much she almost always ends up 'gagging' before spitting the food out. The only stuff she likes is very sweet foods from a jar. Even my own apple puree or mashed banana is rejected.

Cyn

My daughter is almost ten months old and has become a very fussy eater. I couldn't even tell you what she likes or dislikes because it varies from day to day. Mealtimes have become a real battle and I often get very frustrated. My only comfort is knowing that this is a phase that most kids go through.

Amymum

My little boy goes through food fads. At one stage he went off everything except toast and Vegemite. I just kept trying him on a range of stuff and eventually found his new fad. Whenever he goes off something, I panic and wonder what he will eat now but it doesn't take long to find him a new favourite. I just have to keep trying a bit of everything.

If my son refuses to eat something it usually means he doesn't like it. We don't eat things we really don't like, so why should we expect him to? If I offer him a new food, he usually tastes it and then either eats it or pushes it away with a 'no more, all gone'. If he's tried something but doesn't seem to like it, I give him an old favourite and then try the same rejected food again every few days to see whether it was just for that the day or not.

If we seem stressed or concerned that he isn't eating, he eats even less or not at all. If we pretend we don't mind whether he eats or not, he is much keener to eat. The important thing is not to panic and to remember that no child will starve themselves.

Chelle

> **Mumsnet tip**
> If you look at what your children eat day by day, it doesn't look so balanced, so take a longer view and instead consider what they've eaten over a week.

My fourth son was an absolute pain when it came to solids. He started to lose weight and would only accept about one baby spoonful of stewed fruit. He is now ten months and still a pain to feed. It's very hit and miss, some days he eats until he's sick and the next he barely has anything, but since he is happy and crawling, I try not to worry too much.

Foureyes

I'm just back from a few days in the country with my folks, where my son ate like a pig. He loved trying new dishes – plaice and spinach in cheese sauce, chicken, courgettes, grapes and lovely lentils. Now we're back in the smoke and his appetite has disappeared. I've stuck to the same food and routines, but suddenly that mouth is tightly shut and the little hands are pushing the spoon away. So far I've stayed relaxed, but it's very frustrating.

Maximsmum

What the experts say
As important as ensuring that the food that goes into your baby's mouth is wholesome is ensuring that the atmosphere in which the food is eaten is pleasant and non-combative.

Eisenberg, Merkoff and Hathaway (*What to Expect the First Year*)

Our daughter is eleven months old and has started to refuse foods she used to like, such as fruit, yogurt and favourite jars. Now she is on a very narrow diet – just cheese and fromage frais. She is also drinking less milk and juice than before. She has never been a brilliant eater but at least she used to try things before deciding whether or not she liked them. Now she refuses point blank to let them pass her lips.

Fern

Mumsnet tip
I remember being appalled by seeing babies eating food off the floor, but once I had a fussy eater of my own I could see why the mums didn't mind. I now sometimes put a clean plastic mat down and put my son's food on the floor for him – it's the only way to get him to eat!

You should always try re-introducing things that have been out of favour for a while, you may be surprised that they like them again. I find that when you know they like something you can overdo it because it's safe and then they get bored.

When my daughter is being funny about eating I find that sitting down with her for a 'proper' meal really helps. At the weekend we try and have breakfast together – like poached eggs – and lunch. It's harder in the evening because she has supper at six but I try and have a bowl of yogurt or some fruit or something. It seems to make it more interesting and less like a chore for her. I tried to imagine what it must feel like to have to sit and eat my lunch while someone loomed over me and it didn't seem quite so appealing.

Emmagee

Our little boy used to go in phases about food and I found the best thing was to stop feeding the items he refused altogether for a week or two and then try them again. If I kept trying to shovel stuff he didn't like down him, he would keep refusing it – whereas the break seemed to give him the opportunity to forget that it was something he wouldn't eat. Also, little nibbles, like peas, Cheerios, dried fruit and bits of toast, have always worked well with my little boy when he is feeling a bit picky.

Mumsnet fact
Ninety per cent of children are fussy eaters at some time in their lives.

Junior

At around nine months my son would hardly eat a thing. He'd go for days just eating grapes. I began to get desperate and dreaded meal times. My son also lost weight and was about to be referred to a doctor when, on the advice of a health visitor, I cut right back on the amount of milk that he was having to just two feeds a day. I was still breastfeeding and my son was demanding around five to six feeds in a 24-hour period. It worked immediately and my son now eats loads.

Esme

My daughter is a very fussy eater and I was worried about her nutritional intake. My health visitor suggested I buy vitamin drops and give her these. She is also underweight – less than 9th centile – but I am not going to worry about it. I think you know when your child is healthy and the whole weight thing can become obsessive.

Janus

At one weight check-up my son had lost two ounces in a month. He was a very small eater and didn't have much in the way of solids until he was nine months. He was also very low on the charts but did eventually catch up. I didn't worry about giving him the same thing. My son loved yogurt and I'd often just end up serving that time after time.

Don't go by the book or the calendar – go by your baby – they will take things when they are ready for them.

Eulalia

> **Mumsnet tip**
> Use the juice from cooking vegetables to make something they will eat, for example, sauces and jellies, etc. That way they get the vitamins and minerals that have leaked into the water.

My son refused to eat carrots, but he loves mashed potato and gravy, so I mash up his carrots and mix them in, and pour gravy on top. He's so busy concentrating on the potato and gravy that he doesn't realize that he's eating carrots as well.

Ailsa

My son has always been a picky eater. When he was about ten months old, I used to find that sweet potato (make sure it's the orange-fleshed type) just baked in the oven for about an hour did the trick. Also, try butternut squash, peeled and microwaved for a few minutes, then mashed. I think it was the sweetness of these that really appealed to him.

Huncamunca

> **Mumsnet tip**
> My suggestion for fussy eaters is to try ice-cream. Made the traditional way, it has eggs, milk, cream and different pureed fruit in it. It can be a very nutritious food, with little sugar.

I find that my baby eats more if she can feed herself. I offer her a colourful selection of 'finger foods' like sticks of carrot, pepper, cheese, bread sticks, slices of cooked chicken, perhaps with a dip like mashed avocado. Most of it ends up on the floor, but she enjoys picking up the food herself, holding it and experiencing the different textures.

I also try to eat at the same time as my baby – she seems to enjoy watching me eat and sometimes if she sees me eating something she will want to try it too.

Lou

If your baby suddenly goes off food, forget baby food and give them exactly the same as what you are eating (you should start with easy things like Shepherd's Pie and spaghetti). I remember that mine grew out of jars at around eight to nine months – they just weren't interested in them any more. But they all found grown-up food fascinating.

Javarose

Try the train method: 'here comes the train into the tunnel'. You might feel a bit odd but it can sometimes work. You could also try cutting up pieces of cold meat, cheese and veggies in the shapes of faces or animals.

Tigger

If your baby only seems interested in sweet things, try blending fruit and vegetables or meat. For example, carrot and orange, carrot and apple, duck and orange, pineapple and pork, and roasted yellow or red peppers with tomatoes.

Suew

Mumsnet tip
If you're really struggling to get your child to eat vegetables, try mixing them with a dollop of fromage frais. That was literally the only way my little boy would eat any.

The basic rule for food refusers is if they're putting on weight, don't worry (or at least don't let them see you're worried!). Easier said than done, I know. I've had to walk out of the room before now in order not to weep with frustration at my kids' blithe refusal to eat anything remotely healthy.

I think the way to get through is to develop a genuine knowledge of when they're hungry (a skill I lost years ago!) and not give them the satisfaction of getting a reaction from you.

I don't think I know anyone with kids who hasn't had a few 'issues' with feeding and food.

ScummyMummy

Children do not starve themselves – it is unheard of. I really do think that if you let yourself get wound up by their eating habits at this stage then you are setting the stage for food battles in the future. Once these perceptive little beings know that they can get your full, undivided, concentrated attention by not eating something or playing with their food then that is exactly what they'll do!

Molly1

If you're worried about your baby's nutritional intake, try lots of banana as that's fattening and console yourself with the recent research suggesting that mice who eat less live longer.

Robinw

My 14-year-old son is living proof that it is possible to live on nothing but Marmite, toast and fromage frais in the early years and still get to 5 feet 9 inches (and he's still growing!)

Kia

What should you give babies to drink?

If you are breastfeeding you don't need to give water at all. My baby had nothing but the breast until he was 20 weeks when he had his first taste of solids. I didn't bother with water until he was about six months and he took to it fine. You should stick with water rather than juice as I know some babies that actually refuse plain water because they have got used to juice. Most of the weaning foods are so watery anyway and they take so little to begin with that there is no worry about dehydration.

Eulalia

I gave my daughter water from about 11 weeks – I know there is no need to if you are breastfeeding but she seemed to like the odd drink from her beaker. When I started weaning I had a drink of water handy and gave her a few sips after a meal. I wouldn't start with juice because water is the best drink they can have and they might take a real liking to it, saving you loads of money on cordial in the future!

Lizzer

What the experts say
As soon as your baby is having any quantity of solid food she will need water as well as milk to drink.

Dr Miriam Stoppard (*Complete Baby and Childcare*)

From day one my son wouldn't have water. All he would drink was milk and I started getting worried that he wasn't getting enough fluids so at five months I gave him juice. We give him the one that has nothing added to it, and dilute it. He loves it and rarely has water and I often think I've got a juice addict for a child.

Mazza

Call me Mrs Meanie but I would simply keep offering water. If your child's thirsty enough he'll take it. The alternative is years of your child having juice and refusing water, which, quite apart from the tooth decay risk is just establishing a lifelong habit of only drinking sweet things. It is a habit that is much harder to break when they're older – personally, I'd go cold turkey now.

Amber1

I didn't give mine juice as I just didn't think it was necessary and also I'm too lazy to faff around with bottles and dislike the sticky mess juice makes when spilt. Water is so easy to clean up. A baby can be weaned off juice onto water by giving increasingly diluted drinks.

Baabaa

I give my eight-month-old baby juice every day. I drink it all the time too as I thought it was healthy and full of vitamin C. What is the problem?

Lil

Fruit juice does help the absorption of iron but my health visitor told me that it should only be given heavily diluted with water. Don't forget it's got lots of sugar in it, even though it is natural.

Rosy

What the experts say

Water is the best drink to offer. But freshly squeezed citrus fruits, particularly orange, have a good nutritional value, being high in Vitamin C.

Annabel Karmel (*Annabel Karmel's New Complete Baby and Toddler Meal Planner*)

There is no earthly reason why water should be sweetened with cordials or bottled fruit juices, with all the attendant problems for young teeth and sugar metabolism.

Suzannah Olivier (*What Should I Feed My Baby?*)

My dentist said not to give my children fruit juice because the acid in it corrodes their teeth. It also has lots of sugar in it, albeit natural. It gives them a sugar hit without actually nourishing them much. My kids don't get juice at all, except in other people's houses, and they are more than happy with ordinary tap water. It's also cheap and doesn't make a horrible sticky mess when they spill it. The dentist also said they should drink water after eating fruit, to wash the acid away.

Violet

I do think that juice can be given in moderation, although mine never got juice until they were 18 months old. Before that, they had milk all the time, as I think when their teeth are coming in they should not be bombarded with sugar. Ten years ago though, it was fashionable to give children juice and at that time it was given in a bottle!

Tigger

I give my daughter milk and very diluted 'tooth kind' juice because she just won't drink water and gets constipated when she doesn't drink enough. 'Tooth kind' is especially formulated to reduce acidity.

Robinw

Mumsnet tip
If you're worried about your child's fluid intake, make any solid food he has sloppier.

I just don't see that it's necessary to give babies anything other than milk or water. It's not as though they know what it is until you let them try it, anyway. If you think of the amount of pureed fruit we shove down them I'm sure most babies get enough vitamin C and don't need to drink juice to supplement their levels. Okay, so when they're toddlers and they see their friends having juice and try it out at playgroup then maybe I can understand why you'd start. But before then it just seems unnecessary – people are creating rods for their own backs. I've even seen a baby drinking Coke from a baby bottle – it was all I could do not to snatch it from the poor wee thing's grasp.

Alicer

Messy mealtimes – is there anything you can do?

My kitchen floor resembles the Battle of the Somme after every meal and I have lost count of the times I sweep it every day. Tonight, my son knocked the bowl of fish pie that I had sweated over (while he was having his daily nap) right out of my hand. Needless to say I was stupid enough to have used a breakable bowl so it smashed all over the floor. Everything on the table has to be moved as far away from him as possible or it will end up on the floor. It's even worse now he has worked out how to climb out of the chair onto the table.

Esme

What the experts say
Food will be a plaything, most of which will land on the floor rather than in your baby's stomach, but there's no cause for concern.
Dr Miriam Stoppard (*Complete Baby and Childcare*)

As soon as he has taken the edge off his hunger my son starts to play with his food – mashing it up with his hands, squashing it into the table and then brushing it onto the floor. This means that after every mealtime I have to mount a huge clean-up operation. He does continue to eat while he's doing this, though. We are all crowded down one end of the table to stop him from getting our cutlery/plates/food/drinks and he sits at the head of the table in splendid isolation.

Worlass

From when she could first pick things up our daughter has been desperate to feed herself. For the past few months she has refused to let us feed her anything at all, and the mess has been incredible. We decided the only thing to do was to put the highchair on a large waterproof mat, stand well back and let her get on with it   and try at least to be thankful that she's so independent! Yogurts are interesting, home-made soup needs to be thick enough to stick to the spoon and eating out is a challenge, but she'll get there eventually. On the plus side we've some lovely photos to embarrass her with when she's older (Auntie Jean's chocolate pudding last Christmas particularly springs to mind...).

Azzie

The solution we found was to buy a chair that looks like an adult's but is higher. Suddenly our son thinks he is grown up and copies all we do at mealtimes.

Clairgod

Our son is only six months old and has been 'feeding' himself for a few weeks now. At first we thought he was just gnawing on the spoon to help his teething pains, but it started to look like he just wanted to feed himself. We bought him a high chair, which seemed to make him more determined in his quest for independence.

Axel

> **Mumsnet tip**
> Put a few pieces of pasta/rice/potato on the high chair tray when feeding young babies – chasing the bits of food keeps them occupied while you get on with the job of feeding them. As a bonus they start to learn to feed themselves with finger food.

My youngest is ten months now so I empty the jar into the bowl and hand her a spoon. It's very messy but she is surprisingly adept at getting it into her mouth, one way or another, and yes, she uses the spoon. And she thinks she is really clever.

Emmy

I found most baby dishes useless and instead opted for a very heavy earthenware bowl. This bowl is too heavy to be thrown onto the floor and because it is deep it is actually easier to scoop food out of it. To prevent too much mess I only put a small quantity of food into it at a time.

Eulalia

> **Mumsnet tip**
> Instead of laying down a plastic mat on the floor, put down newspaper. You can then chuck it in the bin after the meal.

I think you should encourage self-feeding as much as possible. It might be messier and take longer now but it's much better in the long term.

Try using a small fork – a real one, not a silly plastic one. It takes some getting used to but my boys had much greater success than with a spoon. French set yogurts are easier to self-feed than many other types and pasta in a thick sauce is probably the easiest dish to self-feed.

Scally

The first thing my daughter ate by herself with a spoon was apple crumble with egg custard.

Javarose

I found anything with mashed potato in it quite good as it's sticky and stays on the spoon – so Fish Pie, Shepherd's Pie (I added baked beans to it) or just mashed potato with cheese – all worked well. Fish fingers chopped are also good as you can have a good stab at them with a fork and they tend to stay on.

Aliceb

The best discovery we made was pelican bibs (the plastic ones with the curled-up bit at the bottom). These are just wonderful. They catch loads of the food that's dropped and then our children can have a 'second try', scooping it out of the bibs. It's messy – but better in the bib than wasted on the floor.

Another tip is to save the really messy stuff (like yogurts) until the evening meal so you can throw the baby straight in the bath afterwards.

Hmonty

I think that you have to start thinking about food from a child's perspective. Food is pretty much the only thing they are allowed to put in their mouths, so it's only natural that they are going to want to play with it, put it in, spit it out and mash it about. Our little boy likes certain foods one week and doesn't the next. He will use a spoon and a fork very proficiently one day and then only his fingers the next. Some days he can't get the food in fast enough and others he just isn't interested at all. I just let him get on with it. He is bibbed up and placed where it really doesn't matter what he does with his food. I praise any good eating behaviour and ignore the rest. If he throws something on the floor, then it is removed and not given back.

Molly1

Annabel Karmel – helpful hints or one big guilt trip?

I've found Annabel Karmel's *Baby and Toddler Meal Planner* absolutely brilliant for ideas for food. There are lots of things that you wouldn't necessarily think of doing – like really tasty savoury dips. My nine-month-old will demolish just about anything that we make from it.

LB

I found Annabel Karmel's recipes for four to 12-month-olds fantastic – my boys both adored them. Some of the recipes were fairly time-consuming but if you do massive batches and freeze them, it works pretty well. But it must be hard with a fussy eater – my boys have always eaten virtually anything offered to them, and in vast quantities, so it is quite rewarding to cook for them.

Scally

> **Mumsnet tip**
> When using ice-cube trays to freeze babies' food, use rubber ones, as it saves breaking your fingers trying to get the frozen food out.

I'm not a good cook and was thrilled when someone gave me Annabel Karmel's books as a birth present – it all looked so easy and exciting! In reality though, although some of her tips were useful, too often something that she says takes 20 minutes took me hours and was then rejected – all very frustrating. Just having the book in the kitchen glaring at me, unopened, from the shelf made me feel guilty every time I went for a jar.

Biza

Where Annabel Karmel really helped me was in giving a timetable of what kinds of things your baby can have and when – especially useful if you are a first-timer. I cribbed all her menu tips but didn't always have the energy to follow the recipes. Luckily, as I had twins, I didn't feel guilty cheating a bit.

Berta

Every one of my friends has the Annabel Karmel bible in their kitchen. I assumed this was the only way! I thought the timetables were excellent. I had no idea how to wean a baby or how much to feed them and I couldn't have done it without her help. The meals, on the other hand, were way out of my league. I hate cooking and my son lives on fish fingers, scrambled eggs and baked beans!

Lil

I don't enjoy cooking at all and have had to make a real effort for my 11-month-old boy. I decided that paranoia and guilt were futile and have relaxed about it now. I use jars for busy days and on quieter days I try to cook a batch of something and freeze meal-sized portions.

I bought the Annabel Karmel book because my health visitor recommended it. The book suggested a few purees I hadn't thought of but after that I decided that Annabel had got too much spare time on her hands – some of the recipes for nine months onwards are far more laborious than is really necessary. The meal planners were entirely inappropriate for my son. I think that with a little patience and flexibility a routine works itself out eventually.

Late3osmom

My son eats what we do, but in a format he can manage. I know from experience that he will eat when he is hungry and if he doesn't want it, it just goes in the bin. To make him laugh, sometimes I'll put a smiley face on his scrambled egg with tomato ketchup, or make ketchup hair on his Shepherd's Pie. I'm amazed that people need to refer to a book to make vegetable and fruit purees – blimey, I'm no gourmet, but it's not rocket science blending up carrots.

Emmam

My younger son couldn't eat dairy products, so he had a different diet from what we normally ate. There are loads of other things I wouldn't want a baby eating as well. It's all very well saying they can eat the same as you, but often they can't. Getting the processor out to blend up one meal is such a hassle. They want their food lukewarm and we want ours hot, not stewed into oblivion while waiting for theirs to cool down. From four to ten months my boys ate almost exclusively from Annabel Karmel's book and we have always eaten meals together as a family.

Scally

I worried myself silly about how to feed my son once he passed the puree stage, believing myself to be useless in the kitchen. I bought jars, but felt guilty about not giving him wholesome home-cooked food, so thought I would give Annabel Karmel's book a try. He happily ate more or less everything I made for him but it would take me three times longer than the time stated to cook anything – I could never just rustle something up in 20 minutes. I ended up spending my precious evenings cooking huge batches of food to go in the freezer, so that didn't last long.

Donna1

I bought Annabel Karmel's book and haven't cooked any of the recipes apart from the baby purees. As soon as I thought we could get away with giving our son our diet mashed up, I switched to that. Even if what you are offering from Annabel is better than what you eat, I tend to think that giving children the message that they eat one thing and grown-ups another is not good long-term. The obvious exceptions being large quantities of chocolate and gin, of course.

Clare2

4

Baby's Health

Introduction

Sometimes it seems that being a parent is all about worrying – and there's nothing guaranteed to worry you more than your precious baby's health. If you thought you had concerns before the birth, just wait until afterwards. Every cough, sneeze, pimple and rash is a potentially life-threatening illness when you're a new parent. Just knowing when to call the doctor out or go and see them is hard enough, but you can bet that if you weren't on first-name terms with your doctor prior to having kids there's a good chance you will be by the time they hit six months.

The list of potential childhood ailments seems endless, from the minor irritation of cradle cap through the pain and guilt of nappy rash to the endless tears and misery which may or may not be teething. What's the best way of surviving these inevitable difficulties?

Some things aren't easily explained by medical science – colic, for example – a term that seems to be bandied about by parents and doctors alike without much recourse to medicine. Nevertheless it's an excruciating and exhausting reality for thousands of parents. Who cares if there's no medical definition when you're wearing out your carpet and yourself attempting to soothe an inconsolable baby at all hours of the day and night? Does anything really help and if not, how long does colic last? Is cranial osteopathy an answer to this and other common ills or is it best to opt for tried and tested prescription or over-the-counter remedies?

Then there's the minefield of vaccinations: should you or shouldn't you? And if you do, how do you best prepare yourself and your child to cope with the jabs and their after effects?

Complex decisions aside, there's little that makes a child more miserable (or an adult for that matter) than the common cold. As it's estimated that by the time your child is one it will have had between six and eight colds (*Practical Parenting*), it's worth investigating what remedies have worked for other people. Do you load up with Calpol, demand antibiotics or opt for the alternative approach? And what about the modern plague – eczema? Recent surveys estimate that one in five children will be affected by this horrendous condition and there's nothing more heartbreaking than watching a baby tearing at their own skin – but what, if anything, can you do to help them?

It's a sad but inevitable fact that most babies will suffer some illness in their first year, some more than others. Dealing with these illnesses requires a mixture of instinct, medical science and a healthy dose of tried and tested advice from those who've been there before you – other anxious parents.

When should you take your baby to the doctor's?

I took my first child most weeks it seemed, but have tried to hold back a bit with my second. They both had permanent coughs almost from birth but it seemed that apart from advice on how best to help them breathe there was nothing the doctor could do.

If I'm in any doubt I'll call and ask if it would be possible to speak to either a doctor or a nurse to check whether they think I should come in. I often think an hour or so waiting in a germ-infested surgery, especially with a toddler in tow, will do my baby (and me) more harm than good.

One tip, if you think your child has chickenpox, call first – my doctor did a phone diagnosis and was keen for me not to bring the virus into the surgery.

Biza

I usually wait until my childminder starts moaning about my son's cough and then take him to the doctor's in order that I can reassure her that he's okay.

With tummy upsets in a young baby, I'd give it perhaps a couple of days. Any unexplained rashes or spots and I'd take him as soon as possible – partly for my own reassurance, but also to find out whether he is contagious and a threat to other kids who go to his childminder. If he had a temperature, was hard to wake, floppy – really out of kilter, then I wouldn't hesitate to ring the doctor whatever time of day or night, or even take him to hospital.

> **Mumsnet fact**
> Health has overtaken porn as the top internet search question.
> *Practical Parenting*

I've also used an internet site where you ask a doctor a specific question. I asked about an ear infection that didn't seem to be bothering my son and was told that I should take him to my doctor, which turned out to be the right thing to do as he needed antibiotics.

Don't let a doctor's attitude put you off – if you are worried then get your child looked at or at least phone. A two-minute telephone conversation can be very reassuring and doesn't waste anyone's time.

Emmam

I've used the NHS Direct service when I haven't wanted to call on my doctor. Both times it was the dead of night: the first time because of a really high temperature; the second, a really high temperature and spots. On reflection, the advice I received was all the standard stuff that I knew anyway, but it was reassuring to talk to a professional (the high temperature and spots turned out to be hand, foot and mouth). It calmed me down, like talking to a more experienced mother. I did, however, find the endless questions about my postcode very irritating as all I wanted to do was scream, 'Is my baby going to be okay or what?'

Charliesmummy

I've also found NHS Direct very useful for reassurance. The first time I used them was when my daughter was seven weeks old and crying non stop – it was just good to have someone to talk to. Plus if I try to get an appointment with the doctor and say that I have called NHS Direct then I don't feel like a time-waster.

Minky

A doctor once told me to treat the child and not the symptom, so if my child had a persistent cough, for example, but was otherwise well I would do nothing. I generally feel that with perhaps the aid of some targeted homeopathy or added vitamins, kids get over most things in time.

Lill

I've got several medical books which I'd recommend. These days I would also look up problems on the net before going to the doctor. Our main problem has always been ear infections – my GP didn't want to prescribe antibiotics and my daughter always needed them. Then one time I didn't go straight away and when I finally got there it was, 'Why didn't you come sooner!'

Robinw

These are my criteria for judging whether to go: light cough and runny nose, no doctor. Chesty cough, getting worse over 24 hours, doctor. Temperature, doctor. Vomiting with no temperature, probably no doctor, if this happens just the once. Vomiting with no temperature, but more than once, possibly doctor, but would cut out hard-to-digest food and drinks first. Vomiting with temperature, doctor. Extreme crying, obvious distress, suspected earache, lethargy or other unusual behaviour, doctor.

What the experts say

A doctor's reassurance that your child is well and normal can be just as important as her confirmation that your baby is sick. So feel free to call your doctor whenever your child looks or acts differently.

Signe Larson and Kevin Osborn (*The Complete Idiot's Guide to Bringing up Baby*)

I tried to take my second child less often than my first as I didn't want him dosed up with antibiotics all the time. However, from six months he was being cared for by a childminder. I often found myself at the doctor's surgery to satisfy her worries more than mine.

Frank1

I was advised always to take a child with breathing difficulties to the doctor. Likewise, a listless child who has had a high temperature for a day or for no obvious reason needs to be seen to rule out a urinary tract infection. As for vomiting and diarrhoea – if it doesn't go away or is bloody or the child looks dehydrated (dry tongue or concentrated urine) then you should see your doctor. Chesty coughs and sore throats should be judged by how well the child is coping and how unwell they actually seem, though often there's nothing a doctor can do.

Bon

These are my 'guidelines' for when to call a doctor: fever over 40 degrees, call immediately. Fever between 38 and 40 degrees, call within 24 hours if there's no improvement. Low grade fever with general flu or cold symptoms, make an appointment if no improvement within three days. If the fever is also accompanied by any of the following: limpness, lethargy, convulsions, inconsolable crying for hours, crying, moaning, purple rash, severe headache, drooling, neck stiffness or severe dehydration – call immediately. For a cough, if it is wheezy, around for more than two weeks, disturbs sleep or contains yellow or green phlegm (sorry!), go to the doctor during normal hours. If there is blood in the phlegm, or the child is having trouble breathing, call immediately.

What the experts say

You must start off believing that most doctors won't mind if you consult them for reassurance...a mother usually knows instinctively if her child is well or not. And if any sensible mother feels strongly enough that her child is unwell then a doctor ignores this at his or her peril... your guideline should be 'when in doubt, call a doctor'.

Dr Miriam Stoppard (*New Baby Care Book*)

As mothers I think we can sense when our child is really unwell. We also know how one child can be really sick and cope and the other is laid out for days. So if all else fails, go with your instincts! The worst that can happen is that they think you're paranoid and you waste time in a doctor's waiting room. The alternative – not going to the doctor's when you should – doesn't bear thinking about.

Mollipops

Colic – what can you do?

My first daughter suffered from colic from three to 14 weeks. We were miles away from family, I hadn't any close friends as I'd been working in a different town and I was coping alone with the screaming for the eight hours that my husband was at work. I thought I was going to go mad. Luckily I had help from a health visitor and I'd recommend talking to someone about it, ideally someone who can give you a break. I used to get so upset because I wanted to delight in my new baby, but in fact I was just hanging on until the first months were over. Swaddling and back patting worked to some extent, but the memory of it is still with me 15 years later!

Minou

My baby was extremely colicky from about four to 12 weeks. It's heart-breaking watching them scream, while being unable to comfort them. The classic symptoms are bringing the knees in towards the chest while crying and tending to have a 'worse' time at one point of the day – usually, but not always, the evening – which can last several hours. I was advised not to drink caffeine or eat too much dairy as I was breastfeeding but I'm not convinced that helped. I was also advised to wind the baby after every feed, but the main thing that I think helped her was colic drops.

Lizzer

I found massage helped a lot – colic drops on their own weren't a cure. You can learn the special anti-colic technique from a baby massage book or go to a class. It's a miserable time but it will end.

Late30smom

I've been told that frequent feeding can exacerbate colic. I managed feeds every two and a half to three and a half hours while breastfeeding by working hard to keep the baby awake during the feed. It was difficult, but it did help.

Amber1

What the experts say

These babies all seem to have one thing in common: they are being fed on demand. Feeding this way all too often leads to the baby having another feed before the first one is digested, one of the reasons that I believe may cause colic.

Gina Ford (*The Contented Little Baby Book*)

If the cause of colic could be pinpointed, it could also be treated and perhaps even cured. Unfortunately no one knows the cause.

Signe Larson and Kevin Osborn
(*The Complete Idiot's Guide to Bringing Up Baby*)

Babies don't stop having colic attacks because people try to comfort them, but they scream a lot less than babies who are left on their own.

Penelope Leach (*Your Baby and Child*)

A lot of people I know have found that colic eases a bit after six weeks and should be gone completely by 12 weeks. My daughter used to scream until 5 am for weeks – we couldn't believe it when it stopped.

Two things helped. One was meeting other mums who'd been through it. The other was swaddling the baby (wrapping a blanket or sheet fairly closely round) then holding her against my shoulder and patting her back slowly. Apparently if you pat every second it reminds them of the heartbeat in the womb and the swaddling makes them feel secure. This calmed her down at times when nothing else worked.

Joanne

Mumsnet tip
If you're breastfeeding try drinking lacto bacilli (you can get it in the Actimel drink). I'm sure it's helped cure my baby's colic.

My son had chronic colic for five and a half months. I felt very alienated by a lot of new mums when my son was screaming – they'd pity me for a bit then give me that 'I wish you'd make him shut up' look. If you've never had a colicky baby you'll never understand. I eventually went to a cranial osteopath and wished I'd gone in the first month – two sessions and he was cleared. I can't recommend it highly enough.

A temporary emergency measure is sugar water. It sounds daft, and I was reluctant at first. I assumed that an over-the-counter remedy was bound to be better, but having tried them all I was prepared to try anything (if you'd have told me that dancing naked round a flagpole at midnight would have helped, I'd have stripped!) To make 120 ml/4 fl oz of sugar water, dissolve one baby-spoon of sugar in fairly warm water that has been boiled. My son usually drank the whole lot and then drifted off to sleep.

What the experts say
Many academic doctors find the whole concept of colic beyond them. The descriptions are too vague, there is no pathological explanation and it can't be measured by blood test or any medical machine.

Dr Christopher Green (*Babies!*)

Most importantly you need to know that there is light at the end of the tunnel: it does go away and will not rule your life forever.

Bruntwig

My daughter had colic for four months and the only things that worked were cranial osteopathy and a homeopathic remedy called Colocynthis. I also found that a swinging motion soothed her and, since swinging her in her car seat was killing my back, I went out and bought a swinging seat. It was the best money I ever spent. It calmed her right down within minutes every time (as well as giving me a break from walking around holding her 24 hours a day).

Roz

I found a dummy really helped. With my first child I was very against them and thought they looked horrible. He had colic for three months and it was so awful I can hardly bear to remember it. My last baby started being colicky at about three weeks. I reluctantly bought some dummies and used them every evening. We still had to carry him about sometimes and rock him – we also had to hold the dummy in a bit if he cried a lot (which wasn't as cruel as it sounds). It really worked – and the best bit was that he only used them for about two months and then stopped of his own accord. It saved us and I would recommend them to any parent who's in the middle of colic hell.

Keziah

Our little boy had colic for three months and my husband and I nearly died of exhaustion. We took him to a cranial osteopath but it made no difference. I tried all the remedies in the chemist, diffused dill seed oil and massaged his tummy with a specially prepared aromatherapy massage oil. I made huge efforts to feed him every three hours, even when he was hungry sooner and it made no difference. He was getting a mix of breastmilk and bottles and we did notice an improvement when we switched formulas.

However, the only really soothing thing was for him to be swaddled and then put up over our shoulders and walked around the house. My husband and I took it in half-hourly turns for five hours every evening for three months – then it finally stopped.

Molly1

> **Mumsnet fact**
> Statistics indicate that anywhere from 16 to 26 per cent of babies are considered as having 'infant colic'. www.bbc.co.uk

Colds – what can you do?

The first 12 months were terrible, my son always seemed to have a snotty nose and his first winter was just one long cold and cough. The good news is that now he's older the colds have become less frequent. I don't think you can really avoid a cold but you can help them through it. In the first couple of days I always give him a little dose of Calpol and put a drop or two of eucalyptus oil on his teddy in the cot. I find the vapour more intense than some of the chest rubs and it really helps unblock stuffy noses. It may not be suitable for babies under three months, so check on the bottle. I also put some eucalyptus oil in his nightly bath.

Emmam

We used a nasal aspirator – a little rubber bulb thing that you stick into the baby's nose to suck out the mucus. It was very effective but she hated it, so I stopped using it in the end. I never found any of the various vapours to be much good. My eldest two children had so many colds in a row as babies that I gave up counting a couple of winters ago, but the great thing was that they've hardly had any since, and no really heavy ones. It seemed as though they had all the germs at once and thereby built up some resistance.

Javarose

We had cold after cold with our daughter in the first year, too. We used the nasal suction things to great effect – though don't put them through the sterilizer as the plastic melts. I found that the small, non-chain chemists stocked them rather than the big stores. Also saline drops worked really well for us. You can buy small bags of saline solution and little bottles with pipettes. Just squirt a bit up each nostril and it loosens everything up. Be prepared for a bit of a struggle, though – understandably it's not something a baby takes kindly to.

Berta

> **Mumsnet fact**
> A child with two or more episodes of runny nose before the age of 1 is at half the risk of having asthma diagnosed by the age of 7 than a child with one or fewer episodes.
>
> University Children's Hospital, Munich

I'm a recent convert to homeopathy. I have started using it in conjunction with, rather than instead of, conventional medicine. I've discovered that the homeopathic remedy pulsatilla will clear a stuffy nose and allow my daughter to sleep.

Jaykaye

It's worth trying the homeopathic teething granules. Safe for even the smallest baby they contain xylitol (an antibacterial natural ingredient) and chamomilla, which is a general soothing and calming homoeopathic remedy. We use alternative remedies whenever we can, but I really would not stint on the Calpol or Ibuprofen (within recommended dosage) as it's such an effective and safe way to reduce a child's fever.

> **Mumsnet tip**
> To help with blocked noses and nasty coughs, invest in a humidifier that has a reservoir for essential oils/decongestants. Start the humidifier about five minutes before putting baby to bed and add three drops Myrtle and three drops of Pine Needle to the reservoir.

Our son had constant colds during his first winter at nursery and it was very depressing at times. We put Olbas Oil under his pillow and burn lavender oil, which is very soothing – and he also has echinacea drops (two weeks on, one week off) and a Swiss herbal tonic in his porridge all winter. Chances are, if your child's sick, you will be as well so we use all the same remedies for ourselves and add in some rum and hot lemon, too.

Clare2

> **Mumsnet tip**
> Keep the baby sheets from your Moses basket and lay them under an older baby's head when they have a cold. You can just change this daily instead of the whole sheet, if it gets dirtied when they have colds.

I've got a book on natural remedies for babies and children and there are some great concoctions in it for colds and runny noses! For babies with a stuffy nose mix two drops of peppermint oil with some almond oil and add this to baby's bathwater.

Mollipops

For coughs associated with colds we hang a wet towel over the radiator (which we leave on quite late) in the baby's room and that seems to help moisten the air.

Maisy1

I'm usually philosophical about colds, but recently my son had three in a row so I refused to visit a house where I knew a child had a streaming cold – I just couldn't cope with any more sleepless nights.

Nancy

> **Mumsnet tip**
> Put a couple of books under the head end of the cot. It stops them getting too congested and really seems to help.

Apparently, children can get up to eight colds a year when they are little as their immune system is so new. My son is at a nursery so is rarely without some complaint or other. My reasoning is he might as well go through it now rather than later when he goes to school.

Lil

If a child has just had a cold it's unlikely they will catch another one straight away. However, sometimes it can be best to be on the safe side and keep away from those you know are infected. On the other hand, you don't want to keep your kid cooped up in the house, either. Playgroups and the like can be a breeding ground for germs but usually the benefits of socializing outweigh the risks of catching colds.

Eulalia

Cradle cap – what can you do?

Cradle cap is particularly vile and unsightly and the only babies that don't seem to suffer are the ones in baby adverts. Mine didn't have it too badly and as they had quite a lot of hair it didn't really show but it was still a complete shock to me. It gradually got better and by about nine months it was gone completely. What I really hate is when mothers start picking at their babies' heads – now I'll admit to some private picking but not in public, please!

Alex2

My health visitor and doctor said mine would grow out of it and there was not a lot I could do. I tried all sorts of things on my first baby: creams, lotions and shampoos, and none worked and indeed, at times caused red raw skin. In the end, with my second baby I discovered olive oil did the trick. I put a lot on before her bath, occasionally using mild baby shampoo to wash it off, then gave her a nice gentle rub with a soft towel afterwards. Easy.

Maisy1

What the experts say
It is tempting to want to pick off the greasy-looking crusts, but it is better to use a special cradle cap shampoo which you can buy from the chemist to remove the dead skin cells more easily. Olive oil is a simple home remedy, though it has no active ingredient and merely softens the skin making the scales easier to remove. Some creams containing salicylic acid and sulphur cream can prove more efficient than shampoos.

Dr Hilary Jones (*Your Child's Health*)

Brush the scalp with a very soft toothbrush when shampooing. This will get rid of it. Then carry on once a week or so, and it won't come back. It's the only thing that worked for my four – cradle cap shampoos just seemed to make it worse.

Sc

It's important to brush the scales in the 'wrong' direction so that they are sticking up and not lying flat otherwise they just accumulate even more, then rub aqueous cream into the scalp gently. This can be bought over the counter at any chemist and is cheap. This worked really quickly for my son.

Seh

If your kids have got hair, try the plastic nit detector combs (you'll need them in later years anyway!). I found just rubbing the oil in the night before and then gently combing through with the nit comb worked best.

Scooby2

I used grape-seed oil, which is much lighter than olive oil. Again, as suggested before, rub it on at night and it will moisturize the dry flaky bits so that they can be washed off the next day.

Willsmum

I tried olive oil and brushing, and neither seemed to work. In the end I bought some cradle cap shampoo, which helped, although it did seem to take a while to shift.

Lisaj

Another vote for cradle cap shampoo. It worked very well for my son. My daughter had lots of hair when she was born, and so I didn't treat her cradle cap at all, because it couldn't be seen – and it went away on its own. It's so easy to worry about the cosmetic side of cradle cap, especially if others comment on it. But does it really matter?

Jmt

I tried zinc and castor oil 'bottom' cream and it worked better than olive oil. Rub it in, then rub off with a towel.

Beelzebub

My daughter started with what seemed to be cradle cap at around six weeks. We tried all the usual remedies but it got worse. Eventually we took her to the doctor, who diagnosed infantile eczema and an infection, which was treated with hydrocortisone and antibiotic ointment. Looking back, we should have noticed that what she had was different – regular cradle cap doesn't bother most children, it just looks a mess, whereas she used to cry, scratch at it and break the skin (hence the infection). If your child is disturbed by the condition, it's worth taking them to the doctor's to be checked out.

Biza

How do you cope with eczema?

The amazing thing about eczema is everyone's version is different and different things will work for different folks. My daughter had severe eczema from six weeks. Mittens sewn in everything or blood everywhere. It really is awful and anyone who hasn't suffered doesn't really understand. I tried to cope without steroids for ages (trying everything from homeopathy to cranial osteopathy) but gave in eventually. We only had to use hydrocortisone for a short time, though. The doctors claim that once the skin heals with steroids it should start to heal itself – controversial, but it worked for us. What also seemed to help was a short trip to the Mediterranean (literally three days) when she got a bit of sun and lots of sea water (we took a washing up bowl to the beach and filled it with sea water and sat her in it under an umbrella).

> **Mumsnet fact**
> The more often children have their faces and hands washed, or are bathed and showered, the more likely they are to develop eczema and wheezing. Institute of Child Health

As for food allergies, we had all sorts of private tests done that said my daughter was allergic to milk. Everyone was sceptical as she'd actually never had cow's milk or formula (only breast) and could tolerate butter. I finally went to an NHS paediatrician who put a few drops of full-fat milk on my daughter's cheek. Within ten minutes she had a sort of nettle rash. So, no milk products for her (though she still had butter). You can do the same with egg. The good news is that at three and a half she's free of it all (and has been since she was about 18 months) and eats cheese and yogurt.

Biza

My son had eczema until he was about one and a half. We had to use an extremely strong steroid ointment to clear it up, but that only took a few days. To keep his skin clear, we wash his clothes with special baby detergent, give him a bath every night with hypoallergenic baby bath and before he's completely dry slather him up with a hypoallergenic lotion. If he gets a rash we immediately use a hydrocortisone ointment. If you can, do try to go and see an allergist. It helps to know what is and what's not causing it. My son is allergic to milk and peanuts, although they weren't the cause of his eczema – allergies are so weird!

Jj

Our daughter has suffered with eczema since birth. The best thing for her skin is mild baths and lots of lotion, bath preparations and shampoo specially formulated for eczema. If it gets bad we use aqueous cream that you wash off, as an alternative to bath solutions. We have also found that sun creams have a very bad effect as they block the pores, so instead we use UVA suits and big sun hats if she has to be in the sun for extended periods of time.

Mj

What the experts say
Most cases are made worse by frequent bathing and the itching will increase in hot conditions.

Karen Sullivan (*Commonsense Healthcare for Children*)

My son had eczema for three years from when he was six weeks old. It now appears to have gone. The best treatment was lots of sun and sea water.

Nicks

I feel like I have spent the first couple of years of my son's life in a blur of specialist appointments and home nurses, who helped me bandage him from head to foot (with a mask at night). We had a delayed weaning programme, which introduced one food group at a time and discovered a multitude of food allergies and intolerances – nut, dairy, egg, berries, all leafy vegetables (I could go on). He has always drunk formula soya milk and we were advised to use special eczema preparations to wash him. We used steroids and emollients under the bandages. For washing clothes we use a special non-everything powder.

We found that hard water made things worse, as does hot weather when he gets sweaty and scratches. Gloves on sleep suits were good, but swaddling in a sheet also stopped him getting at himself quite so much at night. The good news is he is now totally clear.

I was advised to go on a restricted diet while pregnant with my second child and took supplements to fill the gaps. He is only allergic to egg and the second time around I feel much more aware of the signs, which means I can be proactive.

Modaddy

Mumsnet tip
If you think hard water is exacerbating the eczema problem, try an oatmeal bath. Put some oatmeal into a muslin nappy and tie the corners. Hang the 'bag' over the taps and let the hot water run through it. The resulting bath is very soothing.

Chinese Medicine seems to have worked for my nine-month-old. After four weeks her eczema is almost completely clear with no itching at all. It's quite expensive, though, and involves boiling up vile-smelling herbs every few days.

Josie

We tried Chinese herbal medicine, which seemed to work amazingly well – and fast – with no discernible side effects. The pong of the soup (mixed with breast-milk/formula) and the appalling nappies were pretty scary, though.

Fish

It's worth trying Chinese medicine but do try and get a recommendation for a practitioner if you can. In cold weather try putting bowls of water around the house near radiators, etc, to re-moisten the air. Also, consider putting in a water softener. It really helps and although it's expensive, it can save you money on washing powder and electricity.

HuncaMunca

I don't want to scare anyone off but you should realize that Chinese herbs can be risky because the strength of the medicine may be poorly controlled. Many Western doctors are very much opposed to their use, citing cases of liver and kidney damage. When we used Chinese medicine we saw our regular doctor every week and he checked our daughter's condition carefully – and it worked for us. One other tip: a lot of young children find aqueous cream an irritant to their skin. If this is the case try one of the other, more expensive, preparations (free on prescription).

Numbat

My three-year-old son had dreadful cradle cap and associated eczema from about three months old and I thought the problem was there to stay. The doctor prescribed a mild steroid which 'blitzed' it when it was at its worst, but I was dubious about using it for obvious reasons. I tried cutting out dairy products in my diet and his, but over a period of three months this made no noticeable difference. I was recommended a very heavy emollient cream, which I can get on prescription (handy as it's very expensive) and it seems to work.

Helento

Mumsnet tip

If you have a baby who won't stop scratching at night, try safety pinning a pair of socks over their hands. Fold the sock back over the safety pin to avoid accidents.

I understand people's reluctance to use steroid cream, but the one they give you for babies is usually very weak, and you can use it for a couple of days (very thinly) to get rid of a bad patch and then try the aqueous cream to keep it away. Another tip is to make sure your child wears only 100 per cent cotton next to their skin.

Janh

My latest discovery is 98 per cent organic cotton socks. They really help as my daughter's ankles are now her worst bits. Babies scratch mitts sewn on everything are also a good idea or if you want to dress the child in short sleeves, try socks pulled up to the elbows.

Babsa

A pair of girl's cotton tights cut to the gusset and put on as long gloves helps my son to stop breaking the skin when scratching at night. It might sound a bit harsh (or uncomfortable) but he seems to tolerate it well. It also means that I can put lots of white paraffin cream on without it going all over the place!

Ceejay

I have found that all the eczema creams/emollients only work for so long – a baby's skin seems to get used to the ingredients and then you have to move on to another, so it's worth swapping and changing if the eczema starts to get worse again. Also, don't have the heating on in the bedroom or have it on really low – it made a huge difference to us.

Delilah

We use special bath preparations, aqueous cream and emulsifying ointment – all on prescription. Liberal coatings of these generally keep my son's skin under control but the really bad patches are treated with a steroid cream. Unfortunately, every time we feel his skin is improving he starts to cut another tooth and it gets worse again. Five teeth down and lots still to go!

Late30smum

We were told to try for at least two ten-minute baths a day. This loosens the patches of eczema and allows the creams to penetrate beneath them. Also, try using a moisturizer in the bath, but no soap. We use an emulsifying cream, which seems to do the trick, but sometimes you have to go try a few before you get the right one. Moisturizing seems to be the key – we had to completely cover our daughter three times a day (yuk), and we still do it morning and night. Hydrocortisone creams (1 per cent) are useful when the eczema is under control as you can use it as soon as you spot a flare-up.

> **Mumsnet fact**
> If both parents are affected by an allergy, their child has a 60 per cent risk of developing the same allergy. British Allergy Foundation

Our daughter was tested for allergies, and was found to be allergic to house dust, and mildly allergic to dairy products. The dairy is easier to get rid of than the dust! Try avoiding furry cuddly toys. Anything that cannot go in the washing-machine should go into the freezer overnight (in a plastic bag) every two weeks.

We were prescribed a combined antihistamine and sedative for night-time, which stopped all the scratching and gave us our first nights of sleep for years. We found that our daughter's eczema was controllable, but it did take hard work and at least six to eight months before we really understood what we were doing and when to use which creams. She now has flare-ups which generally don't last longer than a week, and when they start we get very strict about the regime again.

Scooby2

My daughter had eczema from birth. It started as cradle cap – she used to nearly tear her ears off scratching. We were also prescribed an antihistamine syrup, which was fantastic – the itching stopped and we got some rest. She also had a milk allergy until she was about 18 months old and because of this I had to introduce each new food separately, a week at a time. I found that yogurt and bananas were the things that set off the eczema – not typical problem foods – tomatoes are one of the more common ones.

The water in my area is also said to be bad for this condition and, spookily, we went on holiday to Ireland for two weeks and the eczema cleared completely! It did return mildly when we got back but she now has the most beautiful skin without any signs of having had such a bad start.

Binza

> **Mumsnet tip**
> Calendula cream, although not great for the really cracking and bleeding variety, works a treat on small patches of eczema.

The local water does seem to make some eczema cases worse, particularly if it is very hard and has lots of lime in it. Unfortunately, my son scratches like mad in the bath. I use fairly tepid water – no soap-only prescribed products – even mitts taped onto his hands, but the water still drives him mad. It breaks my heart to see him suffer like that, especially when most babies enjoy bath-time so much. The only thing that works for us is steroids or a visit to my parents in Dorset, where the water is softer and has less lime. When we're there his skin is like silk after a few days.

Pj

My son had eczema when he was three months old, even though he was 100 per cent breastfed. My homeopath suggested that I 'clean out' my body with a weekend diet of only raw vegetables and rice (it was hell, but worth it!). He improved in two days. I then dramatically reduced my dairy intake and he stayed well. When he chose to stop breastfeeding, I tried regular organic milk and the eczema started again – but he had no problem with goat's milk. It won't work for everyone, but it worked for us.

Pupuce

One ongoing treatment is to give your baby flax-seed oil in his daily diet. You can get it at most health food shops and mix the oil in any cold foods (it can't be warmed as it goes rancid).

Jus

I think one of the hardest things to cope with is the frustration when things that worked for other people just don't work for you. I keep meeting parents of non-eczema kids who offer the latest theories (usually the ones you've tried already) and it feels like they're implying that if only you'd tried this or that your child would have perfect skin just like theirs (of course they're just trying to be helpful).

Also, being told your child will grow out of it, though probably true, doesn't much help when you're living through it. Living with a child with eczema is really hard – sleepless nights (you can't do sleep training or let them cry because irritation makes the skin worse), journeys are a nightmare (you feel guilty in case you've been feeding them the wrong thing, or guilty for giving or not giving them steroids).

Apart from all the treatments (hydrocortisone and lots of moisturizers worked for us), I found one of the best things was just talking to others who'd been through, or were going through the same thing – there's even an Eczema Society Advice Line. It's not life threatening, but at its worst eczema can ruin family life and just having that acknowledged can sometimes help.

Longjohn

Teething troubles – what to expect and what can you do to help?

My son is now seven months old and he still has no teeth even though we have had all the signs since he was three months: disturbed nights, dribbling in excess, red cheeks. He seems to go a few nights where he cries out and we put his dummy back in and he's okay, and then the fun begins for a few nights. Our last stint lasted about two weeks, some nights we were up every 30 minutes and little we did seemed to help. I find trying to guess the cause of his discomfort one of the most frustrating parts of motherhood.

Jps

> **Mumsnet tip**
> To cope with all the dribbling teething brings, put a very thin layer of barrier baby cream or petroleum jelly on the baby's chin. It stops that awful red, chapped look.

We use the homeopathic teething granules. Rubbing them into the gum can offer some relief and just offering a gum massage is supposed to help. It's hard to know whether it's definitely their teeth bothering them, though and I always wonder whether I am using it as an excuse for everything. Some babies suffer more than others and some don't seem to suffer at all.

Qd

I also found teething powders quite good as well as those gels that you rub into the gums, but unfortunately I had to resort quite often to baby Ibuprofen, which I found worked better than paracetamol. The good news is that not all teeth hurt equally and bizarrely, my daughter's front teeth were awful, but her first four molars came through without any problem at all. So if the first few cause problems, don't despair.

Elliesmum

What the experts say
Many babies suffer virtually no pain from teething until their first molars (some time after their first birthday). Don't assume that your baby is teething just because she is cranky, and don't assume that she'll be cranky just because she's teething.

Signe Larson and Kevin Osborn (*The Complete Idiot's Guide to Bringing Up Baby*)

Inflammation is the protective response of the tender gum tissue to the impending tooth, which it considers an intruder to fend off. It causes seemingly unbearable pain in some babies, but almost none in others.

Eisenberg, Murkoff and Hathaway (*What to Expect the First Year*)

I've found teething granules worked best cumulatively and so I gave a sachet every few hours on bad days. When things get really bad, especially at night, I give him teething linctus, which seems to work for my son, calming him down and presumably helping with pain. The makers claim that it also clears the congestion that comes with teething, which is great as he also gets cold-like symptoms when teeth are coming through. The only problem is that it's not that easy to find.

Incidentally, my first child had at least two teeth at six months, but the second had no teeth until nine months.

Janei

> **Mumsnet fact**
> US research has shown that teething can cause a temperature of up to 102 degrees. *Practical Parenting* magazine

Don't worry if teeth arrive early or late. My son has four teeth at 22 weeks old! The bottom ones came at eight weeks and the top ones have just arrived – thankfully without too much pain – and there are two more are on the way. My first son had no teeth until he was a year old.

Delilah

> **Mumsnet tip**
> Always keep in stock some ice-cream, fromage frais, Smash and anything else soft or cold for those days when the teeth are coming through and anything requiring chewing will just not do.

Our daughter has just produced her first two teeth at nearly six months old. She became hell to live with for about two days, which was a real change of character: very gripey, vocal and babbling a lot throughout the night, red cheeks, and a slight cough. Calpol helped. Once the teeth came through the gum, she returned to her old self. She enjoyed teething on a small clean wooden spoon as she seemed to like the slightly rough texture.

Newdad

My son, now six months, has had 'teething' symptoms for the past three months. He lost his appetite for anything but soggy rusk and fromage frais but three teeth have appeared over the last ten days. We're hoping for a bit of peace now.

Dm2

Don't underestimate tooth pain. I had problems with my wisdom teeth when my son was about four months and realized how crabby I was when I was in pain – and I knew what was happening to me, he didn't. Half an hour after taking something, I felt better. So, if half an hour after applying teething gel I had a happier baby, I knew he must have been feeling his teeth and I gave the recommended dose of Calpol.

Our son started drooling at Christmas and finally cut his first tooth in late April when he was about seven months old. I think teething's like colic, nothing works for very long but it's worth trying everything. Small ice-cubes had a surprise factor and the vibrating teether was another distraction, though if your baby is too small to work it alone you get finger cramp holding it. Peeled cucumber and frozen carrot sticks are other suggestions. Incidentally, warmth can increase the blood supply to the mouth and give an extra kick to the pain, so going off food or crying when feeding (even when hungry) is possible when teething.

Malmomum

My eight-month-old has recently been existing on yogurts, mashed banana and homeopathic teething remedy. I wondered if it might be heat causing trouble and have started to give him his savoury stuff straight from the fridge which seems to have worked.

Emmagee

My daughter always had bad nappy rash, unusual pooh and a runny nose when teething – not pleasant but at least it gives you some symptoms to look out for. I only used Calpol occasionally when she had a high temperature and found it worked very quickly. She also needed a lot of TLC and was very clingy. I know some people who have used ice-cold vegetables (but make sure they're not so cold, they're sticky) as teethers.

Minky

---

what the experts say

It is important to realise that the symptoms of teething do not include bronchitis, nappy rash, vomiting, diarrhoea or loss of appetite. These are symptoms of an illness, not teething and should not be treated as such.

Dr Miriam Stoppard (*New Baby Care Book*)

Both my boys get upset stomachs when teething and they also seem much more likely to succumb to any bug or virus which is going round, which sometimes requires treatment separately. So, if your baby is unwell, make sure you visit the doctor and don't just put all the symptoms down to teething.

Scally

Nappy rash – what worked for you?

There's a brilliant cream for nappy rash called Metanium. It comes in a tube, is very cheap and should be available in your local chemist's. You should only use a small amount and only need to spread it thinly over the affected area. The instructions say to do it so you can see the rash through the cream. We found that with one application overnight the rash cleared. We no longer use anything else and the one tube has lasted us for two years!

Debster

My son had a terrible nappy rash at the weekend: bright red and burning – we tried Metanium and it worked by the next day.

Maisy1

Metanium cream, available from pharmacies and used sparingly, often clears up persistent nappy rash where other creams don't work. It's also worth switching nappy brand. If there are white, curdy spots on the rash it might possibly be thrush. There are other things it could be, so if it won't go away it's worth going to see a doctor.

Clare2

Nappy rash can be caused by teething – my son has it every time a tooth comes through. I use nappy cream and leave my son without his nappy twice a day for at least 30 minutes a time.

Pupuce

I also found teething brought on nappy rash as it tended to result in runny, acid diarrhoea. Make sure you change the nappy straight away and leave it off as often as you dare. I also found some brands of nappy more likely to bring on a nappy rash than others, so if your baby's suffering it's worth trying a different make.

Nancy

What the experts say
Switch, at least temporarily, from disposable to cloth diapers (or vice versa). The change may make a big difference.

Signe Larson and Kevin Osborn
(*The Complete Idiot's Guide to Bringing Up Baby*)

Nappy rash is common and usually unmistakable and occurs whatever type of nappies you use – disposable or reusable fabric ones.

Dr Hilary Jones (*Your Child's Health*)

We found putting a thick layer of nappy cream with a layer of Vaseline over the top at night-time really helped. He was better the next morning. Whichever nappy cream you decide to use, keep with the same one for a few days as constantly changing to different brands can upset the skin balance and hinder healing.

Dixie

We did much the same, but put Metanium on top of the nappy cream. It had been getting worse for a week, but once we started doing this it started to get better.

Biza

We found that the best cure for nappy rash was olive oil. Dab cotton wool into a bowl of olive oil and spread it generously on the baby's bottom – it works miracles! It works especially well when left on overnight.

Emilys

Another old fashioned remedy that worked for us was to separate an egg and wipe the egg white onto the area affected by nappy rash. This forms a breathable barrier while the rash heals and is more natural than nappy creams.

Benjie

If you're using real cotton nappies, silk liners are very good – just line the nappy overnight with no barrier cream and this will get rid of it.

You can also make your own remedy. Take a quarter of a muslin, soak it in chamomile and honey tea, then use it instead of a liner. It's weird using something damp to cure nappy rash but it almost seems to cure it overnight. Chamomile is excellent on sore skin – if you can get some as an essential oil. Tea tree and lavender have very similar effects, so you may only want to use one or the other – though please read the instructions about diluting and strengths carefully.

If the nappy rash is caused by teething, midwives used to recommend lemon barley water as it reduces the acid in the urine that causes the reaction.

Wends

> **Mumsnet fact**
> You will change more than 7000 nappies (per child).
> Signe Larson MD and Kevin Osborn
> (*The Complete Idiot's Guide to Bringing Up Baby*)

I found a herbal cream called calendula. It works amazingly well and it doesn't block the pores like the zinc-based barrier creams. It seems to deal with the irritation and discomfort very quickly.

Emmagee

I found that soon after my daughter was born she started getting the most awful nappy rash. It got so bad that it was raw and bleeding, and it even got infected. I tried all the usual things to clear it up but I noticed that certain things made it worse, like wet wipes and baby lotion, so I stopped using those and switched to cotton wool with warm water.

Mumsnet fact
Up to 35 per cent of babies suffer from nappy rash
Eisenberg, Murkoff and Hathaway (*What to Expect the First Year*)

It started to clear up but still would not go away completely. It turned out that she was highly allergic to lanolin, which is in just about everything, including the lotion contained in her nappy (which was released when she peed). I switched brands, the nappy rash cleared up and she has not had it to this day.

I can't begin to describe what a treat it was when the extra sensitive wipes were brought out. She is fine with those, too.

Pie

Vomiting – what's normal and what can you do?

There are two types of vomiting: possetting and reflux, and they're frequently confused. Possetting is when a baby burps and some milk comes up with the wind. This normally stops once a baby is on solids.

Reflux is a medical condition, which is caused when the sphincter at the top of the stomach is weak. It's actually weak in all babies, but weaker in some than others, hence reflux comes in varying degrees. Usually, though not always, a baby with reflux will be sick with or without burping, because it's not wind related. Babies with reflux are also sick much more frequently.

What the experts say
[pre 12 weeks]
By far the most common reason for babies to vomit is if they have been fed too much.

Dr Yehudi Gordon (*Birth and Beyond*)

Possetting is due largely to a floppy valve at the junction between the lower end of the gullet and the stomach which allows swallowed milk to come up again. As the child grows older, the valve becomes tighter and more efficient, so possetting eventually stops.

Dr Hilary Jones (*Your Child's Health*)

It can happen to breast and bottle-fed babies and isn't caused by over-feeding. It's practically impossible to overfeed a baby. Unless you're applying pressure to squeeze the milk down its throat, they naturally stop when they're full. Likewise, the build of the baby makes no difference, though for some reason, reflux occurs more frequently in boys.

Treatments are available but it's important to go and see a doctor to get a firm diagnosis. Eventually babies do grow out of reflux as the muscle strengthens naturally over time.

Drjake

People who haven't dealt with a child like this cannot appreciate how wearing it is. My eldest son was very sick after every meal, and sometimes up to three or four hours after a meal, until he was six months. It took years off the life of my washing machine. It wasn't until I had my second child that I realized quite how bad my first had been. They do grow out of it, and there are no long-term effects.

We did try limiting my son's feeds, and this seemed to help a little. In retrospect my second child winded far more easily, and much more convincingly, so possibly this was the route of the problem.

Scally

My seven-month-old son has been sicky from the day he was born. I know it's all down to a weak muscle but it seems to be worse for the poor mums than the babies. it's not helpful to be told not to worry when you spend your life washing your clothes, their clothes, bedding, towels, carpets! Solids didn't help either.

My doctor got me to keep a 'vomit chart' for a week, keeping track of when I fed him, when he was sick, and how much. He took me seriously when he saw that sometimes it was 25 times a day. We saw a paediatrician, and I've now been told that the problem is probably acid related, so I have an antacid to give him three times a day.

> **Mumsnet tip**
> If the baby's possetting a lot and is bottle fed, it's worth trying to 'split' a bottle, feeding half then the other half about an hour later. Another thing worth trying is to change the brand of formula – this worked for me. Also, wind them often.

The paediatrician also gave some practical advice. If you're not averse to them, a dummy can help as the baby keeps swallowing, thus strengthening the offending muscle. After the baby has been fed, don't lie them flat. Either hold them in a semi-prone position, or prop them up on pillows (gravity helps to keep the food in the tummy). If you're bottle feeding, there is an anti-reflux milk you can get, which basically thickens up once it's been drunk, making it more difficult for it to come back up. Finally, rest assured that if your baby is putting on weight well, is meeting the 'milestones' and is happy, there isn't a serious problem.

Kanga

I found my son stopped being sick at around nine months after I took him to a cranial osteopath. She manipulated his diaphragm, back, neck and head over a course of three sessions. His appetite improved dramatically and the vomiting stopped. I remember distinctly this almost immediate improvement. I actually took my son to help sort out his sleeping problems, so this was an added bonus.

Emmam

What the experts say
If you are getting worried about the amount of food your baby is losing, try spilling five millilitres of milk on purpose to give you a standard of comparison.

Penelope Leach *(Your Baby and Child)*

A friend's child had reflux, but it wasn't diagnosed until she was nine months old. She had been told by a health visitor to wean early because her daughter wasn't gaining weight and didn't seem to eat much. In retrospect she wished she'd stuck to her guns and demanded to see the doctor earlier. When she was eventually prescribed heartburn medicine, the change was quite dramatic. She started eating twice as much as before and put on weight – she must have been in so much pain before. She tells everyone to follow their instincts and make a fuss if they think something is wrong with their child.

Biza

My daughter has reflux – it does tend to be at its worse around three or four months then it starts to settle down – she's now ten months and is only sick around once a day. Having tried heartburn medicine and milk thickener, the hospital did a PH probe, where a probe was inserted up her nose and into the stomach. This measured the stomach acid over 24 hours and confirmed that her reflux was quite severe. It was a fairly unpleasant procedure, but the hospital insisted on it before they'd give us any medicine. At first, she was on medicine seven times a day, but now she only takes it twice a day.

I don't like her taking so much medicine, but reflux can make a baby very uncomfortable and cause scarring of the gullet, if left untreated. The only consolation is that it's not caused by anything serious and it will get better in time.

Sometimes you have to persevere with your health visitor if you feel there's a problem – they do tend to be a bit dismissive of reflux because they see it a lot.

Joanne

Meningitis C – should you have your children vaccinated?

My daughter had the Meningitis C vaccine and I am afraid to say she was not a well girl afterwards. I had a one-year-old with 'PMT' for two weeks and a constant cough. She has now had 14 vaccines injected in her little life and I am saying enough is enough so I am not taking her for her MMR.

Blt

My daughter missed her Meningitis C vaccine as a baby, and now, aged 4 I don't feel inclined to have it given to her. Babies are not capable of telling parents or carers when they have a stiff neck or feel ill but at three years plus my daughter is no longer mouthing toys and can describe symptoms.

Suew

The evidence seems to show that the Meningitis C vaccination programme has already had the effect of lowering the number of youngsters contracting the illness. My four children all had the jab, and only one had any obvious side effect, namely a sore arm, which was hard and hot where the needle entered the skin. You would not have known the others had had an injection at all. However, I have read that the health department is doing a follow-up on the side-effects, due to numerous reports of headaches, dizziness and sore arms. I think, like many parents, that meningitis is so horrific that I am glad they can be protected from one strain at least.

Minou

> **Mumsnet fact**
> Since the meningitis C vaccine was launched, cases in 15 to 17-year-olds have fallen by 77 per cent and in babies by 73 per cent.
>
> The *Guardian*

I agonized over the MMR jab but eventually went with it. Any perceived problems seemed to be caused by the combination of all three at once. So when it came to Meningitis C vaccine the risks of the disease (for me) outweighed the risks of the vaccine.

Emmagee

I had meningococcal septicaemia (basically Meningitis C with blood poisoning thrown in) a few years ago and nearly died from it. As an adult, I was lucky enough to recognize the seriousness of the symptoms (my doctor certainly didn't!) and managed to get an ambulance to take me to hospital, where I was on an antibiotic and saline drip for weeks. I now have a six-month-old son and couldn't wait to get him vaccinated. To my thinking, if a doctor struggles to recognize the symptoms in an articulate adult, he might not manage it with a child. I will do everything in my power to make sure that my son doesn't have to take that chance. Meningitis really, really kills – and quickly.

Alli

> **Mumsnet fact**
> Meningitis C is most common in babies and is the commonest cause of death in children aged 1 to 5 years of age in the UK.
>
> Department of Health

My husband is a doctor and our eight-month-old daughter has had and will have all the vaccinations offered to her. We don't know a single doctor that doesn't do the same. People don't always realize that meningitis can kill a baby within a few hours. A toddler might not be able to tell you what's wrong. We have the chance with the Meningitis C vaccine to offer children and young people immunity against this illness, and as responsible parents it really is our job to take this chance.

Fp

We are living in a much more complacent era than, say, our own parents or grandparents. Most of us don't know the heartbreak of losing a child to diphtheria or measles. I think this clouds our view of vaccinations. We are now all more concerned with the side effects of the immunizations rather than the effects of these horrible illnesses.

My son has had all the vaccinations offered to him since birth with no side effects whatsoever. I could never forgive myself if he wasn't vaccinated, caught one of these illnesses and died from complications.

My sister-in-law had a very worrying time during her early pregnancy when she came into contact with a child with German measles. She had to have repeated blood tests and spend a week off work. Fortunately, everything turned out okay. So please, don't just think about whether your child may be ill from the vaccinations, but think about the effects on others, too – pregnant women and children who, for one reason or another, are unable to have the immunizations and so are at greater risk.

Of course, I'm only human, and I too worried about the side effects of the vaccinations on my child. But remember, for every horror story, there are a thousand or more good ones!

Emmam

> **Mumsnet fact**
> The Chinese were the first to practice an early form of vaccination called variolation, which was carried out as early as the 10th century.
>
> www.immunisation.org

The MMR jab – should you or shouldn't you?

My son had the MMR jab at 13 months – no reactions, side effects, nothing. He didn't even cry when he had the injection. He also had the meningitis C jab at the same time. Thousands of children are immunized annually with no ill effects. Sadly there are always examples of things that go wrong. We all hope our kids are not the ones who suffer the side effects, but statistically, the MMR jab is less likely to harm a child than a car.

We are extremely lucky to have an immunization programme. If everyone took up the vaccines then in time we may actually be able to do away with them, as the diseases are eradicated from society. Polio is practically non-existent now, thanks to the immunization programme.

Emmam

I agonized about MMR but went for it in the end because the link with autism wasn't really convincing and my doctor had her children done. The illnesses are very serious: mumps for boys, rubella for girls, measles for both.

I did leave it quite late though, on the grounds that an older child might cope better with a large dose of vaccines – but this was just instinct, not scientific fact, I freely admit.

Javarose

> **Mumsnet fact**
> In 1999, following a high-profile vaccination programme, only 2,500 people contracted measles in the UK. In 1998 86,000 were affected and 16 died. *The Times*

I have a close friend whose nephew has suffered something which is potentially linked to his MMR – a condition that has gradually led to the decline of all his senses. Obviously this has caused great distress to his family and since no doctor can assure my friend it is not linked to MMR, her children have not been vaccinated. I know two doctors have not vaccinated their children. In spite of this, I still feel that generally vaccinations are a good thing – just that people should know there are risks and do their best to minimize them. For example, I will do everything I can to ensure my daughter gets her next set of shots when she is at the best of health.

Suew

I don't think anyone would deny that there is the chance of a child having a
bad reaction (and yes, this can be anything from a rash to, in extreme cases,
permanent disability) but this needs to be put into context.

There's nothing wrong with wanting to know the facts but the problem with
the MMR debate is that the consequences of people not having the jab threaten
society. Measles is one of the most infectious of all childhood diseases and
worldwide is still a major killer of children. There are a number of children who,
for various reasons, are unable to be immunized. What a tragedy if some of these
children end up deaf, blind or dead through needless exposure to the virus. The
consequences of rubella for pregnant women are, of course, well documented.

What the experts say
Mumps can cause viral meningitis and is a major cause of permanent
deafness which can be sudden in onset and affect one or both ears. Before the
introduction of a vaccine there were epidemics every three years in the UK.
                                                              Department of Health

Mumps vaccines have a chequered history and most experts believe that the
condition is not serious, provided it is acquired before teenage years.
                              Karen Sullivan (*Commonsense Healthcare for Children*)

I took the view that the vaccine probably did have a small risk attached to it, as
does virtually everything to do with health. However, this risk in my view is
outweighed by my overall social responsibility. A child I was at school with died
from complications of measles. It's all very well to say people are entitled to their
view – let's just hope that view doesn't lead to the death of somebody else's child.
                                                                        Croppy

Our son had his MMR jab, there was no question about it. I have a lot of deaf
friends – all the same age – who all lost their hearing after contracting measles
during in a major outbreak of the disease in Cardiff and Newport.
                                                                       Bruntwig

All three of my children had MMR jabs and are fine. I too, worried about them
having the vaccine, but decided on balance that I would prefer them not to suffer
the illnesses.

                                                                      Chanelno5

> **Mumsnet fact**
> Ninety countries worldwide are now using the MMR vaccine and no coun-
> try is recommending the use of single vaccines over MMR.
>
> GlaxoSmithKline

If us mothers could only have the jabs for them it would be so much easier! I was particularly nervous about having my son vaccinated. He got a fever after 48 hours but it was short-lived.

Amber1

I dithered for a few weeks wondering whether to have single or triple vaccinations, then my daughter developed a horrific rash one weekend. I was convinced she had something terrible like measles and felt completely sick. Luckily, it turned out to be a strange virus. She had her MMR jab as soon as she was fit again. Believe me, the utter horror of thinking my child had got something dangerous because I hadn't immunized her was sickening and, if she had had one of the illnesses and been seriously ill, I would have had a very hard time living with myself.

What the experts say
One in every 2,500–5,000 cases of measles cases proves fatal. Worldwide, measles kills more than a million people each year.

www.immunisation.org

Measles are still common, but it is no longer as severe a condition as it once was. It can be safely and successfully treated with natural remedies and the best advice is to avoid the jab if you can.

Karen Sullivan (*Commonsense Healthcare for Children*)

The MMR jab was fine, she was off-colour for about a month – which my doctor failed to warn me about – but I feel much better now knowing she is protected. I'm trying to understand that everyone has a choice but if, God forbid, anything happened to your child, could you live with the guilt? As we have seen before, break-outs of these diseases will occur, so how can you run the risk?

Janus

Both my sons have had the MMR jab and have had no side effects. My eldest has just been diagnosed with aspergers syndrome (a form of autism) and now everyone is asking whether it was because of 'that' jab. In my opinion he has shown this behaviour since he was a baby.

Loobie

It's not just our son that I considered when he had his MMR jab but also the welfare of the other children with whom he comes into contact and the expectant mothers that he may encounter as he grows up (not least me, should we have another child). The consequences of measles and/or rubella on a child and on others can be devastating. It's not just the fact of dying but dying a long and lingering death with the complications of encephalitis. I have personal experience of this and can't imagine the selfishness of leaving either my child or someone else's open to that kind of risk.

Harrysmum

Mumsnet fact
In the past ten years the US National Vaccine Compensation Programme has paid out over $1 billion in payments to vaccine damaged children of which a 14 per cent share has been paid out for MMR or its components. www.jabs.org

I've decided to miss out on the MMR jab at least for a while. My main reason is that as my little boy has egg allergies – and so I was recommended that he be given it in hospital in case something goes wrong. Also, my husband had a very bad reaction to the measles jab as a child (involving paralysis of his lower body for a few days). Doctors seem to give different advice – some say don't have the MMR if your child has major allergies, other say go ahead. I've decided to err on the side of caution. If he has outgrown his allergies by the time he starts school – and advice seems to be that he will – then I'll get him done then.

Lizp

I am terribly torn about whether or not to have my daughter vaccinated with MMR. I wasn't and have grown up pretty healthily. The reason for my hesitation is that my daughter has reacted badly to vaccinations shortly after receiving them. She suffered terribly with whooping cough symptoms after her second jab. She was also very ill after the meningitis C vaccination – not as ill as if she had had meningitis C – but fairly debilitated for several weeks. She also has a mild allergy to eggs. I worry in case my daughter gets measles and dies, simple as that. I worry in case my daughter suffers a terrible reaction from the vaccine and lives.

My middle road, at this stage, is to give her a homeopathic nosode, which can reduce the chances of her catching measles, should there be an epidemic, because if she is going to have the vaccination I would rather wait until she is older.

The Government pays out several million pounds annually to families of vaccine-damaged children. Vaccines are safe, though – the government says so.

Blt

> **Mumsnet fact**
> With the MMR vaccine there is a risk of 1 case of febrile convulsions for around every 1000 doses given. The risk of convulsions from measles is 1 case in every 200.   Department of Health

A good friend of mine didn't have her son vaccinated for fear of complications, and shortly afterwards he was diagnosed with an autistic spectrum disorder. If he had been vaccinated, I imagine she would have spent years wracked with guilt, thinking her decision to have him vaccinated was the cause.

Steve

When you're faced with articles claiming that there could be a link between MMR and autism – no matter how slight – of course you're going to agonize over decisions. I would have my child immunized against these diseases if I can have them administered separately (even if it's just for peace of mind).

Joz

> **Mumsnet fact**
> Over the last two years the UK's Autism Helpline has had more calls about where to obtain single vaccines, than about whether to vaccinate.
> National Autistic Society

I took the decision to go for single vaccines after a chat with health professionals. Their main concern was that all three of these illnesses have the potential to cause brain swelling-type complications in some cases. They thought that immunizing against all three at once was a bit of a viral overload on a small child and that spacing the jabs out over a couple of months reduced the slight risk of those kinds of complications.

I do think it's possible to be concerned about vaccine safety without compromising 'herd immunity' and putting others at risk. As our son is in daycare with other children, I felt it was our responsibility to have him immunized, but I certainly don't assume he is now completely safe from any of these illnesses. The Dublin outbreak of measles a few years ago affected several fully-immunized children in its case list. And one little guy at our son's nursery got a nasty dose of rubella only nine months after his MMR. So we will be off to the doctor's pronto if he develops any feverish rash symptoms.

Junior

> **Mumsnet fact**
> Eight out of ten parents believe the NHS should offer a choice between the MMR vaccine and three individual jabs.

Incidentally, in retrospect I would also have asked for the tetanus part of the tetanus/diphtheria/whooping cough jabs to be given once my son was mobile. Your chances of getting tetanus lying in a Moses basket in a flat 50 feet above garden level are remote, but when you start walking and heading eagerly for the rose garden in the park, then you need some protection.

Clare2

The argument against the triple jab is that it bombards the immune system so that it cannot create its own immunity to all elements of it at once. This is why the booster is necessary, in order to pick up the five to ten per cent of children who do not gain immunity from the original jab. By giving the single vaccine, the immune system can concentrate on generating immunity to one vaccine at a time. The downside to this is that some side effects exist with the single vaccines, too.

There are always risks, but whereas I know what the risks are if my child contracts any of the diseases in the triple jab, I do not know what the risks are if they have the vaccine.

Berries

This is such a personal issue that all we can do is recognize that, as parents, we make our decisions, right or wrong, for our own reasons. Sometimes I wish I had blind faith in the medical profession so I could let them make the choice for me, because it's a minefield out there!

Lill

5

Your Health

Introduction

The bundle in your arms may be priceless, but that doesn't mean it comes without a cost – not least to your health. Unless you're one of the lucky ones who squeeze out babies effortlessly, the chances are that childbirth has left you with some scars, either mental, physical or both.

Perhaps you're one of the many (one in five according to the Department of Health) women in the UK who have a Caesarean. The fact that it's an increasingly common procedure is scant comfort when your belly's been rummaged about in as if it's a voluminous handbag. Whether it's elective or emergency, the aftermath of a C-section can leave you exhausted and in pain. Add to this a small creature that needs feeding, changing and cuddling almost hourly, and it's no wonder women struggle to cope. So what can you expect when you have a C-section, and what can you do to make life easier?

If you had a vaginal birth you now understand all those references to inflatable rubber rings and valley cushions. The jokes about 'leaking' when you cough aren't so funny when it's your private parts that have been ravaged and it's easy to believe that your pelvic floor is damaged beyond repair. Can it be fixed? Around 14 per cent of women have an episiotomy each year in this country (Department of Health), so you're not alone in wondering if the patchwork quilt that was once your nether regions will ever resemble normality and whether sex will one day be something to enjoy rather than to endure.

That's always assuming you can bear to unwrap your body post-birth. There is nothing quite so depressing as being asked when the baby's due months after giving birth. Unless you're one of those irritating types who leave hospital in their pre-pregnancy jeans, chances are you'll need to make at least some effort in order to get back to anything like your normal body shape. What diets work and how can you stick to them when your entire body is crying out for comfort food? And what about exercise, can anything really conquer the most common legacy of childbirth – a saggy tummy?

If and when you do finally venture back into the boudoir, how do you ensure that you aren't going to end up with a little 'accident' nine months down the line? Is there such a thing as the perfect contraceptive method?

And then, as if the birth and its aftermath aren't shocking enough, there's the white-knuckle ride of life with a small baby. Sleep deprivation, isolation – just being responsible for another human being – all take their toll, not just physically but mentally as well. Whether it's PMS, baby blues or full-blown post-natal depression, it's crucial to understand that you're not alone in your feelings of anger, resentment or despair. There are countless others who've felt the same and have suffered, survived and gone on to enjoy their life as a parent.

Post-partum perineal trauma – what can you do to help?

I ended up with a forceps delivery, had an episiotomy and tore. I was incredibly sore and my stitches were pulled very tight. We didn't try to have sex for five months and it hurt me so much that we didn't try again for another two months and even then I found it an uncomfortable experience rather than something pleasurable. My doctor said there was still some scar tissue healing internally and suggested doing some internal massage to help it to break down. I reckoned sex was probably similar and did find that eventually things got more comfortable to the point where it even became enjoyable again!

Molly1

In my experience it can take about a year for an episiotomy scar to heal. I had a horrid episiotomy: the stitches were too tight and then the midwife loosened them, only for the whole lot to come apart. I was advised to just leave it and have it repaired after the next baby. It took ages to heal, weeks on a rubber ring and unable to walk properly and sex was very uncomfortable for months. However, it did get better and it's amazing how such a delicate area can repair itself in time.

Jessi

> **Mumsnet tip**
> If you're suffering with stitches or a tear after giving birth, invest in some baby wipes. They're far more soothing than ordinary toilet paper.

I had an episiotomy with number one, a second degree tear and stitches for number two and another episiotomy for number three. My nethers now resemble a patchwork quilt! It takes a surprisingly long time for things to feel more comfortable in this department, and they never do feel exactly as they were before. I don't think that my first episiotomy was sewn up very well, but did feel slightly easier after my second baby – perhaps because everything was even saggier and more stretched. The episiotomy for my third birth was sewn up really well by a doctor and hasn't given me as much trouble as number one.

Chanelno5

I had an episiotomy and quite frankly I found the stitching up far more stressful and traumatic than the actual giving birth. It took nearly two hours because they kept undoing the stitches as they felt they wouldn't heal right. When I felt brave enough to get a mirror and look I was horrified and I'm sure it has psychologically scarred me. A friend of mine eventually got the doctor to recommend hers was re-done and said it was worth it. Everyone I've spoken to has taken time to get over having an episiotomy so I'm not alone, but if I'm honest I still feel a bit uncomfortable about sex – though I'm not sure if that's a psychological or physical problem. One bit of advice I would give is don't look down there!

Selja

What the experts say

About one in four of us has either had an episiotomy or a natural tear at some stage during the process... however, the healing process is quite remarkable and normal sexual activity is likely to be resumed sooner than you think, even if things do feel a little different at first.

Penny Wilson (*Wipe: Survival Tactics for Parents with Attitude*)

I looked, too, and it freaked me out completely. This was after the midwife described me as 'the lady with the pucker'. I would recommend a warm bath with lavender oil as often as you possibly can and, gross as it sounds, drying yourself with a cool hairdryer rather than a towel (hones,t it works!). Mine took about a year to feel 'normal' again.

Candy

> **Mumsnet tip**
> I really recommend lavender oil – it's brilliant for speeding up healing.

I had my first baby nine months ago and ended up having a forceps delivery – they had to turn him as he got stuck with his head sideways while he was still quite high up. Needless to say, this involved a 'generous' episiotomy – it's generally okay but I'm still sore around the scar. Sex is uncomfortable and doesn't seem to be getting easier with time. However, having a look and seeing how long the scar actually is did make me realize that it would take a while to settle down.

Ouch

With my first child I had an episiotomy plus a third degree tear, so there were a lot of stitches. Sex afterwards was always painful, to the point that I went to my doctor about it, but didn't have much luck. Sex only really stopped being painful after the birth of my second child five years later when I tore slightly again and was re-stitched.

Lou33

> **Mumsnet fact**
> It is estimated that over 85 per cent of women who have a vaginal birth will sustain some degree of perineal trauma and of these 60–70 per cent will require suturing. www.2womenshealth.co.uk

I had an episiotomy and a lot of stitches the first time around. Sex was incredibly painful and this put a strain on our relationship. I was prescribed a gel that actually acted as an anaesthetic to the painful area. I also used KY Jelly and it really helped the problem. After the birth of my second child I also had two tears and quite a few stitches, but I couldn't believe how quickly I recovered and had sex after a couple of months without any pain.

Glitterbabe

I tore badly and, like many others, ended up with (what felt like) a patchwork quilt, plus a lot of pain and discomfort. It turned out that part of the internal wound simply hadn't healed properly. I had it cauterized twice (not nearly as bad as it sounds!) and eventually had surgery to remove the 'bad' patch. It's not a difficult procedure at all, though it's done under a general anaesthetic, but you're back home the same day. It's worth being prepared with a valley cushion and a comfortable chair!

Wmf

> **Mumsnet fact**
> As many as 40 per cent of first-time mums still feel pain during sex six months after the birth. *Baby*

I too found sex very painful after my first baby. My doctor checked me and said the stitches had left a nasty scar that would need time to heal, but if the pain didn't stop I could have surgery to remove the scar tissue. She told me it would be like having the stitches done all over again! However, we went on holiday soon afterwards and I got drunk and we managed fine! But then when we tried when I was sober it hurt again. This convinced me that most of it was psychological. So I recommend KY Jelly and a bit of Dutch courage.

Rhubarb

I had six months of painful sex which turned out to be the result of a cyst on my episiotomy scar (very common, apparently). I had a simple (and quick) operation to remove it (under general anaesthetic) and was pain-free within a week or two. The cyst feels like a small but painful lump.

YumMum

I clearly remember my midwife having a look at my stitches a week after I'd given birth, tutting and saying 'now that looks a bit brutal'. If anything was guaranteed to give me a complex, that was!

Enid

Caesareans – what to expect afterwards and what helps

I had an elective C-section and was out of hospital in three days. Looking back, I thought that I was a lot fitter than I actually was, though. However, I got around really well and didn't really do anything different to people who'd given birth naturally. I had a spinal, which is easier to recover from than a general anaesthetic. One thing I would have asked for was for the midwives to look after the baby on the first night. I was in a communal ward so every time a baby snuffled I thought it was mine and struggled out of bed, discovered it wasn't my baby and got back into bed. Also half my scar was red and lumpy for around two years but it did eventually fade and the itchiness and lumpiness subsided.

Paula1

> **Mumsnet fact**
> In 2000–01 over 21 per cent of deliveries were by Caesarean section; more than half of these were emergency Caesareans.
>
> Department of Health

I felt far less tired after my elective C-section than my emergency C-section – the emergency came after several hours of labour and it isn't called labour for nothing! The elective birth experience was fantastic in comparison – no pain, quick, calm and lovely. However, although I seemed to have made a quick recovery – home in two days and then out at a party – but I think I took it too fast and my surface wound started gaping after a week. I had steri-strips put on it and had to lie down for a few days. So, even if you feel great, don't try and do too much too soon. One positive thing I found was that my husband was very involved in all the baby care right from the start. He did the first bath and all the early nappies because it was just much easier for him to get around and carry the baby. He enjoyed it, it helped him bond and feel involved, and I got some rest.

Bizu

What the experts say
Post-operatively these four remedies are invaluable, each taken in 200c potency, four times a day for three days, then three times a day for four days...Arnica...Hypericum...Bellis perennis...and Calendula...Moving and walking realigns the cut sheath and can help to diminish the pain.

Dr Yehudi Gordon (*Birth and Beyond*)

The first night, the hospital offered to take the baby so I could rest. I said no, feeling I wanted her right by my side. It was hard to sleep and I had to call a nurse anyway if she cried, so with hindsight, I should have let them take her.

Sjs

Keep one changing set upstairs and another downstairs so you don't have to go up and down all day. Take it slowly: you think you're fine and then overdo it slightly and the stitches and cut really don't thank you.

Even quite a while after the birth I found Hoovering problematic – so that's one excuse to either get a cleaner or someone else to do it – or live in dust. If I overdid it, it would ache quite sharply, so much so I thought I had an infection, but it was okay.

> **Mumsnet tip**
> Take all the pain relief going, sleep as much as possible and accept all the help on offer. Don't do anything but look after the baby and yourself (just think what you would normally do if you had had major abdominal surgery!)

The best advice I got was to wear 'granny pants', the big ones that come over your tummy and hips so they don't hurt or restrict your scar. Looked great on the washing line! Also take all the painkillers on offer. With regard to driving, they say if you feel you can manage a hard emergency stop then you should be okay. I could drive after five to six weeks, but before that I would have been afraid of pain or injury if something difficult had arisen. It helped to have a car with power steering.

Maisy1

I found holding my relatively heavy baby to breastfeed put pressure on my scar and hurt – so one of those 'v' pillows in front of me for support was a great help. I ended up wearing my Lycra aerobic shorts under some jogging pants if I had to move around much or go out, but it's also important to get air to the scar too, so I tried to wear looser clothes when I was around the house.

The thing I was most worried about was how the scar would look, but two years on, mine is very pale and not massively noticeable.

Motherofone

I came home from hospital after three days and was out shopping the day after that. It wasn't a pleasant experience, I was frightened to stand up straight in case my belly popped open (of course it didn't, but it felt it might at the time) but despite that I would definitely opt for another one.

Kid

> **Mumsnet tip**
> After any birth, but particularly a C-section, online supermarket shopping is a godsend. You can order what you want, however heavy, and get it all delivered in the next day or two. It's worth signing up in advance as the first order takes some time to set up.

I think I was lucky as I had no problems at all after my C-section, apart from the first couple of days in hospital when I was a little drowsy (probably the general anaesthetic). I have a very modest scar and experienced no real discomfort. I stayed in hospital for five days, mostly due to my son losing weight so we weren't 'allowed' out. I was home on day six and cooking lunch for guests on day seven. I was also driving quite quickly because when I checked with the insurers I was told there was no 'six week rule' for insurance purposes – more for medical reasons and as I felt so well I assumed it would be okay.

Lindy

As soon as I had the operation I started taking arnica and I am sure this helped me heal better. Within a day I was walking, holding and feeding my baby and had taken a shower. I was in hospital for three days altogether, but was really scared about going home. My partner couldn't take more than a couple of days off work and I lived in a flat so I had to climb up and down stairs, which I did very slowly. I used to get twinges for quite a while after my C-section – I saw these as warning signs that I was doing too much.

Batters

I've had four C-Sections and healed quite well after all of them, though I did find the scar tucked in further every time!

Janh

> **Mumsnet tip**
> I was given peppermint oil in warm water by a doctor after my C-section. It really helped when my bowels were in spasm and causing pain.

I was amazed at how long it took my scar to heal and my middle to feel normal after my C-section. I felt bruised and very sensitive for about six months. My scar itched for at least 12 months and three years on it's still a bit red and lumpy in places. I also felt very numb internally, as if I'd lost control of parts of my body. Now I know a vaginal birth is no walk in the park but Caesareans are no picnic, either.

The catheter and drain for the wound after the operation was not a pleasant experience, either and I also suffered from appalling wind for days afterwards (fairly common I've since discovered). That's something they don't tell you about.

Berta

I had pain for quite a few months after the operation – a sharp internal ache, higher than the scar and a strange tingly numbness, too. According to a friendly doctor the internal stitches were pulling on muscles which in turn were affecting nerves and I was advised to take pain killers and wait for it to pass.

Dm2

I had numbness after my C-Section with number one and it lasted six months. With number two there was no numbness at all.

Rosebud

I had a Caesarean eight months ago and my scar still itches at the wrong time (like when I'm shopping or when friends are visiting!) and was painful for several months after the event. The pain has now passed, though and hopefully the itching will, too.

Lj

Mumsnet fact
Between 1997–98 and 2000–01 the Caesarean rate increased from 18.2 per cent to 21.5 per cent.   Department of Health

I was really concerned about looking after an energetic two and a half-year-old and not being able to lift. But a few nights without a bath didn't kill him. With hindsight I think as long as you can ignore all the housework and enjoy just spending time at home with the children it can be a great time. Keep expectations low as regards going out and about. You usually have lots of visitors anyway, so encourage them to do a bit of Hoovering while they're there!

Elvis

I just told my two-year-old that mum couldn't pick him up for a while because I had a sore tummy and he seemed to accept that. We got a plastic step to help me get into the bath. I would also suggest getting some paid or family help for the first few weeks if possible.

Sophy

After niggling pain for nearly a year after my Caesarean I finally read that having pain for this length of time is common. Now, sixteen months post-op, I really don't get anything worth mentioning any more, just a bit of tight pulling on the scar.

The hardest thing is having to stay in hospital for five days (the norm) especially if you have children at home. What really helped me was having friends and family who popped down to the shops for all the things I'd forgotten. The best advice is to walk a little, rest a lot, don't stretch too much and allow others to pass the baby to you and put the baby down again in the first 24 hours (I breastfed lying flat on my back within hours of our children being born). Even though it's a major operation it's amazing how quickly you recover and are able to start caring for your baby yourself. I was on my own from the third to fourth week.

Rivi

Pelvic floor – can you fix it? (Yes, you can!)

My incontinence started in pregnancy but after the birth it was just dreadful, completely ruining the first couple of months with my daughter. I was utterly shocked and devastated. If you have serious pelvic floor damage, like me, there is an operation you can have, but I've been told that as I'm only 25 I will have to wait until I'm older and have completed my family as any subsequent child would ruin the surgeon's handiwork. Every time I've asked a specialist 'this is quite common, isn't it?' they've looked at me with a mixture of pity and bemusement, and said, 'No, we've never actually come across this before'.

Bee100

Mumsnet fact
Seventy-five per cent of women questioned in the largest study on health after childbirth accomplished in Britain still had symptoms of stress incontinence a year after the birth of their baby, with few women seeking medical advice for their condition even though it inevitably modified their lifestyle.   Kate Figes (*Life After Birth*)

I'd really recommend Pilates, which I've found excellent for my pelvic floor and my stomach muscles, too (as well as my general posture and my back). Although it's tricky at first, it gets easier to pull together the various elements like breathing, 'zipping up' the pelvic floor and other movements over time.

You need to be sure to find a good instructor – one who keeps on talking you through the exercises and describing what you should be feeling. My instructor is always coming up with new similes for what 'engaging the pelvic floor' should feel like. Her latest one is 'it should feel like sliding doors coming together'. Now that I've got used to the feeling, I often do variations of the exercises during the day – even while sitting in traffic jams!

JanZ

As a physiotherapist, I can't recommend Pilates highly enough. I use it as part of my post-injury rehabilitation programmes. A lot of my patients find it very difficult to feel anything happening to begin with, but this usually means that their 'core' muscle groups are very weak and just aren't giving them any feed-back. It does comes with time, though and it's really worth it.

Honeybunny

What the experts say

Pelvic floor muscles – like other muscles in the body – can be affected by strong emotions. When a woman is depressed, it is not only the muscles of her face that sag, but also those of the pelvic floor.

Sheila Kitzinger (*The Year After Childbirth*)

If you're really determined to work out then just begin with the pelvic floor... if you ever want to sneeze or go on a bouncy castle with any degree of confidence and dignity again, they're an absolute must.

Penny Wilson (*Wipe: Survival Tactics for Parents with Attitude*)

I had been feeling really smug about the fact that I had managed, on and off, around 50 pelvic 'squeezes' a day after my daughter was born. At my six-week check, when my doctor was doing the internal exam, she asked me to squeeze my pelvic floor muscles, which I duly did. Then she said no, could I squeeze my pelvic floor muscles? She hadn't felt a thing. I'd been squeezing the wrong end, so to speak!

Blt

I had my pelvic floor wrecked by two long labours and two ventouse deliveries, resulting in complete incontinence after my second child – leaking steadily throughout the day, not just under stress. I was told I was a pretty unusual case, as I was only 35 and most women don't experience real problems with incontinence until their muscles get further softened by the hormonal swings of menopause.

The upshot was that I had to have quite a major abdominal operation to stitch up my pelvic floor and haul my displaced bladder back into position. I also have a vaginal prolapse and uterine prolapse. So I guess it's my punishment for having laughed at those adverts for 'small bladder problems' you see on afternoon TV. I was given the option of having a temporary ring inserted around my urethra to boost control, which may or may not have worked and of having my prolapse repaired and a bit of support work done, which would have been temporary, but I opted for the colposuspension, which has about a 98 per cent success rate. I had a week in hospital then a six-week convalescence, but it was worth it.

I saw an incontinence nurse for six months who gave me lots of electric stimulation of the muscles to try and kick-start them into life again. She also got me onto the cones – and they work, I can vouch for it. I do them every day and have worked my way up from the large cone with no weights inside to the small one with a 30 g weight inside. So all you people out there contemplating further babies, let this be a cautionary tale, and look after your pelvic floors!

One extra tip, if the doctor seems uninterested in your pelvic floor or incontinence problems, just make sure you cough lots and wee all over the surgery floor. Then you might get the attention you need.

Grizzler

> **Mumsnet tip**
> Quick tip for remembering to do your pelvic floor exercises – do them whenever you take a drink. Remember what goes in must come out!

After I had my son, I went to post-natal exercise classes run by a physiotherapist and she showed us some really good pelvic floor exercises. I think that exercising these muscles is essential. Initially it can be really difficult to do it on your own because the muscles are weak and hard to isolate. Physios have techniques to help find all the muscle groups and also give you different ways of exercising them. For really severe damage you can try a plastic cone-shaped pod, which you can put different weights in and then insert as you would a tampon. The idea is that you start with a light weight that starts to tone your pelvic floor muscles (you have to tighten them slightly to keep the cone in). You can buy them from large chemists.

Molly1

> **Mumsnet fact**
> One in four women will, at some point in their lifetime, suffer from urinary or faecal incontinence. The prevalence of incontinence peaks around 45–55 years of age, but many younger women suffer too, especially during or after pregnancy because of pelvic-floor damage. It is twice as common in women than men.
> Royal College of Obstetricians and Gynaecologists

I had 9 lb 8 oz and 9 lb 12 oz babies born a year apart. There were no stitches or tears but they played havoc with my pelvic floor. I have tried cones but am not disciplined enough to use them everyday. I have now invested in a pelvic floor exerciser that emits a slight electric shock. It looks a bit like a vibrator! I've convinced myself it was so expensive that I'll use it. I slip it in and leave it while I watch the news every night. According to my husband it's beginning to work!

Alibubbles

A friend used cones to build up the muscle tone she had lost after three closely-spaced pregnancies and said they really worked. Unfortunately, while lifting the rear car seat to make room for the shopping her cone fell out and slipped down her trouser leg, landing on the floor between her and the bemused assistant who was helping her. They both stared at it before my friend grabbed it, muttering, 'I think this must be mine'!

Minou

Getting back in shape – what exercises work?

I have a sad, wrinkly, sagging stomach despite twice-weekly visits to the gym. My hairdresser (you laugh, but she recommended an excellent osteopath) says the Power of Yoga video worked for her sister, but I'm having trouble braving the ridicule of my kids and husband. My stomach bugs me because I'm quite fit, just locally destroyed by two kids in quick succession.

Dannie

I have one of those rocking, sit up things, not too expensive and very easy to use – probably about five minutes a day suffices. I had a toned middle pre-pregnancy and am working on getting it back!

Peanuts1

Although I managed to go from a size 18 to nearly a size 12, my tummy just didn't seem to be shrinking at the same rate as the rest of me. So a friend suggested I use a gym ball – a large burst-proof ball which you can use for doing sit-ups (among other things). It's the best money I've ever spent. After eight weeks my waist is two inches smaller and my 'pouch' is seriously reduced (although not yet gone). My diet has been 'flexible' of late but I'm still losing weight so it must be exercise that's making the difference. The balls come with a list of exercises and really work – I could only do ten sit-ups on it to start with, even though I could do 60 or more in the normal way.

What the experts say

For many women it's not pregnancy pounds that keep them looking pregnant; most are shed without much effort in the first six weeks postpartum. Rather, it's the stretched out abdominal muscles that stand between those new mothers and their old pre-pregnancy silhouettes.

Eisenberg, Murkoff and Hathaway (*What to Expect the First Year*)

Personally I have my figure back, it's just not the one I recognise from before.

Penny Wilson (*Wipe: Survival Tactics for Parents with Attitude*)

If you still need convincing, every toddler that has entered our house has found some use for it, too! One word of warning though, make sure you're alone with the curtains drawn until you are confident you have sussed out your balance.

Twink

Try tummy tucks – holding your tummy in as you breathe deeply – while you sit in the car. Even one journey each day would be enough to make a difference. My other top-tip for tummies is not to do loads of crunches – what people normally do – mostly incorrectly. Try standing up in front of a mirror with your arms hanging by your sides. Pull your tummy in and keep it pulled in as you lean down to one side, ideally until your fingertips reach your knee. You must, must, must keep your tummy pulled in and you must not lean forwards. Do this on each side about 15 times, very slowly and you'll feel your muscles the next day. It's a really good exercise for waist definition.

> **Mumsnet tip**
> Instead of flopping on the sofa when it's your turn to do the dawn start with the baby, buy or borrow an exercise video. I dug out an old yoga video and found doing it even when exhausted improved my mental and physical health and kept my son (and any early morning passers by) thoroughly entertained.

Another good exercise is to get down on all fours with your arms and your back straight, (neither humped nor curved, it's a good idea to check in a mirror). Let your tummy flop down and then pull it back in, keeping your back completely flat all the time. Do this exercise about 15 times and then pull your tummy in and hold it in for as long as you can manage. Very easy, not sweaty and effective.

Molly1

I read a magazine article a few weeks ago about using kids' toys to get fit. A few people have already suggested hula hoops, which you could even do in front of the telly. You might feel a bit silly, but so what? Also suggested were skipping ropes, space hoppers and pogo sticks for a cardio-vascular workout. Much cheaper than going to the gym and more fun too!

Stompy

Walking, walking, walking. It worked for me. Every time you go to get the car out, think about taking the pushchair instead. It doesn't cost anything, burns calories and you can even feel virtuous about helping the environment. Double buggies not only give your heart a workout but tone your arms, too.

Biza

Keep exercising all the time – not necessarily heading for the gym every five minutes but running upstairs rather than walking, dancing around the living room to the Teletubbies and pushing that pram! I've gone from a pre-pregnancy size 16 to a size 10–12 after two babies – it's a new lease of life!

Clary

Losing weight post-birth – how do you do it?

Everyone says that you'll lose weight if you breastfeed, but that wasn't the case for me. I didn't lose my post-baby weight until I had given up breastfeeding, then it all seemed to come off – with some effort on my side. I had porridge for breakfast with a spoonful of maple syrup, beans on toast (no butter) for lunch and something from a low-fat cookbook for supper and no alcohol. I exercised with a yoga video and went for long walks with the buggy. I managed to shift a stone and a half of stubborn post-pregnancy fat over about four months.

Enid

I went to a slimming club – the support and advice from others made me feel normal for a change. It also helped me rethink my eating habits and look at food in a different light. I love recipe books and I enjoy eating from them now because I know how to adapt high-fat food into low-fat versions, which I can eat freely. It's good to have the permanent support of the class and know that others struggle, too.

Crunchie

I'm a Weight Watcher. It's expensive but I seem to need the public humiliation to diet. My tip is not to expect the weight to come off quickly. I knew it would be a long haul and didn't give up, even after the Christmas, Easter and birthday binges and I still treat myself to some chocolate on Fridays.

AtkinsB

> **Mumsnet tip**
> A Weight Watchers trick is to start each day with hot water and a slice of lemon. It cleanses the system, brightens the skin and somehow keeps constant sweet cravings at bay.

I believe that the old adage 'nine months up, nine months down' is very true. Don't force your body to lose weight – mine just seemed to want to hang onto that last half a stone even though I ate healthily and exercised regularly. I highly recommend Weight Watchers (At Home) – I did an eight-week plan when my daughter had just turned a year and lost a stone.

JudeB

Vegetables don't count, so eat as many as you want. Keep some chopped raw in the fridge to nibble on (go on, pretend it's exciting). Make a massive vegetable soup. You can freeze it, puree it for babies and kids love it. Have it for lunch or as a starter at supper to help you eat less of your main meal. For dessert, a low-fat plain yogurt mixed with two teaspoons of low-calorie drinking chocolate is yummy.

Maisy1

When I first got pregnant I was huge but the weight fell off during the first few weeks following the birth – probably due to constant breastfeeding and absolutely no sleep. With my second pregnancy, I only had a discreet bump, but my daughter turned out to be the most placid baby ever and by the time she was six months I had put on nearly two stone! The moral of the story is, watch those chocolate biscuits and make yourself go for at least a half-hour walk every day from as early on as possible.

Mopsy

It's important to have a healthy lifestyle rather than going on a diet because it's impossible to diet for the rest of your life. So, eat plenty of fish, chicken, vegetables, and fruit, pasta and rice, and not too much red meat – everything in moderation. I find I need to eat well during the morning when I'm hungriest and not eat too late at night. I never cut down on the wine – a girl's got to have some pleasures and I think it aids digestion.

Exercise is key. I went out walking with my daughter every day for at least an hour in the morning when she was little. She would sleep and it helped shed the initial weight when I didn't feel ready to start going to the gym.

Tillysmummy

> **Mumsnet tip**
> A trick that sometimes works is to decide that I've had enough to eat and go and brush my teeth – it puts me off scoffing any more!

After I stopped breastfeeding I went on a low-calorie diet and did some gentle stretching exercises every night. I ate lots of lean chicken, baked potatoes, tuna fish and coleslaw, gave up chocolate and went to the gym as often as I could. I lost two stones in two months. I still want to lose another stone – but then I always did.

Sobernow

Eat less when you stop or cut down on breastfeeds! I was relatively happy with my weight when fully breastfeeding twins – the babies seemed to be absorbing all the extra calories I was shovelling in – but larded up once weaning began.

Scummymummy

Each time I stopped breastfeeding, my clothes became noticeably tighter. I estimated I was approximately 10 lbs over my pre-pregnancy weight. The good news is my weight returned to its pre-pregnancy level without dieting. The bad news is it took two years for this to happen. I went through a very active phase when my sons hit toddler-hood – surprise, surprise! Running around after them got rid of the excess pounds in no time.

Frank1

I just can't get on with diets and loathe the gym, so all I did was banish all the chocolates, cakes and crisps from the house (huge willpower involved) and switched to low-fat or fat-free dairy products and salad dressings. And I walked, walked, walked everywhere with the buggy.

Donna1

When my daughter was seven months old I joined a gym that had a crèche. I really enjoyed getting out and doing something for myself while knowing she was happy playing. It helped my self-confidence and I also managed to tone up and lose a bit of weight.

Lizzer

I have this deal with myself that if I drink three glasses of wine I have to burn the same number of calories. So I walk fast for 25 minutes or run for 15. If I drink it, I make sure I work it off the next day.

I hardly put on weight while pregnant but despite breastfeeding for a year managed to pile it on afterwards (walking to the bakers with pram does not mean you can eat three cream cakes). I got rid of the weight by following a low-fat eating plan plus loads of exercise. I'm now hooked on the exercise and doing a 5 km charity race which keeps me focused – I've told everyone what I'm planning to do so I can't give up now.

> **Mumsnet tip**
> I used a rule that for every biscuit, crisp or sweet I ate, I had to throw one away. That drove me nuts because I hate waste and I just had to eat less junk food.

If you're exercising to lose weight, measure your body all over – not just the obvious three points: waist, hips and bust, but also the tops of your arms, thighs and just above your knee. Have a check every month and you'll be able to see the inches disappearing even if the scales are being unfriendly. You can improve your overall muscle tone and shape without any decrease in weight.

Twink

I lost two and a half stone by going on an ultra low-fat diet and signing up for a charity cycle ride from London to Paris. Telling everyone I was doing it and paying my registration fee gave me the motivation to get out and take plenty of exercise.

Azzie

Re-evaluate your targets regularly, aiming for a little at a time to begin with and stepping up the exercise when you feel as though you are hitting a plateau. I've changed my personal focus to fitness rather than 'thinness', hoping the former will automatically lead to the latter!

Suew

I tried the GI (glycaemic indices) diet. I lost weight and I never felt hungry. I remember drinking vast amounts of apple juice and having at least five meals a day. It's not the easiest diet as far as willpower is concerned as you can't have 'a little of what you fancy' without messing it up. In the past I've done calorie-counted diets and found them much easier to follow as you can 'sin' and still lose weight, but the GI diet is the first one that's made me feel better as well.

Dm2

I followed *Dr Atkins' New Diet Revolution*, started walking instead of driving (when possible) and going to the gym regularly, and I lost a stone in a month. I like to comfort eat, which is okay on the Atkins diet as long as it's the right sort of food. Typical low-fat, calorie-counting diets have not worked for me, so I'm pleased to have finally found something that does. Also, it doesn't leave me feeling starving all the time. I get my kicks from going down a notch on my belt, rather than the quick buzz of having a bit of chocolate in my mouth. I'm also enjoying exercise, which is a miracle. I don't wish to sound like I'm gloating, but if I can do it, anyone can!

Chanelno5

Post-natal depression (PND) – can you get over it and what helped you?

I fell pregnant when my first baby was only four months old. I thought I was just tired and run down. Everything was a trial. Just getting out of bed and getting washed and dressed would take forever. I wasn't sleeping and felt exhausted to the point of dropping. I didn't want to see anyone or even talk to my closest friends. I didn't want to go out but didn't want to stay in either and spent hours walking with the pushchair. When I finally admitted there was a problem my son was 13 months old. Now I look back on his first year with horror at how depressed I was. The best thing I did was go to the doctor and get anti-depressants and counselling. I would urge anyone to seek help. There is life after PND, I now have two happy toddlers and a happy husband. Talk about it – you will feel such a release.

Ursie

I was totally and utterly opposed to taking anti-depressants before I started taking them so I tried everything else first. In the end, I was so desperate and so ill that they really were my last hope. I understand when people say that pills aren't the answer, but I'm afraid sometimes they are the only answer. It's taken me a long time to accept this but I was very seriously ill because of a chemical imbalance in my brain. There was nothing wrong in my life and ironically I had everything to be happy about and to live for.

Kizzie

What the experts say
The exact cause of post-natal depression is unclear, but as with baby blues it seems to be related to the stresses and hormone changes of birth.
Dr Christopher Green (*Babies!*)

Depression can overwhelm a woman after adopting a baby, too. Further evidence that depression after birth is not hormone-related.
Sheila Kitzinger (*The Year After Childbirth*)

I suffered bad post-natal depression after both babies. For me, it meant not being able to sleep or eat, feeling terrified and crying all the time, hating my children, wanting to run away and hide and wishing for my old life back. These feelings then receded into just feeling low, lethargic and grumpy. The first time I did not receive any medication. It was not until I had my second baby and the same symptoms returned that I was given anti-depressants. They took about a week to work and the effect was amazing. I started to feel great again and realized that I had been down for so long after the first birth that I'd got used to feeling that way. I weaned myself off the pills after about seven months. I so regret that I didn't get help after my first child as it tainted my first few years of motherhood.

Lauraw

After the birth of my second child I would cry about anything and nothing and felt I couldn't cope. It wasn't until I moved house when my son was ten months old and changed doctors that I got the help that I needed – weekly visits from the health visitor and bi-weekly visits to the doctors. After much discussion I decided to go on Prozac, and it helped a lot.

When my third child was four months old we moved house again and I was determined not to go back on Prozac. But again, I found that old feeling of not coping creeping up on me. The final straw came when I threw a (full) box of baby wipes at my husband. It sounds funny but I will never forget the feeling of not being in control and needing to hit out. Again, help has come in the form of Prozac (happy pills my husband calls them!).

There is light at the end of the tunnel. I've been there before and got better and I know given time and the right help I will be better again.

Andie

> **Mumsnet fact**
> Known as 'the silent epidemic' post-natal illness affects between 70,000 and 100,000 women and their babies in the UK every year.
> The Association for Post Natal Illness

I took Prozac, but found it suppressed every emotion. I didn't enjoy being a zombie.

Maisy1

I had two children a year apart and became weepy, emotional and irritable. I went to see my GP, who gave me anti-depressants. I didn't realize how bad I had been feeling until I started to feel better. I took them for ten months and weaned myself off them very successfully. I discussed counselling, but decided I didn't need to talk to a stranger about my problems, in fact I didn't have any problems, I just needed something to help with the physical aspects of my illness. I had everything I wanted and needed but I was depressed until I received treatment.

Alibubbles

I found that the best thing I ever did was admit to my friends and family that I was depressed – I find it so much easier to cope with my 'black days' now. Depression is like alcoholism – often hidden from others. But recovery cannot start until you admit you have a problem and I think it never truly goes away, even if you haven't had an attack for ages.

I no longer take anti-depressants as I've found that having a support network of close family and friends works far better for me. And a really good crying session once in a while does you the world of good – even if you haven't got a clue what you are crying about!

Snugs

> **Mumsnet fact**
> In a study of 139 health visitors, just over 50 per cent were confident in their ability to identify PND, but collectively they failed to identify 50–80 per cent of cases. Eighty-two per cent of health visitors think a validated assessment tool would be useful in identifying PND.
> Nottingham Community Health NHS Trust

Eight weeks post-birth I completely changed. I was moody, cried at stupid things and began to have panic attacks in shops. I went to the doctor and was told to start taking anti-depressants straight away. The drugs had an odd effect on me, so I stopped taking them and went to see my health visitor. She comes round every week to have a cup of tea and a chat and I think in the end that was all I needed. Although I have lots of friends, I just needed to talk to an outsider so I could say everything I wanted without offending anyone!

Delilah

I was very moody and depressed post-birth and was prescribed Prozac – although I only took one and that was under pressure. Eventually, Social Services arranged eight hours of childcare for me and this helped enormously, though the depression has come and gone ever since. I've been taking St John's Wort, a herbal anti-depressant, for a while. I don't take the full dose, but generally I feel more able to cope with the world. It should not be taken if you are taking any other medication (including the pill) or are breastfeeding.

Bj

I had some loopy moments in the year after our son was born and I found that a liquid St John's Wort supplement helped. I also talked to the doctor and a psychiatrist. It was really helpful to have a good chat and get stuff out in the open.

Molly1

I've found St John's Wort very effective for stress, although the only problem I've heard about is that it can make you more sensitive to the sun. I've also used Bach Flowers rescue remedy – even if it's just the placebo effect my mind thinks something has worked!

Candy

I started suffering from severe panic attacks a year after my baby was born. I have been taking Kava Kava and vitamin B, and forcing myself to go out whenever possible to face the fear. My doctor said that it was hormonal and very common after the birth of a child and promised me that the attacks would go away. He prescribed tranquilizers that I don't take, but just knowing that I have them makes me feel better. I found that Bach Flowers rescue remedy seemed to help, and alcohol exacerbates the problem.

Caznay

Mumsnet fact
Around 15 per cent of new fathers suffer depression when their partner has a baby. *Scotland on Sunday*

My depression came to a head when my friend told me that my behaviour was unacceptable. I hadn't realized it but I was becoming more and more withdrawn from all my friends and family. I couldn't sleep for longer than five hours and didn't want to go for shopping or take the kids to playgroup and I hated my husband touching me in any way at all. I went to my GP and cried for an hour. She prescribed an anti-depressant which helped me sleep and I gradually started to feel better, though I still have days when I want to be on my own and do nothing. Someone who will listen is the best remedy of all. My advice is to set yourself the goal of a place to go and really go for it, even if it's just to the park or play area. Do not, and I cannot stress this enough, feel ashamed to cry. Crying is like opening a release valve, you can open it a bit or you can open it all the way, but do not cry on your own.

Tigger

I was in a dreadful state after I had my second child but I didn't want to start taking anti depressants as I had watched my mum fight addiction to Valium. My doctor and I concluded that I needed space (amongst other things). The only way I could get any 'me' time was to go to a local gym. I was overweight, overwrought and definitely overwhelmed, but it was the best thing I've ever done. The first weeks in the gym were very embarrassing – not being able to cycle more than ten minutes or hoping it was sweat when I got off the rower (not anything to do with my pelvic floor), but it worked.

Kia

Mumsnet tip
I have found that the homeopathic remedy sepia lifts the gloom and exhaustion a bit, and helped me when I was complaining of panic attacks and depression.

My PND started with really terrible headaches, not sleeping, having awful thoughts about things that could happen to my daughter, crying all the time and not wanting to go out. I didn't let anything go like the housework and cooking – everything had to be done every day. I tried not to let my daughter see how upset I was and put a brave face on things. I eventually saw the doctor, who wanted to put me on anti-depressants but I wanted to sort myself out without the use of drugs. I saw a counsellor for six sessions, which was excellent, and went to a health shop and got some Bach Flowers recovery remedy, which I find helps at stressful times. I still have my down days, but generally I am a happier person.

Dolphin

I suffered from very severe post-natal depression after the birth of my twin sons. It was devastating and I don't think I'll ever be able to forget the fear and trauma it caused me and my family. I felt tormented and terrified. I don't say these things lightly. I had to have someone with me 24 hours a day and my husband wasn't able to work. I went from being a confident, outgoing, happy person to someone who couldn't bear to be in a room on her own. I couldn't read a newspaper or watch television, I didn't eat or sleep for months. But, although I never believed I could get better, I did. I'm back at work now and still taking a small dose of anti-depressants, although I know I'm not addicted. I love my children to bits and I can't believe it ever happened to me. You can recover.

Twinsmum

Having had little success with my GP, I saw a homeopath who listened to me for over an hour and said I needed to give myself permission to feel the way I do. After all, no one can be upbeat all the time, it's only society that pressurizes us into thinking we have to be. It also turned out that delayed PND is possible – I had tried so hard not to be depressed after the birth that I had suppressed it. She gave me Bach Flower Remedies to take and I haven't looked back. Although I wouldn't say I'm cured, I certainly do not need the rescue remedy every day and I'm coping with my stresses a lot better. There is light at the end of the tunnel – it's just that there is no map to tell you how to get there, just the odd signpost now and again. Everyone reaches it from a different angle!

Blt

Contraception – what works for you?

I was on the combined pill quite happily for several years, but with a family history of breast cancer I was advised to come off it. I used the cap (diaphragm) for a couple of years but we found the spermicide made everything a bit numb (not something anyone had warned me about!), plus it doesn't allow for much spontaneity and I'm convinced it was responsible for recurrent cystitis. I finally plucked up the courage to have an IUD fitted (my doctor prescribed Valium as I was so nervous) and it's fine, except I now have periods that last about eight days and are very heavy for about four days. For a long time we used 'safe sex' (non-penetrative) but I'm not convinced how 'safe' that is in terms of pregnancy!

Hollee

Isn't it amazing that contraception choice is still so limited? The doctor put me off the combined pill with tales of clots and cancer scares, so I opted for the mini-pill and I'm feeling very low, though it's hard to say if it's the pill, or exhaustion.

Jayc

> **Mumsnet fact**
> In 2000 doctors prescribed the contraceptive pill to 2.6 million women in the UK. Department of Health

I had really bad problems on the combined pill, I was like Jekyll and Hyde! I would start feeling low, then the slightest thing would set me off and I could become violent. I self-harmed and hit my husband – all things I am ashamed of now. As soon as I stopped taking it I felt 100 per cent better. It's scary to think that hormones can have such an effect on your personality. I am now on the mini-pill and feel fine.

Lisa

After the birth of my first child we decided to try condoms. We weren't very successful so after the birth of my second child (soon after the first!) I decided to try the mini-pill. It was ideal as I was still breastfeeding. The only 'problem' I had was that I didn't have any periods – a great 'problem' to have. Once I stopped taking the pill it took three months or so for my cycle to return to normal.

Hmonty

I used to take the mini-pill – it was very effective but you have to be very accurate about what time you take it or it's not safe. The only problem I had that I didn't have with the combined pill was that it made my skin spotty. The only other time I had that was during the first trimester of pregnancy.

Fran

I took the mini-pill for three months and bled most of the time. In fact, I was only averaging one bleed-free day a week!

Curly

> **Mumsnet tip**
> If you have problems remembering to take your mini pill, keep the packet by your toothbrush or the kettle or wherever you automatically go every morning!

I have been taking my contraceptive as an injection – you have it in your bottom every 12 weeks – for over two years and can't recommend it enough. You do not bleed at all, except for when you first start to take it and when your body is adjusting. It's great not to have to worry about taking pills or using condoms.

Rosebud

When I used the injection I bled for six weeks at a time and it made me feel really horrible. It took my periods nearly six months to settle down after coming off it and I've got friends who also had problems. I now use the mirena coil which is like a normal IUD but releases progesterone. Having it fitted was no worse than having a smear test –though it was a bit uncomfortable for a while afterwards – and I was in and out of the doctors in 25 minutes.

Tigger

I had a contraceptive implant and bled more or less continuously after it was put in. I've been able to take the mini-pill though, with absolutely no side effects.

Lindy

I had an implant when they first came out and had no problems with it until I wanted to have it removed – apparently some doctors have been sued by patients who have had permanent scarring after heavy-handed removal so others aren't keen to do it. I eventually found a doctor who would remove it via my left hand and was left with a virtually invisible scar.

Sweetie

> **Mumsnet tip**
> If you're stuck for contraception ideas it's always worth going to a family planning clinic – after all, they're the experts and if all else fails you can pick up some free condoms while you're there!

I use a mirena coil. It was very uncomfortable but not painful during the fitting but I felt as if I'd got bad period pains for a few days afterwards. I bled a lot for three weeks, which was a bore as I was told not to use tampons until it had been checked after six weeks. The bleeding is very light now. Mood-wise I don't think

I'm any better or worse than before, although I haven't dared stop the starflower oil. I can't feel it at all and my husband says he can't either (but I made sure they trimmed the strings as much as possible). I'd definitely recommend it.

Twink

I've had a mirena coil for three years with no problems at all. I bled loads for the first three weeks but now don't have any periods to speak of at all, which saves a fortune on tampons. Fitting is uncomfortable but considerably less painful than a contraction! I remember my doctor saying that the amount of progesterone in the mirena was the equivalent of taking a mini-pill two or three times a week.

Salalex

I'm now on my second mirena IUD (I had the first removed in order to have a baby) and I would recommend it to anyone. It has none of the side effects normally associated with IUDs (heavy periods, pain). I was also impressed by the fact that I returned to full fertility as soon as I had my previous mirena removed.

Starling

I got a mirena coil after having an IUD removed because I had periods that lasted for three weeks. The only side affect I had was being spotty for the first couple of months, so I wouldn't recommend having it fitted just before the Christmas party season. On the plus side, it has regulated my heavy periods. The worst bit about the fitting was having my cervix wiped with antiseptic – it was freezing cold!

Scooby2

> **Mumsnet fact**
> If 100 couples have sex for a year using no form of contraception, statistics show that 85 of the women will become pregnant. By comparison, if the same 100 couples were to consistently and correctly use the pill or a condom with spermicide, only one of the women would become pregnant.   www.Voters4choice.org

My friend used contraception by the stars – she got pregnant within six weeks! I am using a coil – not the one with hormones. I really like it. Having had a disaster with the morning-after pill and broken condoms, this seems the best option. I have no side affects, I hardly know it's there and have managed to get to my fourth child's second birthday without getting pregnant (a record!).

Countrybumpkin

I've had my coil in for three years now. The side effects are nothing compared to those I had after taking the morning-after pill when the condom broke (hence the coil fitting!).

Berries

I had an IUD fitted some years back, soon after the birth of my son and as soon as I stopped breastfeeding I got pregnant again, with the coil still in place. Based on my experience, I wouldn't recommend an 'ordinary' coil to anyone!

Debsdebs

We very successfully use NFP (Natural Family Planning). By keeping an observational chart every day and noting the type of mucous you produce you know when you are ovulating and can avoid making love during that time. You can also use this method to plan your family.

Kirsty

But does NFP really work? I've got two kids already (born quite close together) so I can't afford an 'accident' and I have friends who swear they got pregnant during their period. I also know women who got pregnant while using Persona (the automated version of NFP).

Rara

NFP can be very difficult. Many things can upset your cycle, from stress to a cold. It must also be remembered that sperm can live in your body for about three days. So even if you have not ovulated they can hang around until you do!

Kate71

What the experts say

With unrestricted breastfeeding that includes at least one night feed, and if your periods do not start again, there is a 98 per cent chance that you will not conceive during the first six months.

Sheila Kitzinger (*The Year After Childbirth*)

Since ovulation can quietly precede your first post-partum period, you can never be certain as to when the protection you've been receiving from breast-feeding will cease.

Eisenberg, Murkoff and Hathaway (*What to Expect the First Year*)

I don't trust NFP. Quite apart from the fact that nature will make you horny at your most fertile time, it must quell your sex life somewhat. I used the mini-pill after having my daughter and it was a great success although you have to be careful because it affects people so differently. As soon as I stopped breastfeeding I changed back to my combined pill, with no problems. I would never go for the coil as I had a friend who had one and ended up pregnant for the fifth time with the coil still inside (not a nice thought).

Embloomers

I know I don't want any more children, not even if I found myself meeting a new partner through divorce or bereavement, so my husband had a vasectomy. I think perhaps you need to wait until your children are at school – the second child starting school seems to be quite a trigger for some women to start wanting number three. In my husband's case there were some complications and it was pretty unpleasant at the time, although he is okay now. I certainly haven't noticed any loss of libido – quite the opposite.

Rosalind1

Mumsnet fact
Eighteen per cent of British men who are of reproductive age and with a partner opt for a vasectomy. The *Evening Standard*

My husband had a vasectomy but he had it reversed two years later. Despite being sure we only wanted two, we've found we very much want a third child. We've been told the reversal was a success but must wait and see what happens. I'd advise taking a long time deciding whether it's the right thing for you – the reversal was extremely uncomfortable but hopefully it will be worth it.

Snick

After our third child I knew I didn't want any more and to avoid temptation I got sterilized, even though I was only 29. The only problem was, they didn't warn me about the heavy periods, although they improved over time. I have never regretted it but of course it is very final. We used condoms in between our children, which was fine – until we ran out!

Violet

Mumsnet fact
In 1999, 41,300 women were sterilized by the NHS in the UK with 500 reversals of sterilization. Department of Health

I got sterilized at 30 and have no regrets at all. I have two children 13 months apart. I knew I didn't want any more and felt if something happened to me I would want my husband to be able to marry again and, if necessary, have children – so no vasectomy. The sterilization was very simple, in and out of hospital the same day and all done under a local anaesthetic, no after effects at all.

Alibubbles

I've known three couples who decided to have another baby after one of their children died, even though they thought they would not want another child. This makes me wary of sterilization.

Numbat

I use Persona – you take a urine sample eight times a month and the monitor tells you when you're ovulating, which days are 'safe' and which aren't. I used it for two years before switching its function to aid rather than prevent conception and have returned to it after having our son. I find it more reassuring than the natural way and it's nice not to be taking drugs or inserting foreign bodies into myself. Used correctly the failure rate is supposedly the same as condoms, but I would only use it if you're not going to be too upset at becoming pregnant.

Prior to this, I had a coil fitted, which led to a lovely exchange between me and the doctor's receptionist.

'I need to see Dr X today, my coil has come out.'

'What do you mean "out", how "out" is it?'

'It's wrapped in a piece of tissue on the bathroom window-sill. Is that far out enough?'

Late30smom

My advice is to only use Persona if you want a baby! It is a cheapish way of finding out when you're ovulating. It sounds wonderful and completely natural, but I used it correctly for six months and got pregnant (which wasn't what I was aiming for at all!). I'll always remember the chief midwife saying that Persona was on special offer and her staff would look forward to lots of overtime in nine months time.

Batters

Parenting

Introduction

So now you're a parent. Never mind the fact that you've just experienced the most traumatic hours (days even) of your life, there's no time to dwell on it. You've got responsibilities to face up to, burdens to shoulder, decisions to make. And we're not just talking about whether you plump for sunflower yellow over pistachio for the nursery.

'Too often they (parents) are confused by an avalanche of contradictory advice from well-meaning doctors, books, and friends, and try desperately to adhere to some particular method without thinking of its applicability to their own infant.'

That was the verdict of the *Intelligent Parents' Manual* published in 1944. Funny how little has changed. These days there are even more parenting gurus and a myriad of titles promising all the tricks of the parenthood trade that will render your baby contented, your children happy and your life full of love and laughter. Should you bother reading them? Are they sanity savers or will they just end up making you feel inadequate? And, short of camping out in the library for weeks, how do you know which expert is for you?

Before your pride and joy even entered the world you were most likely faced with some choices that, if nothing else, could have had a momentous effect on your finances. We're talking four figure sums here. According to supermarket chain, Asda, baby equipment alone for a new child costs around £1,850. Mistakes can be costly. Of the vast array of 'baby essentials' out there, what exactly do you need and what, after one use, will get shoved to the back of your cupboard destined to be untouched by mother or baby again?

Even the seemingly straightforward issue of what to name your precious new bundle can be a minefield. Can you go for the same name as a friend has chosen for her child? What about the politics of using family names? Will Granny be offended if she doesn't get a mention – and should you be worried if the names you plan will consign your child to a set of initials like MAD or PMT and a lifetime of cheesy jokes?

From then on, the parental brain-teasers come thick and fast. Are you going to be a strict routine parent or a go-with-the-flow type? Should you tempt your wee bairn with a dummy or bridle at the mere suggestion of it? And what if your baby isn't sitting, crawling or standing at the same time as his peer group? Should you be worried – and what can do to get him moving if you are?

Of course there are a few 'naturals' out there – those perfect mothers who are all too keen to marvel publicly at their perfectly sleeping, feeding angelic first-borns and surviving these paragons in the early months can be every bit as challenging as coping with a newborn.

Last but not least there's that thorny problem of parental guilt to overcome. How do you know if you're a good enough mother, whether you love your baby enough, or spend enough time with her?

Read on to see how thousands of others negotiated all of these prickly issues and more that arose in the first whirlwind year of being a parent.

Mums' Dictionary

Amnesia: Condition that enables a woman who has gone through labour to make love again.

Dumbwaiter: One who asks if the kids would care to order dessert.

Family Planning: The art of spacing your children the proper distance apart to keep you from killing them.

Feedback: The inevitable result when your baby doesn't appreciate the strained carrots.

Full Name: What you call your child when you're mad at him.

Grandparents: The people who think your children are wonderful even though they're sure you're not raising them right.

Hearsay: What toddlers do when anyone mutters a dirty word.

Impregnable: A woman whose memory of labour is still vivid.

Independent: How we want our children to be, as long as they do everything we say.

Ow: The first word spoken by children with older siblings.

Puddle: A small body of water that draws other small bodies wearing dry shoes into it.

Show Off: A child who is more talented than yours.

Sterilize: What you do to your first baby's dummy by boiling it and to your last baby's dummy by blowing on it.

Top Bunk: Where you should never put a child wearing Superman pyjamas.

Two Minute Warning: When the baby's face turns red and she begins to make those familiar grunting noises.

Anonymous

Choosing a name – what should you consider?

Two friends of mine had babies within about six months of each other and called them by the same name. It caused untold hurt to the friend with the first baby and the mother of the second baby won't even talk about the matter. These were friends who saw each other three to four times per week and it has ruined their friendship.

Paula1

If you don't use the name you'd always wanted because a friend has already used it, you might resent it later. If your children grow up to be friends they'll probably like being called the same thing. Do watch out for initials, though. My husband's are PMT and as everyone in his office is known by their initials (on emails and circulars), that's what he's called day-in, day-out – good thing he wasn't a girl, really!

Biza

Someone I know has just given her child exactly the same name as my daughter – first and middle name. I suppose I should feel flattered, but I'm a bit peeved.

T

What the experts say
A strong argument can be made against any name.
David Narter (*Don't Name Your Baby...What's Wrong with Every Name in the Book*)

I don't think I'd choose the same name for my child that a close friend had chosen, even if it was a personal favourite – it just doesn't seem very original. It's not that I think it's a particularly big deal, just that I'd want my baby to have a special name – at least amongst close friends. Isn't it amazing how children grow into even the most bizarre names? The first time you hear them, you think 'no!', but a few meetings later and you couldn't imagine them being called anything else. I guess I'd be quite flattered if a friend named their child the same as mine – but I wouldn't think them particularly imaginative.

Alex2

Am I missing something, here? Why on earth should anyone resent someone else calling their child the same name? You don't get a copyright at the christening and it's rather flattering, actually.

Javarose

Me and my husband could only agree on one girl's name so we called our daughter that even though we knew two other couples (who had become good friends) were also going to give their daughters the same name. Our theory was that it was all our own choice, so why change it for anyone else? It is your child, and besides, it wouldn't clash in the long term as lots of people have the same name! Anyway, we ended up sharing a nanny with one of our NCT friends, which was fine when both girls were babies, but as they got older it became a tad more tricky (give that toy back X it's X's!). So I am afraid nicknames are now used. I would not change my choice of name even so as both girls suit their names (and nicknames).

I disagree about originality when choosing names. If you like a particular name, then go with it no matter what the surrounding circumstances. It is your child and your choice!

Blt

My sister (born 1972) was going to be Sarah Louise but a friend of my mum's got there first and so my sis became Sara Michelle. Typically, both families moved away from the area and we kids have never kept in touch!

One thing you might want to do is to check out the top ten names of the year, which are produced by the Office of National Statistics (www.ons.gov.uk), if you want to ensure your choice isn't the most popular name. There are nine boys in my four-year-old's class at school and three of them are called Harry, although I don't know if that name has ever been top of the pops!

Suew

> **Mumsnet fact**
> Jack was the favourite names for boys in 2000, as it has been for the last six years; while Chloe was the favourite for girls for the fourth year running. The *Guardian*

I called my second child Tallulah because it was a name that I loved and also I thought it unusual enough not to hear it that often. However, after she was born, we discovered that there was a child in the next road with the same name. It really shouldn't matter how many children are called the name you pick, as long as you love the name and it suits your baby. The two Tallulah's are almost opposites of each other and it suits them both, mine being blonde and blue-eyed, and the older Tallulah having jet black hair with brown eyes.

Lou33

I called my new baby Sasha. But in the birth announcements in the local paper, which I always check for some reason, there have been another three Sashas (or Sachas) born since my baby. I thought I had gone for something slightly different, but it seems that by the time she starts school she may be one of, say, three in her class. So you never can tell.

Bumblelion

I was worried about my second child's name 'going with' the first one – luckily it was a girl as even at due date we could not decide on a boy's name. I prefer old-fashioned names and ones that don't shorten so the 'going with' bit just made it even harder (so many criteria to fulfil). Anyway, after all that thought we still managed to pick two names that my mother doesn't like!

Clary

Names are such an emotive subject. I spent months agonizing over what to call my boys. I soon learnt that no matter what name we came up with someone was bound to dislike it. Then you have to think about what the name could be short-ened to (I couldn't call my boys Richard as I dreaded them being called 'Dick' – apologies to any Richards out there) and what the initials stand for (I have a friend who's initials were WAS so she was always known as a has been) and then the names have to sound good with the surname. Oh, and don't forget to throw in your favourite uncle's name so he won't get upset. What a minefield!

In the end we stuck to our guns and went for the names we liked. Strangely, once you've lived with a name for a while it becomes much less important anyway. The baby just becomes that name, if you know what I mean.

If anyone picked the same names we've used I'd be really flattered. (After all, isn't this why you name your children after members of your family and friends?)

Hmonty

What the experts say
One in twelve boys born in 1944 were named John.

Emma Merry (*First Names*)

I recently found out that my husband's ex-fiancée (who is much hated in our house) has called her baby exactly the same as ours. Loads of people have asked if I'm outraged. I sort of am but also thank God we were first to have ours other-wise it would have looked like we were copying her! Pathetic, isn't it?

When I was on teaching practice years ago, there was a girl in one of my classes called Bambi. Luckily she was very petite with huge eyes and it suited her.

Rara

I worked for an attorney named Fred Judy, who married a woman named... Judy! So she would call and say, 'Hi, this is Judy Judy' and I would have to try to keep a straight face.

JoAnne427

I knew someone with the surname Commode who called his daughter Honour (I kid you not) – so whatever you plump for, it could be worse.

ChanelNo5

Should you follow a routine or not?

I believe that young babies should be allowed to sleep, feed and play whenever they like – there's plenty of time for structure in the future. I don't think they should be woken to be fed at a certain time because sometimes they may not need it – you know yourself sometimes you can be ravenous after eating a couple of hours earlier and sometimes you don't feel hungry after not eating much. Growth and stimulation can have an impact, too and sometimes the brain needs a little more sleep to cope with the physical changes taking place. A little body is not a clock and I don't believe you should try to set it to GMT that early on. I know it's hard being woken but you just do it because they are gorgeously yours. I remember thinking 'this will never end' but it does and in a few months you'll wonder why you were so worried.

Lizzer

I have three children and the last two babies slept through the night from the age of about one week old. None of them ever had colic, or cried much and all ate well. And all this without a routine in sight.

They slept next to me in bed and I breastfed them if they woke in the night. But they soon got the message that night-time was for sleeping. Take life easily and go with the flow. Mine got everything on demand until they started eating solid food, when I fed them with the rest of the family right from the start. But you don't want to burden yourself with a set of rules for the first four months. It's only for four months anyway. Just enjoy the little thing's company!

I think routines are for control freaks – professional people for whom babies are a job or people who don't know what they're doing and need the comfort of following a set of rules. Children need routine, advice and guidance as they grow to adulthood, not when they're tiny babies.

Javarose

We operate within a society that has moved so far away from natural parenting that it finds it acceptable to impose feeding and sleeping routines on babies often against the parents' better judgement. Each child is different, as is every parent, which is why we need to listen to our instincts rather than the so-called experts. What parent leaves a child to cry without feeling wretched? These are our instincts saying it's wrong for the baby and it's wrong for us. It feels wonderful to sleep with your baby – that's because it's where they belong at first. And breastfeeding makes the mother feel relaxed and the baby blissfully happy – another important indicator that this is right.

Josie

I am a firm believer in routine because it has worked for my little boy. I find that he likes to know where he is and what will happen next. I waited until he was seven weeks old and then for three weeks I noted every time he wanted feeding and every time he wanted a nap and a pattern emerged. That became his routine. He was sleeping through the night from nine weeks and has never looked back. However, I have always made sure that he can nap in the car or his buggy if need be, so that we are not always tied to the house at nap times.

Hels

Mumsnet fact
Children whose days are structured – including regular bedtimes – learn to become more co-operative.
Study by the Effective Provision of Pre-School Education project

It's worth reading the different books and then seeing what makes sense for you and your situation. Almost all the books have something that's worth knowing but you have got to trust your intuition. Doctors know to expect questions from first-time parents too, so don't be afraid to ask! Just from my personal experience I found that flexible routines were great for my son but it's something we worked into.

JJ

The trouble with baby books is that we pour over them when we are at our most vulnerable (when we've just had a baby, everything's new and we're suffering from too little sleep). I don't believe a particular book's routine is the answer. I think that you find one that fits your baby or your family best. I did demand-feed, and for the first three months it was every two hours – hellish. I looked in every book to find if this was 'normal' but did not go to fixed feeds because it was obvious that my son was hungry.

Once you've found your feet, I strongly believe a reasonably fixed daily pattern helps babies feel secure. Of course there will be changes, they may not always want to go to sleep at exactly the same time but so long as there is a framework I think it helps everyone. Just look at the children of people who think they should be allowed to do what they want, when they want – including going to bed any time up to midnight – and you'll see that these 'free' children are in reality quite mixed up and very unpopular in company.

Kenny

Loose or flexible routines definitely worked for us. The key is to find a routine that suits you and your baby. A rigid routine may seem ideal when chaos is reigning but in the end it makes your baby inflexible. Say you are out shopping and you get held up somewhere, it's awful to have a baby or toddler screaming because they are used to a meal at a particular time in a particular place. Our baby was not fussed if a meal was half an hour late or early because she wasn't used to a rigid timetable. It certainly made life easier. Obviously we kept her to a particular pattern of feeds, changes, outings, but it is really great when they fit in with the rest of the family, rather than everything being organized around the baby.

Vicky

I do think that children in some families need to follow some sort of routine – particularly where both parents work. I do not work and therefore don't have a strict routine for my son. As long as you love your child and are consistent in whatever you do, that is enough. My child still breast-feeds on demand at 12 months and is very happy and healthy. I do have meals and bedtime at roughly the same time each day and he naps whenever he feels tired.

Remember that babies change a lot in the first 12 months so routines that are appropriate for a three-month-old won't be right for a six-month-old, and so on. They know themselves what they want, so watch them rather than reading from a book.

Eulalia

I guess it's always going to be different strokes for different folks. I'm delighted with my daughter, love her to death, but believe I'm a better mother for having some sleep myself and for having a good relationship with her father. She doesn't sleep in my room and she does sometimes get a dummy. My husband and I eat together in the evening and get a chance to be partners as well as parents. But it's so hard with all the contradictory advice and people telling you to 'listen to your instinct' – it's not always easy to know what your instinct is.

Molly1

What the experts say

Believe it or not, no matter what the particular issue – feeding problems, irregular sleep patterns or mis-diagnosed colic – a structured routine is often all it takes to solve the problem.

Tracy Hogg (*Secrets of the Baby Whisperer*)

Routines are very helpful for small children and adults, but they have no relevance at all to babies.

Mary Nolan (*Being Pregnant, Giving Birth: The National Childbirth Trust*)

Most babies like routines. It provides them with a sense of security.

Signe Larson and Kevin Osborn (*The Complete Idiot's Guide to Bringing Up Baby*)

I had a premature baby and when she came home after her first three and a half weeks in hospital, she was in an incredible routine – change and feed every four hours. Since then, though, I have tried to adapt her to a completely flexible approach. She has always slept in different houses and travelled and eaten with us at different times. Now she is a very accommodating and flexible three-year-old. Maybe I'm very selfish, but it is great to have a child who can fit around what the family is doing, rather than the other way around!

Dianat

Any routine is prone to breaking down but I try hard for my daughter's pattern not to be disrupted. Some people want to be able to continue with life as it was pre-kids and in order to do that expect babies to adapt to continuously changing bedtimes, places to sleep and so on. Some of those people kid themselves that it is fairer to be so 'flexible'. Isn't it a bit selfish? I have discovered that routines work and if that means I have to sacrifice a few early evening parties or wedding receptions, then so be it. They won't be little forever and of course, come 8 pm, I am free.

I am a believer in routines – surely a little one learns by repeated experience, whether we are talking about language development or bedtime. My daughter has (on the whole) slept through for 12 hours a night from ten weeks of age although, of course, with some breaks. I call what we do a routine but that is really a rather grand term for what most parents with any sense have always done – tea, bath, story, bed. Quite easy, really and she seems to like it. At least we all know what we are doing in the evening.

Elliesmum

Children, even as small babies, love 'joining in' with family and other events. It's these times that enable the necessary socialization to occur. The earlier that children are exposed to other people and normal life the sooner they are able to cope with everything and this makes their lives more enjoyable. The parents, far from being selfish, are providing opportunities to greatly benefit their child's development. I think routines should be flexible enough to allow for this.

Cam

> **Mumsnet tip**
> A friend of ours has just had a baby and asked for my best bit of advice: ROUTINE from day one!

I recommend having a flexible routine and I definitely feel that my baby is happier for it (he is always grumpy at weekends when his routine is disturbed). All it entails is regular feeds (I do not feed on demand) and activities in the same order. I think that routines are about common sense. But don't get hung up about your baby's behaviour. There is too much emphasis on whether or not your baby is sleeping through the night (mine isn't) and a first time mum who lacks confidence can end up feeling guilty and a failure. Try to find a comfortable routine but be prepared to follow your instincts. And, most important, learn from others but do not be hard on yourself.

Minnie

At five weeks old my son decided his own routine for the evening – a bottle at around 4 pm, a bath, cuddles, another bottle at 6.30-ish and then bed. He slept through the night from six weeks old. He showed us what he wanted and we kept to it as much as possible. Yes, there were times when the routine changed due to social engagements, but we usually took his carrycot and he'd happily go to sleep in that. I think each baby has different needs. Over time you will spot the routine your baby wants. No book can teach you that.

Lisab

Do I care enough?

I was overjoyed when I fell pregnant and though I was never very interested in other people's children I thought that it would be completely different once I had my own. I can't deny that I love my baby but I'm not sure I love him enough. I don't gush about him like other mothers do about their children and I don't think I feel as much for him as they seem to about theirs. If he is under the weather, I don't fret and rush to the doctors, hearing him cry doesn't always tug at my heartstrings. Since I have been back at work I don't find that I miss my son, even though I don't see that much of him. However, I do always want the best for him, whether it is food, education, clothes or anything else and I breastfed him for longer than any of my friends breastfed their babies. I just don't feel that he is always my number one priority although he is always one of my top priorities. I haven't yet experienced that all-conquering love that a mother is meant to have for their child and I'm worried that I never will.

Worried

I felt so much like this when I had my son. I had him in my mid-thirties, so I was used to living a happy life without children. I didn't feel maternal even when I was giving birth. I felt I was entering strange, unknown territory. I go through huge swathes of my working day without thinking fondly of my children or violently missing them. I am still a separate entity, much as I love them.

What the experts say
So many factors influence this bonding process, from the birth itself to your new baby's temperament and the support you receive, that there can be no 'average' experience.

Jan Parker and Jan Stimpson (*Raising Happy Children*)

Personally I think it's difficult to feel that all-conquering love before your child begins to show his or her personality and can respond to you in a thought-out way, as opposed to the early baby reflexes. For me that process began when my son was about 14 months. The older my children get, the more I love them – because, frankly, there is more of them to love.

Frank1

I too was like this. Not rushing to doctors or doing the 100 mph dash to the nursery room when he cried. When I returned to work I found I didn't 'miss' him, but I did clock-watch. I mentally made a note of when he'd have his bottle or when he should be going down for his nap now. I became worried that I didn't love him as I should. However, he was very young and had no personality. But then as he got a bit older and his personality started to show through, it crept up on me. I didn't even realize the bond had developed. I remember him getting badly hurt and having to rush to the hospital. I howled and screamed 'my baby, my baby'. I would have traded places with him in an instant to take all his pain away. From that point, I realized he is the most important thing in the world to me. Some women bond differently and some, like me, don't even know the bond is there until something drastic happens.

Dixie

I had my son at 43 after 13 years of marriage – I had a very full life before motherhood and, although I really enjoy it, it does irritate me when people assume we were 'trying' for years and have only now become fulfilled in life. There are many aspects to one's life and for me, being a mother is just one of them. I stay at home but I make sure I have a wide range of friends and activities organized, I just do not want to talk babies all day long. I too do not rush to pick up my son when he cries and have no qualms about leaving him with responsible babysitters. I am amazed when I hear about couples who haven't had a night out for years and are too nervous to leave their babies. I also do not experience any emotional feelings about breastfeeding. I do it because I know it is best for him (and for my figure).

Lindy

It took me quite a long time to feel the fierce love that I do now for my son (he's just over two). Just because you don't fret and rush to the doctors for every minor ailment it does not make you uncaring or unloving, it probably means you are able to keep a cool head. Also, not everyone waxes lyrical about their children but again it is not symptomatic of missing love.

Molly1

> **Mumsnet fact**
> Ten per cent of new parents say they have contemplated running away forever.   NCT survey

At first I felt an overpowering need to protect and look after my daughter but I did not feel the overwhelming love that I feel for her now. It just sort of crept up on me. You can talk about a baby all day long, but it isn't talking that means you love them, it's what you do for them.

Batters

I questioned my love constantly for a long time. I also obsessed about the fact that other people could 'see' my thoughts and I felt so guilty. I would try and say the gushy things I thought I was supposed to, but rarely felt them inside. Now I realize that we are all made differently and can only love in the way in which we feel comfortable.

Peony

I spent ages worrying about whether there was something wrong with me because I wanted time by myself. But now I just accept that I love my son and wouldn't want to be without him. I'm not a 'natural' mother – I find it very hard to sit down and play with him. I went back to work recently for three days a week and love it – it's time not being a mother and having something else to talk about. At first I felt guilty that I only saw my son in the morning to dress him and at night to get his tea and put him to bed, but he loves the nursery and I think we both benefit from the break from each other. I don't think any single approach to motherhood is 'right', it's just what works best for the mother and baby.

Selja

After my first baby I was in shock, I felt so numb and confused. Where was the bond everyone talks about? Why did I feel so separated from everyone and everything? I later found out I had mild PND, which lasted about 12 months. Anyway, how can you measure something like love in terms of how much is 'enough'? I think it's great to place yourself high on your list of priorities, along with your baby. Too many women think that when they become mothers they need to become these amazing selfless, driven women with boundless energy, patience and enthusiasm, and it just isn't possible for most of us mere mortals!

Mollipops

I went back to work full-time when my son was four months old – and didn't have a single qualm about doing so. I enjoyed my time 'off', but I also looked forward to the company at work (it got lonely at home!) I enjoy getting home in the evening and spending that time with him.

The bond grows as your baby develops more personality. My son is now changing and developing so fast and starting to interact so much more with us, it's a pleasure to get home every night.

Janz

My son wasn't a planned baby by any stretch of the imagination and I don't think that I am a hugely maternal person. Going back to work was a huge help because I now look forward to the more limited time we have and I am motivated to do things with him and enjoy them. I had a big crisis when we went on holiday and spent a long time sobbing because I was at the end of my tether looking after him, accommodating him and hating that everything was dictated by having a baby. That sounds quite selfish; it was, and is, but it happened. I sometimes worry that wanting the best for him is different to loving him. We wouldn't be without him (as a person) now, although sometimes I would happily not be a parent (does that make sense?). It's not something I admit to anyone other than my husband.

Harrysmum

I had my baby when I was 32 and she is now 22 months. She was planned and we were delighted when I found out I was pregnant. After she was born, I was concerned that I didn't experience the rush of love that other mothers spoke about, and I kept waiting for it to happen. It never did. I did not particularly enjoy the time when she was a small baby and my favourite period has been from when my daughter reached 18 months or so. I look back to the first six months and I can remember absolutely hating it. The loss of freedom, the crying child and the boredom of being stuck at home. I went back to work when she was eight months old and I have no guilt about it. She is well looked after, I go to a job I enjoy and we have a nice time in the evening and at weekends. I would like another baby, but next time I won't be waiting for this huge rush of maternal love to appear. I'll just get to know my baby and grow to love it. I can honestly say I love being a mum, but I love being me too – a separate individual who goes to work and has a life outside of motherhood.

Evesmum

What makes a good mother?

I've thought about this a lot over the years and I don't think I'm any nearer the answer. Being a 'good mother' is such a nebulous thing. I'm sure we can all say what a 'bad mother' entails – abusing a child, starving them, beating them – but merely *not* doing these things doesn't automatically turn someone into a good mother. It's bit like people saying that X, Y or Z isn't a good reason to get married/have a baby/change your job but somehow, no one ever seems to tell you what is a good reason.

> **Mumsnet fact**
> Fourteen per cent of readers in an Irish magazine poll voted Sir Bob Geldof as 'best mum'. *Junior*

Sometimes I come across women that strike me as wonderful mothers, who make me feel I am short-changing my family. But I still find it so hard to define their qualities. One friend had a seriously sick child in hospital, yet still managed to make chocolate brownies every morning before school with her other children, one of which was still a baby. (I would have just been moaning on about how life was so unfair and pull the blanket over my head to shut out the world!) But what does my example mean? Was she selfless, was it a matter of time management, devotion to duty, or what? I wish I knew!

Baabaa

A good mother is happy with herself and the way in which she is bringing up her children and doesn't listen to other people's opinions of what a good mother should be!

Emmam

Oooh...does this person really exist? I think I fail based on that definition.

Hmonty

I struggle all the time with this idea. The 'good enough' mother is a comforting concept but whenever stuff goes wrong (as it always does) it's very easy for me to let that little word 'not' slip in before the 'good'. There's so much pressure to do everything perfectly. My only source of comfort is knowing that whatever I do, I do it because I believe it to be in my children's best interest. I don't like the idea that to be a good mother you have to be happy with yourself because most of the time I'm not.

Cela

> **Mumsnet tip**
> Don't feel guilty – when you sense yourself entering the downward spiral of guilt, please remind yourself that everyone would really hate you if you were perfect!

My own mother, having raised five children (although that doesn't automatically qualify her), has told me that I am a good mother. I suspect she says that because I'm lucky enough to have a very easy-natured little boy. I wonder if things would be different with a more demanding baby? I would be very wary of labelling anyone as a good mother or otherwise.

Tel

I am utterly unable to even say 'I am a good mother' without silent 'buts' creeping in. I can say, quite happily, that I am a nice mum and a good parent. But stumble on the overloaded phrase 'good mother'.

Allie

> **Mumsnet fact**
> Only 25 per cent of dads read to their baby. *Junior*

After one of my sons broke his leg on Sunday I took his brother swimming today. When we got home his lips turned blue, he started shivering and became delirious. After NHS Direct told me to keep him warm, the doctor said he had a temperature of 40.5 degrees and told me to 'GET THOSE CLOTHES OFF HIM'. He'd got a throat infection but after a few hours his temperature started to go down. So does that make me a bad mother – two children unwell or injured in the same week? Or a good mother – I realized both needed treatment straight away? Or just like everyone else – trying to muddle through as best I can and trying to do the best I can for my boys?

Twinsmum

I think love, affection and encouragement rate pretty highly in making a good mother. When my brother and I were children we received quite a bit of criticism, so we both grew up lacking self-esteem. I can see clearly now how much praise and encouragement can help a child. My goal is to try and instil confidence into my son so that he will be able to do whatever he wants in life. I also think it's a great thing to be affectionate with children and let them know how much they are loved – little boys are often very loving and I believe this is a quality that should be nurtured in them.

LiamsMum

I think an essential quality for good mothering is me-time. You need this to enable you to devote quality time to others. Also, being able to count to ten and breathe deeply when your child is kicking off at 3 am!

Monnie

I work with parents and young children who are having difficulties and I also have quite a few friends and acquaintances with kids. So, I meet and hear of lots of families, one way or another. It's extremely rare to find mothers who don't want the very, very best for their children. I suppose, if I'm honest, it was a bit of a revelation to me. I can't tell you how many times I've walked into very grim homes (badly maintained, poorly furnished, postage stamp-sized places, often housing people with profound health, emotional or social needs – homes that are in essence the 21st-century equivalent of the hovels of Dickensian disgrace) which are leavened only by the love and care lavished on the children.

I've met some superb mums in this way – people whom I admire immensely. I've also met a small minority of people who were on the cusp of being unable to be good parents because their situation was so unbearably overwhelming for them that they could not cope with their child(ren).

Mumsnet fact
Thirty per cent of British children are below the poverty line.

The *Observer*

I believe being a good mother is sometimes about there being suitable conditions for a parent's natural wish to love and nurture their child to flourish – having decent housing and support, access to a good education, good health care, not living in poverty to name a few. Once these things are in place we can argue about Gina Ford or not, private versus state education, smacking or not, Caesarean sections versus natural birth leading to a sore fanny, breast-feeding versus bottle-feeding, authoritarian rule-setting versus permissive wishy washiness until the cows come home. We can have great fun speculating about how all these affect our children and our status as good mothers. The truth is that some of these probably don't affect it very much at all. Why? Because mothers who are worried about these things are obviously interested in their children and in childhood issues generally. Their kids will get the chance to bask in their parents' love, howsoever this may be expressed, and grow up great.

ScummyMummy

To me, loving your kids unconditionally is the crucial thing. Even when they've misbehaved and have to be disciplined, they need to know that no matter what, they are loved and cherished above all else.

Donna1

I think a good mother needs to be a mind-reader as all children have different physical and emotional needs and the 'good mum' has to work out what they are and meet them. Then, just as you start to pat yourself on the back for being so good, the child moves on and gets a new set of needs...

Sis

Being a good mother involves letting up on yourself a little. Stop worrying about what you are not doing, what your friend up the road manages to do and concentrate on what you can do. Your child needs you and your skills. I may not have as clean a house or be as fancy a cook as someone else but in not obsessing about these things I have more time for my child and also more time for me to re-charge the batteries before the next onslaught!

Demented

What the experts say
The fact is that child rearing is a long hard job, the rewards are not always immediately obvious, the work is often undervalued and parents are just as human and almost as vulnerable as their children.
Dr Spock and Stephen Parker (*Dr Spock's Baby & Child Care*)

I also think it is important not to lose sight of the fact that often what children want from you more than anything else is simply your time and attention.

Ringer

Infinite patience, time aplenty, the ability to do at least a dozen things and to be in at least two different places at once, eyes in the back of your head, speed-reading skills (to absorb all the parenting books available), the ability to survive on only three hours of sleep a night, stain-removal knowledge second to none, empathy and sympathy galore, a psychology degree, a first aid certificate, the ability to problem-solve and resolve arguments in any given situation and an understanding of the developmental ages and stages of children, including possible gender differences.

Mumsnet fact
The average stay-at-home mum does 67 hours per week cooking, cleaning, shopping, ironing, washing, childcare and chauffeuring.
The *Observer*

There is so much pressure on mums to be 'perfect', when all we can really hope for is to be 'good enough'. So for those of us who are mere humans, here's some more realistic goals (though still far from easy to achieve): to give affection and love, be a good role-model, give praise and encouragement, be as patient and resilient as possible, keep a sense of humour, listen, set limits and provide consistent discipline, be respectful, give choices and responsibility, and be realistic. And I agree, me-time is very important because an unhappy mum can't really be an effective mum.

When my kids are grown up, I'd like to think they will look back and say I was a good mum. Sometimes I wonder if that will be the case – will they just think, she was always cranky, too tired, too busy or will they remember the love, the hugs and kisses, the fun we had? Guess I'll just keep doing my best, and hope that in the end it will be 'good enough'!

Mollipops

What the experts say
You will never be the perfect mother, your child will never be the perfect child and that is as it should be. Burden yourself with unnecessary guilt or unrealistically high expectations of your achievements... and you risk focusing on what isn't happening rather than what is.

Jan Parker and Jan Stimpson (*Raising Happy Children*)

When I asked a woman I know how the breastfeeding was going with her newborn, she replied blithely: 'Oh, I just couldn't be doing with that. I'm bottle-feeding all the way!' I was a little taken aback that she hadn't even given it a go but actually I found myself thinking that her sheer confidence in her parenting skills was long-term probably an even better gift to her child. So many of us spend too much time second-guessing ourselves and it was refreshing to find someone who just took a decision and got on with it.

Amber1

I think being a good mother is also about keeping a distance. Keeping your identity, finding the energy to make new friends, cultivate interests, study – whatever makes you happy with yourself. My sons may not see the importance of this now, but as they grow older, I hope they will. I want them to feel they have a happy, interesting mother, with lots going on in her life, growing old gracefully, full of independence as well as love for them.

When my sons are asleep, looking like angels, fleetingly I think I am a good mother. When they are awake, I don't have a minute to think such thoughts!

Frank1

Parenting gurus – who would you recommend?

In my view each child needs its own individual manual. They're all completely new models, straight off the production line. As for Penelope Leach, she states categorically that a baby with only one tooth can't bite when you breastfeed. Has this woman ever had a razor sharp-toothed six-month-old attacking her nipple?

Beelzebub

You cannot know what having a child is like until you have one. It's the one area where I think that experience does count. We all know we are different people as mothers than we were before. When you don't have children you are full of bright ideas about how everyone else should bring up their children. And then you have them and realize life isn't so clear cut after all. My whole mindset is different now. It's like a switch that's been turned on and now I am stuck in mother mode.

Lil

Most of these so-called 'experts' do not have a clue. I never thought about reading one of their books as I think that they are living on another planet. What do they know about your child? In a nutshell, nothing. It is up to each parent to decide what is best for their child. The most helpful advice you will get is from another mum, who is about the same age as yourself with a small child, as things change so quickly. I was told with my first one: 'Only feed every four hours and if she is not awake then wake her up'. I fed both of them when they were hungry and found that they slept better during the night as they had stored up enough food during the day. As my granny always says: 'They'll eat when they are hungry, drink when they are dry and sleep when they've had enough of the big folk'. At the end of the day, it's what you think that's best.

Tigger

What the experts say
The more people have studied different methods of bringing up children, the more they have come to the conclusion that what good mothers and fathers instinctively feel like doing for their babies is usually best after all.
Dr Spock and Stephen Parker (*Dr Spock's Baby & Child Care*)

For me, the most useful thing about childcare books is that they confirm that I'm not alone. My personal favourite is Dr Christopher Green – sensible but in an approachable and rather light-hearted way. I also gained much comfort after the birth of my first child from reading Simon Brett's *How to be a Little Sod* and subsequent titles – hilarious and so true.

Helento

I **avidly read many** books before my little boy was born, thinking that this would equip me to be a mother – what a huge mistake! I was so confused by the different advice that I didn't have a clue what I was doing. I learnt Gina Ford's routines by heart and spent a few desperate weeks trying to ignore my poor little chap's cries for milk because it was before the three-hour feeding time. I was convinced it had to be something else: over-tiredness, wind, wet nappy, just wanting to suck and every time it was because he was hungry. Now, I so deeply regret those weeks where I ignored my instincts. I was so stressed and I'm sure my poor little boy must have been, too!

I **think** *Raising Happy Children* by Jan Parker and Jan Stimpson is one of the nicest and most helpful childcare books. It is not prescriptive or full of soft focus pictures but just has lots of helpful suggestions. Any book that contains pictures of glowingly-beautiful made-up mothers and cherubic babies should immediately be disregarded. I was stunned to find out that newborns are pulpy and red looking and they don't like opening their eyes that much. Subsequently, I realized that a lot of these books don't use newborn babies for newborn pictures but babies that are more like three months old.

Molly1

I **really needed the factual stuff** for newborns (information on possetting, temperature of bath water, skin problems and so on) but personally I have little time for parenting books as such. I have never sought out books by people like Steve Biddulph and whilst I know he has a devoted following, I struggle with his views. I don't get, for example, how he can say that the mother should stay at home with the child for the first three years. Surely that depends on the mother, the child, the family, the reasons for her working and the consequences of her not working, the quality of childcare and a myriad of other issues? It seems to me that nothing to do with children is black and white and the only thing many of these books do is engender guilt.

Having said that, the one book I have read and absolutely loved was *How Not to be a Perfect Mother* by Libby Purves. I would highly recommend it.

Ringer

How Not to be a Perfect Mother kept me amused in the last week before delivery, gave me some really practical advice and didn't try to make me feel bad.

Robinw

Living in the middle of nowhere, I was stuck with Penelope Leach's book and was gutted to learn years later that a nanny looked after her children while she wrote her childcare manual! I suppose I expected her to be juggling everything around the kids like I was and felt that would have made her advice more authentic. When I had my first child there was a move to halt the 'clinical' side of childcare advice and Penelope Leach was, if I remember rightly, one of the first books held out to be 'by a mum for mums' and not by a doctor of child psychology, for example. If I tell you that in the hospital where I had my eldest there was a campaign for the 'right to wear your own nightie during labour', you'll understand why I was looking for help!

Do you remember Dr Jolly and the 'call everything by its medical name' fad? How many oldies were faced with 'Has granddad got a penis?' in front of the sewing circle because of him!

Kia

Must we ignore all that Penelope Leach said because she didn't look after her children full time? Gina Ford never had children and only looked after other peoples' – does that make her unfit to give any advice?

> **Mumsnet fact**
> Seven out of ten people think that parenting is something we have to learn or be taught.   Mori

I have read loads of different books – most before the birth – sometimes you just need to know that you're not alone and that your little darling is doing what thousands of others have done before and will do in the future! I pick and choose between the advice these books offer, friends' advice and what I feel like doing – and what works! Some days I feel strong enough to do sleep training (very rare!) but other days I don't, but mostly I just try to go with the flow and with my 'maternal instincts'!

Emmagee

I don't think it matters what these experts do or whether they're full-time parents or not. What matters is whether you find one that strikes a chord with you and offers you some practical advice. Penelope Leach did that for me, others I bridled against somewhat because they just weren't me – Steve Biddulph, for instance, who made me and my partner feel guilty for not both giving up work for five years to care for our kids.

Nancy

I, for one, felt I really needed a bit of guidance from somewhere when I was allowed home with my newborn premature twins. I was the youngest in my family and none of my close girlfriends had kids, so I knew next to nothing about children. I found the health service was far too stretched to offer more than medical advice. I had a burning desire to read up on things, much as I would if I were exposed to anything of which I had little or no experience.

I found Penelope Leach hit the right note with me and gave me more confidence with my babies. Apart from anything else, all the development stuff is interesting. Although I don't think I have picked it up since they were six months, I'm glad I bought and read her book.

Berta

Although I think Penelope Leach is way off the mark on some things, I've found her books helpful, humane, child-focused and extremely well researched. When I had my daughter nearly nine months ago, I'd never even changed a nappy. This brave new world of motherhood was very intimidating and her book helped. I agree that the development stuff is interesting. I know babies differ, but there are similarities and patterns. To use an analogy, just because each company is different, not all management teaching is redundant!

Jayc

I agree that childcare books can lend moral support. The trick is to find one that more or less goes along with your instincts and disregard the rest! Penelope Leach gave me great comfort at a time when both my mum and my childminder were nagging me about continuing to breastfeed after returning to work. Apparently I was making a rod for my own back and making him too dependent on me.

When these comments were being made I was at my most vulnerable as a sleep-deprived, hormonal first-time mum. Penelope Leach made me feel good about what I was trying to do, Gina Ford made me cry. I'm sure there are loads of people out there for whom the exact opposite applies. I don't have a problem with either of these two gurus not having the same circumstances as me – there is a nice piece in the Kate Figes book about how childless aunties and childcare professionals can enhance a child's experience of adults precisely because they are not mums themselves.

My consistent bible for practical matters has been the fabulous Nikki Bradford and Jean Willis book: *What They Don't Tell You About Being a Mother and Looking After Babies.*

Clare2

All the research suggests that mums and dads get their skills, confidence and competence as a direct result of practical experience of childcare – the more you do it, the better you become.

Tom

I don't think there are really any childcare experts. I've been caring for children for over 13 years and one important thing I've learnt is that every child is an individual – no two, even twins, are exactly the same. Some children are easy going, some are monsters. While it is possible to write about child development, it has to be generalized as children do not conform to any set manual on childcare.

If you feel the need to consult one of these so-called 'manuals' written by a childcare expert, then it's far better to go to a parent and toddler group or NCT coffee morning and talk to other parents as nothing beats practical experience.

Babynick

I think the best thing is to read a good selection of books and get as much advice as possible from everyone else – and then follow your instincts.

javarose

We are all doing our best, and should try to see these 'experts' for what they are – writers trying to sell books!

Minou

Gina Ford – how was she for you?

I've never tried her routines, although I have skim-read her books to see what all the fuss was about. My main thought is that Ms Ford's expertise is not that of a parent. Rather, it is based on her experiences as a maternity nurse and nanny to very well-off families. I'm sure that in this capacity she has picked up a wealth of knowledge regarding the needs of small babies. However, I feel she has rather less insight when it comes to considering the lives of ordinary families.

I think her advice is particularly poor when more than one child is factored into the equation. Say you've got a child at school, a toddler who attends a drop-in nursery and a newborn baby. The only way you can deposit your baby in the correctly darkened room at precisely the right time is if you forget about taking your older child to school and your toddler to the nursery. She forgets practical realities like this because she's never worked with normal families. The very rich folk, from whose offspring she has gained her baby-taming credentials, don't have to worry about this sort of thing because they hire Gina to look after the baby and an additional nanny to do the school run and take the toddler to the nursery.

What the experts say
We would not advocate feeding babies by the clock except in very specific circumstances.

Jan Parker and Jan Stimpson (www.mumsnet.com)

From my own experience of looking after other people's children I can say it is different from looking after your own. Studies have shown that if a baby starts crying, its mother's blood pressure will go up in response, while other people nearby remain unaffected. Gina Ford has not experienced this and so she is able to be very rational about what babies, in her opinion, need. This is obviously attractive when people feel overwhelmed by the demands of their babies. A legion of fans testify to her popularity. However, as I've said, I personally am not convinced either that she really understands the parent-child relationship in all its subtleties or that she has much notion of how the other half lives.

Scummymummy

While pregnant I read Gina Ford's book (*The Contented Little Baby Book*) at least twice and was very enthusiastic about following her routines. (I had also read the laudatory reviews on Amazon's website.) In practice, I found them far too regimented. If you can imagine having an old-fashioned nursery nurse looking after your baby then you'll understand what Gina Ford is like. It is so restrictive that you couldn't possibly go out and meet your girlfriends, for example, for fear the baby would fall asleep in the car on the way home at the wrong time of day.

Minnie

We have moved from having an demand-fed, wriggly little baby in our bed from birth, to a baby who goes down in his own bed and sleeps through until morning without having to use rigid routines. I knew I could not make them work because of the sort of person I am. It has taken a lot of patience and many gradual changes to his bedtime routine but we've got where we want to be regarding sleep and without what I know would have been a destructively stressful experience for us all. So, if you're like us and worried you couldn't see Gina Ford through consistently, rest assured, things do settle down well in time anyway.

Clare2

I too thought that rigid routines were both unnecessary and unrealistic... until I had my son. I tried having a flexible routine – letting him determine the time of his morning and afternoon naps, letting him sleep as long as he liked each time, with an attempt at a regular routine before bedtime and he was miserable. He appears to be a baby that is totally incapable of setting his own routine satisfactorily. I totally accept that many babies can do this as I have seen it for myself. If your baby can do it, I don't see any need to put the extra time and effort into following a Gina Ford routine. But my baby could not. He fought sleep for hours. He never slept for more than 45 minutes at a time and usually not for more than 20 minutes (at two months old). At the age of four months, he was getting about six to eight hours sleep in every 24 – which is nowhere near enough. He was fractious, restless, clingy and demanding... he would just cry and cry and cry unless he was being held by me. It was an awful, awful, awful time. I was constantly thinking about how nice it would be to get hit by a bus so I'd at least get a few quiet weeks in hospital.

And then we put him on the Gina Ford routine. Within 48 hours he was sleeping better and longer. His personality changed – he was so much happier and calmer. He started to have decent naps in the day so that I got a little break every now and then. Life was transformed. So you can see why I am a fan. If recommending the book, I always point out that it is rigid and it may suit people better to pick and choose.

As for Gina Ford herself, as far as I know she has had no children of her own and maternity nurses usually do not have any formal qualifications. She points this out in her book. However, I fail to see why this disqualifies her from parenting advice, given that her job for many years has been to give full-time care to hundreds of babies. Frankly, she has more experience with babies than you or I would get in a lifetime.

Amber1

Gina Ford suits me. Two friends who are expecting their second children and didn't follow her routines with their first had such a challenging experience the first time, they have now bought the book. Having read it they understand some of the 'mistakes' they made the first time around. Both had babies who only slept through very late (after eight months) and when you work, that is a challenge.

Gina Ford may not be a mother herself but she has plenty of common sense recommendations. I feel they have worked for me. I completely respect parents who have chosen not to follow her routines. Some have wonderful experiences, others don't... and it is to those who don't and who are looking for another option that I recommend reading her book. They can then judge whether it is for them.

Pupuce

I was a total Gina Ford cynic after reading her first book – to me she sounded like an army major, which is the sort of thing that sends me back into teenage rebellion mode. However, I had a baby who would not sleep during the day, was tired and screamed for most of the day. I didn't realize that this was the problem because all my books said that little babies sleep when they are tired and can't keep themselves awake. In desperation, I tried Gina Ford's sleeping patterns (approximately). Within a week I had a much happier baby who would nap, as long as I put her down before she showed signs of tiredness as by then it would be too late.

> **Mumsnet fact**
> Gina Ford's *The Contented Little Baby Book* has sold 120,000 copies in the UK alone.

However, our breastfeeding routine was a non-Gina Ford pattern. During the day, she would feed forever (often every 45 minutes, and for 45 minutes) and from 8 pm until 10.30 pm, but then she would sleep until 6 am (at three weeks). I was totally freaked because my other books talked about feeds taking about 20 minutes. As I seemed to be permanently feeding, I thought I must be doing something wrong. Eventually my husband convinced me that my daughter was gaining weight, was relatively happy and slept through the night, so must be okay. I relaxed about it and I carried on breastfeeding her for a year.

Methods don't necessarily work 100 per cent for every baby, so if you find yours does need a 'routine' in some areas, be prepared to adapt things to suit them and don't beat yourself up about it.

Twink

I used Gina Ford with my daughter, who certainly sleeps and eats brilliantly, so in that respect it was great. However, the isolation I felt in the early months when I was desperately trying to stick to her routines made my life much more depressing than it needed to be. I didn't know any other mums who were following Gina

Ford and so I found socializing very difficult indeed. I certainly feel that getting out and about and meeting other mums is equally as important as getting a sleep/feed pattern established. Because of this I won't be following the routines exactly with my new baby (due next year) as I value the times I have at Mother and Toddler and the other classes I go to with my daughter.

Jolly

Whilst there seem to be many 'contented little babies' around, some mothers seem to end up far from happy. Research shows that one of the causes of PND is social isolation, which appears to be a side effect of Gina Ford's regime for babies. Speaking for myself, part of the pleasure of having a new baby is the social aspect and I would hate to have been tied to someone else's idea of what my baby should be doing. As you've probably guessed, I've not used Gina Ford's book, but of my four children, three probably would count as 'contented' babies and just one as less obliging.

Baabaa

I've followed Gina Ford's routines for some time now (though I shrink from admitting to it) but I have to say it does p*** me off when people keep banging on about the rigidity of the routines and their carefree lives which allow them to go where they want when they want with their children. (I very often hear the same people moaning that 'little Johnny was up till 10 pm playing football last night. I'm so tired').

Frankly, I think my children – all children – have the right to a reasonable amount of decent sleep and I don't think you can get that when you're been pushed around in a buggy or whatever. I think you need bed for that. I also believe babies feel more secure with the predictability of a routine. I find that I've had more fun with my babies when I've put them first, we're all well-rested and all of our needs have been given consideration.

Inky

I am following the Gina Ford book at the moment and it works with varying degrees of success. My son is 12 weeks old and is sleeping from 10.45 pm to 7 am pretty much most nights. The problem I am having is that when things don't go the way the book describes (sometimes my son wants to sleep a lot earlier than the routines allow), I begin to feel as if I'm a failure. This is disheartening and sometimes exacerbates my post-natal feelings. I think that if you're not too much of a control freak, can deal with the fact that it doesn't always work and allow for the fact that babies are individuals with good and bad days, the book has some excellent advice. However, today my day hasn't been brilliant and it has got me down a bit.

Alli

I think the key to understanding Gina Ford is to take the spirit of her advice, rather than applying it to the letter. I think she is right about the amount of sleep a baby needs during the day, but I think her approach is too strict. My little boy has the same number of feeds and naps as she recommends and so we have adopted her waking and bedtimes, but we have tailored the timing of what goes between to what suits him and us best.

Hels

My sister used Gina Ford's routines with her three and she swears by them (her kids are really good I have to admit). I chose not to follow them because my baby was so easy, but I borrowed the book when my daughter still didn't sleep through the night at six months. I thought Gina Ford's explanations made a lot of sense and while I didn't follow her routine, I used her advice and within three days she was sleeping through the night – it may have been a coincidence. I think Gina Ford is good for parents who like to lead an organized life, as my sister does. She is a very confident person, she likes things to run smoothly and I have to admire her sometimes because her three children are very close together in age and are very, very easy. They are all in bed by 7 pm, they get up at 7.30 am (later at weekends!) and they eat well.

Valerianne

Bear in mind that Gina Ford's routines are only advice. I found it really helps to know how much a baby needs to sleep. Most of us do have a brain and use the book to base a routine on, but we don't necessarily follow it to the letter. Gina Ford gives a fantastic guide to how to get a routine going. All in all, though, it depends on the child, some are fractious little beasts and some are placid, routine or not.

Crunchie

Dummies – yes or no?

I hate dummies – there, I've said it. I can just about stand seeing them in a tiny baby's mouth, though I prefer to see what the child actually looks like rather than a lump of plastic and two little eyes. I can't stand seeing children over the age of six months with one and hate it when they're trying to speak with one attached or having one shoved in their mouth by their parent. Basically, I wonder why people bother. My daughter was far from an angelic wonder-baby that never cried, she was, in fact, very demanding but cuddles and feeds got us through the early months – would a dummy have made all the difference?

Lizzer

I just cannot bear the look of them. Endless people tried to foist them on me when our son was a baby with my mother-in-law even buying a few for me. Sorry, but I just think they look horrid.

Croppy

I also dislike dummies intensely and swore I'd never use them. But sure enough, when my son was two weeks old and fractious all the time, I was at the shop buying six different kinds! He refused them entirely, so it was his decision in the end. I like to think that I would have weaned him off dummies by around six months, but who knows? Unfortunately for us, the breast never calmed or soothed him either. So we just had a very fractious baby. My neighbour has a 21-month-old with a dummy permanently in his mouth or clipped to his shirt. He has many tantrums and they usually try to head these off by sticking the dummy in his mouth (succeeding about 50 per cent of the time). I really noticed it once, when looking through a roll of film she showed me. There wasn't a single photo of his little face without a big dummy in the middle of it. It seems a shame, but I'm aware that I could all too easily have ended up there myself if they had worked for us.

Amber1

I hate dummies and never used them with my two. We had some tough months at first but they both sleep beautifully now. I suppose I still haven't got my head around why they are needed. Surely if a baby wants to suck then it's better to give them something with nutrition in it to suck on like a bottle/boob? If they're just bored or upset then use some other form of distraction and if they won't settle to sleep, try sleep training. If you never use a dummy, you never have the trauma of getting rid of it. I nearly went ballistic when my childminder used a dummy on my six-month-old. He'd never had one up to that point, so why start then?

Hmonty

Mumsnet fact
Over ten million dummies were sold in the UK in 2000.   Avent

I hate dummies and was livid to find a midwife had shoved one in my four-day-old baby's mouth when I had dashed off to the loo! There were other new mums in hospital with me, who virtually shoved a dummy in their baby's mouth on delivery.

As a result of feeding problems for the first few months, our little boy was also fairly whingey and irritable most of the time. I can understand people wanting to give a dummy at this stage as I was contemplating driving all the way to town at 3 am to buy one! However, with the threat of exacerbating his feeding problems hanging over our heads we persisted and managed to get through. I am glad we did now as I watch a friend's four-year-old son still sucking on his dummy for all he's worth!

Chelle

Most of the people I know who used them did so out of desperation. I can't stand them either, so soldiered on but did envy friends who opted for the dummy and their bedtime peace and quiet, so much so that I did buy a couple to try them out. But my son didn't like them and I really didn't push the issue. I feel strongly about older children having them, too. Soothing a little person off to sleep is one thing, stopping them from interacting vocally with their surroundings is entirely different.

Clare2

Both of mine had dummies but no one ever saw them outside the house. I cannot stand to see children with dummies strapped to them or being constantly shoved in their mouths. My two had them for bedtime and the youngest gave his up at a very early age and found his thumb. In fact, they used to fall asleep with them and then chuck them out of the cot. I have heard of children having them when they go to school, not at school of course, but still having them at bedtime.

Tigger

I hate the sight of them, but my son had one from about five months until he rejected it himself at eight months. The dummy helped us over a difficult patch (including a holiday abroad) when he would wail all the time and I don't think he has been psychologically damaged as a result! Of course all the time he was using it, I felt like an inadequate mother but that just goes with the territory. My daughter, on the other hand, always rejected a dummy, but at two years old is still a frenetic thumb sucker. I'm not sure if that is any better, particularly as I have no control over when she does it or when she'll stop.

Minchen

I was very anti-dummy – no child of mine was ever going to have one. This lasted until we got fed up with sitting with my son at night with a little finger in his mouth until he sucked himself to sleep. The health visitor said, 'What's the difference between him sucking your finger and a dummy?' Answer: an extra half hour every evening for mum (or dad) to relax. So we got a dummy and it worked very well – until my son realized he was being fobbed off and learnt how to pull it out of his mouth and throw it away. So that was the end of that. I don't like to see dummies glued permanently into babies' mouths but I reckon they can have a place in a desperate situation!

Azzie

Excepting the sensible people who seem to manage to tightly control the use of dummies, I think that they're essentially a sign of lazy parenting. For many it seems to be an easy option for anyone who can't be bothered to interact with a child and would rather stick a dummy in its mouth to shut it up. I think putting up with a few grizzly days is far preferable to having a child stuck to a dummy for years.

Harrysmum

After three dummy-less children, including one very unsettled one, I'm afraid I'm with the smug, 'it's just lazy parenting' school on this one: I think people often just shove the dummy in whenever the baby makes a noise and I don't like to see them soothing themselves with a piece of plastic instead of their parents. But hey, maybe if I'd been more willing to experiment with a dummy it would have made life much easier and the unsettled baby's early life more fun, who knows?

Numbat

One of my boys still has a dummy and neither I, nor my husband, are lazy parents. I was totally against dummies before having my twins and refused to buy them. After a few weeks however, I was persuaded to try them by a health visitor because one child in particular was getting himself into a real state by crying and screaming. The dummy soothed him instantly and he became a happier baby. The health visitor advised that it was much better for him to have a dummy than to be sobbing his little heart out. He now has it at night very much in the same way that other children have comfort blankets. His twin brother, by the way, has never had a dummy – he just didn't like them. The vast majority of us are just doing the best we can and whether you do or don't give your baby a dummy, biscuits or put them in bed with you or whatever, then as long as you can manage it with a vague smile every now and again, and your kids get enough cuddles you're not doing too badly.

Twinsmum

What the experts say
If a baby isn't willing to give up a dummy – at any age – I don't think it's right to take it away.

Dr Spock and Stephen Parker (*Dr Spock's Baby and Child Care*)

A dummy can be useful to soothe a colicky baby in the first four months, but it is better to transfer children to sucking their own thumbs after that.

Hilton, Messenger and Graham (*New Baby and Child Care Book*)

The worry with dummies seems to be that people use them to shut their children up instead of getting to the real problem. All I can say is that with mine that wouldn't have been possible (not that I would have wanted to use dummies for that – well, not often!). They want them when they're tired or sick and aren't interested any other time. I too have a horror of children aged five sucking on a dummy. I seem to remember reading that some supermodel still uses one. Like all things to do with kids, I think as long as you have boundaries and set them early on, they are manageable. For us, using dummies for sleep has definitely made life easier for everyone.

Berta

A baby has a strong urge to suck. The natural state would be to get this from the breast, which has the added advantage of providing food. A baby needs a lot of comfort sucking, which for some reason many think is wrong. As many women don't breastfeed or if they do they restrict it to 'mealtimes', then the sucking instinct is not satisfied. Therefore it can be provided artificially through a dummy. It does genuinely comfort them. For bottle-fed babies it can often be the only way to comfort them. There's nothing wrong with this. However, the problem with anything artificial is that it can be misused or overused. Hence you see the older child with dummy in its mouth.

Mumsnet fact
Research from the Netherlands shows that they (dummies) can prevent SIDS (cot death) in susceptible children. Probably because they stimulate the child to suck throughout the night.

Karen Sullivan (*Commonsense Healthcare for Children*)

In societies where women wear their babies strapped onto their bodies, so allowing the baby to suckle at will and breastfeed for longer, thumb sucking and dummies are unknown. Dummy misuse is a sign of our modern society and yes, often they are shoved into babies' mouths to keep the peace. However, they can be used perfectly well without problems.

We tried one with our baby but he spat it out, so for the first eight weeks or so

I just wandered around with my bra open most of the time – fortunately it was a hot summer. I still allow my child to comfort suck and I am sure some people would be horrified by this, but it makes him happy – is it wrong for him to be happy? A child will always give up breastfeeding eventually but the same can't be said for thumbs and dummies and a soft boob will not damage teeth.

Eulalia

Both my sons have dummies. The four-year-old still has one at night, and as long as he sleeps and is happy I don't see it as much of an issue. My two-year-old still has a dummy day and night. At the moment I am not at the stage of saying 'no' during the day. As long as they are happy children I am not at all worried.

Feline

If your children sleep with dummies, be grateful. At 18 months, my daughter still wants mama's breasts to comfort her when she wakes at night. I had a dummy until I was four and it doesn't seem to have had any disastrous effects on me. The next one will have a dummy, whether they like it or not.

Gilly

My two (twins) have always used them to go to sleep (they're 22 months). They don't use them out of their cots and I truly believe they are fantastic things. Partly because of them, in my view, I had children who went to sleep soundlessly in cots by themselves from about four months and slept through so we never had to resort to controlled crying. They're easily washed, easily replaced, better for your teeth than thumbs and what's more, my nipples were used only for feeding. If they'd had to work as comforters as well, with twins, they probably would have fallen off! Having said all that, goodness only knows how we're going to get rid of them... but does it really matter if they only have them in their beds? I think we'll wait for them to stop by themselves.

Clairer

I found with my three children that they gave up their dummies in their own time when they were ready. I see no harm in a child having a dummy for sleep and the longer they have it, the more comfort they are storing up so that they will not need a substitute (like a thumb or blanket) when the dummy finally goes.

Liza

Mumsnet tip
If your child wakes at night because she has lost her dummy, try leaving three or four around the cot. She is bound to find one of them and you might get a few extra hours of precious sleep.

We could not have survived without dummies – my eldest son was extremely fractious as a tiny baby. I remember at the time my husband saying he would pay £50 for a dummy for the peace it bought us when we were at the end of our wits. It comforted our son, soothed him, stopped him crying and sent him to sleep. (It did these things better than breastfeeding.) He gave it up himself when he was 15 weeks old. My youngest son also had a dummy. He didn't give it up himself and so we had to fight that battle when he was 21 months old. I personally dislike dummies for toddlers, especially during the daytime.

Scally

I used a dummy with my son from when he was about two weeks old until we stopped it at around two years. We found it the only thing that would soothe him off to sleep. It allowed him to get used to the idea of getting off to sleep by himself in his cot and he has been absolutely brilliant at sleeping ever since. We thought it was going to be a real hard slog getting rid of it but in fact we just told him he didn't need it anymore, threw it in the bin and after a few minutes grizzling he was asleep. He has not used one since. We only ever used it for bedtime, or if we were in the car on a long journey, and I would definitely use them again.

Debster

We used a dummy for about two days when my daughter was very tiny. The only trouble was it kept falling out and we couldn't tell if she was hungry or not, so we stopped. She quickly became a thumb sucker, which actually does not bother me but does seem to bother a lot of other people, including complete strangers who seem to think it is their right to tell me off about it. My daughter is now three and still sucks her thumb when she is tired or upset. It has not in any way stopped her speech developing or pushed her teeth out or anything like that, but I am not sure how she will ever break this habit. My health visitor actually said my daughter should have been given a dummy because the parents have ultimate control over the use of it, unlike the thumb.

Batters

I am one of five children and my mother said proudly that none of us had one! However, after a few days looking after my first child even she said, 'for goodness sake, just get a dummy'. My eldest was a very colicky and hungry baby for the first four months. I spent all my maternity leave walking, babe in arms, up and down the living room as feeding her constantly made her colic worse. Enter the dreaded dummy! She loved it from the word go and it gave the colic a chance to subside before the next feed. I hated seeing it in her mouth, so as she got older I limited it to sleeping times only and at the age of two, just before Christmas, I told her Santa needed it for another baby. This worked like a dream. Dummies were our saviour at a very difficult time and if it helps then, who cares what others think?

Sporty1

> **Mumsnet fact**
> A primitive form of dummy was made from a knotted rag. In 1859, a woman's magazine recommended mothers stuff the knot with pork fat or rabbit brains. The rubber soothing pad (as it was then called) was first invented in 1882. *Mother and Baby* magazine

I can see both sides. As a thumb-sucker until the ripe old age of thirteen, I'm pro-dummies – unlike a thumb, they can be thrown away. It became such a habit with me that I didn't know I was doing it, so it was extremely hard to stop. I was teased mercilessly if anyone caught me.

Binza

I too used to be one of those (prospective) parents who thought that dummies were horrible and vowed never to let my child have one. But after two weeks of a crying, non-sleeping baby (she once stayed awake from 6 am to 11 pm), I gave in and have never looked back. I don't particularly like my child sucking on a dummy when we're out but I know that anyone who judges me to be a bad parent because of it is not in a position to judge and therefore I don't care what they think. (In fact, it's changed my attitude on judging others about anything, as I have learnt that you can never know how you would act, given the same circumstances). I wouldn't mind so much but it's so unimportant!

Rosy

My son has several dummies and in my opinion they are brilliant. It is his comforter and anything that comforts him is great as far as I'm concerned. However, I also agree that outside the house they are a little strange. For night-time, naps and car journeys they are invaluable. Surely that is what they are made for, to comfort them to sleep, not for when they are out and about, and interacting with people and the world. Most people don't even know he has a dummy unless we go to stay the night.

Jessi

What the experts say
Once the intense need to suck for comfort and food starts to wane around six months you can try to wean your baby off her dummy.
Priscia Middlemiss (*How to get a Whole Night's Sleep*)

If your baby needs the comfort of sucking, by all means introduce a soother (dummy).

Karen Sullivan (*Commonsense Healthcare for Children*)

I've just come back from Spain where every single baby that passed had a dummy, either in its mouth or pinned to its clothes on a little chain – it must be compulsory over there. I'm not totally anti-dummy but the idea of buying one never even crossed my mind before my son was born. As soon as he was, though, I sent my Mum out to buy half a dozen before I'd even left the hospital. Perhaps I was a lazy parent but when you are a new mum your head is all over the place and I don't see what is wrong with calming a fractious baby with a dummy for a while. My son gave the dummy up himself at six months, and now has a 'blankie', which I suppose is just swapping one thing for another. On the other hand, I don't know any young child that doesn't have some means of comfort, whether it's a dummy, a thumb, a teddy or a blankie. Why should we deprive them of these?

Donna1

In the great scheme of things, whether you give your child a dummy or not is really of little importance. Surely what matters is that the child is loved and cared for. If it wants to suck a dummy, or if the parent wants it to have one, then so what? My nephew is 26, sucked his thumb since birth and still does at times. His dentist is appalled and my sister now wishes she had given him a dummy, which she could have taken from him. I have been in France, where my friend was encouraged to give her daughter a piece of washable cloth to suck on by her French relatives. Yuck! Give me a dummy any day. At least you can run them under the tap.

Evesmum

Neither of my sons have had dummies. I liked the sound of their voices too much. Had I felt they really wanted to suck on something, though, I would not have ruled out a dummy. If your baby uses a dummy, what harm can it do to them? So many of us, me included, seem to hate dummies, especially in public. Yet, I can't see why they are so bad. If your child was sucking on a favourite blanket, a toy or a teething ring when you were out (not to mention a bottle or a beaker), would you still feel the same way? You could present a pro-health case for dummies. As a soothing tantrum-stopper, doesn't a dummy score higher in the health stakes than a sweet? Put bluntly, aren't we being vain, shallow and selfish in our condemnation of dummies? Aren't we putting our own wishes about how we present our child to the world above our child's wish for fairly harmless comfort?

Frank1

Late sitting up and crawling – should you worry? Is there anything you can do about it?

Developmental milestones can be very confusing and worrying. Babies are all different. They do what they want, when they want – and definitely not when we want. I still meet up with my NCT antenatal group (all our babies were born within four weeks of each other) and they have all reached milestones at completely different times. There was an eight month age difference between the earliest walker and the latest one.

Molly1

My little one is ten months old and still not crawling. He sits cross-legged like a Buddha then leans forward on to his hands but then topples over and falls on his tummy. I know he will eventually get it – you don't meet many 18-year-olds still sitting on their bums (or perhaps you do but you know what I mean!). It is frustrating having to keep picking him up but will soon be even more frustrating picking him out of the cupboards or video and chasing him all over the place like a demented chicken!

Emerald

I don't think my son sat up until he was around six months and that was after lots of practice with us holding him and lots of cushions to prop him up but he was always much more interested in standing. Now at ten months he doesn't crawl, just rolls around but will happily walk while holding your hand. So he hasn't done things as a lot of people expect but will do things in his own way and in his own time.

Peanuts1

My daughter didn't sit up until she was over eight months old, even though she crawled at six and a half months! My health visitor was so concerned she was thinking of referring her to a paediatrician (slight over-reaction, I thought). Anyway, she's 18 months now and, of course, sits perfectly, although she's still not a sitting still kind of person!

Caznay

My youngest has always done things at his own pace and in his own way. For instance, he was an early walker and his balance, spatial awareness and manual dexterity are definitely better than his brothers were at the same age. However, his talking is at least nine months behind – and his first words were vastly different and a lot less clear. I try and see his development pattern as individual to him – while staying aware of general developmental milestones.

Frank1

My eldest daughter didn't crawl until she was 16 months old. Obviously, she was later walking because of that, but she is no different to any other child now. I have heard it said that heavier babies take longer because they have extra weight to deal with and also, if their head is quite large it is very difficult for them to balance. This seemed to be true for my daughter anyway. Having said that, if you are worried about your child's development there's no harm in talking to your health visitor.

Lou33

My son is nearly 12 months old and is not yet crawling or bearing much weight when we try to get him to stand. My sister, who is a physio, has suggested that I play games with him to stimulate his feet and try to get him to realize what they are actually for. I don't know if the heavier baby thing is true. My son was quite small at birth and is not what I would call a big baby even though he's eating loads and spending all day on his fat butt.

Hilsr

My son never crawled. He bottom-shuffled from ten months onwards and became very good at it! He didn't start pulling himself up until he was about 13 months. Some babies don't even do this, they just go straight from sitting to walking. My friend's child (who's the same age as mine) didn't move at all until he was over a year, then he did slow bottom-shuffling and finally walked at 15 months. There really is nothing you can do except let them get on with it, but for reassurance you can always ask the health visitor or doctor to check their hips in case there's a problem.

> **Mumsnet fact**
> Occasionally some perfectly normal babies never crawl at all; they just sit around until they learn to stand up.
> Dr Spock and Stephen Parker (*Dr Spock's Baby & Child Care*)

I think the subject of crawling and walking is one where old wives' tales abound. I don't think size of body or head, or rate of growth has anything to do with it. A child just does what he feels comfortable with and he does it in his own good time so there's no point in putting them on their tummies to get them to crawl, and stuff like that. I don't believe in baby walkers – they are dangerous because they tend to tip over. Also, it doesn't encourage the child to balance by himself. Some mothers put them in walkers far too young so they are sitting in a bad position. At the end of the day all normal kids walk eventually, so why worry?

Eulalia

If your child is getting really frustrated at not moving, think about getting one of the new-fangled stationary devices that are similar to walkers but don't move.

One of mine was late with all her physical development – I can't remember when she first sat but she didn't move herself until her first birthday and didn't walk until she was 18 or 19 months. Her elder sister sat at six or seven months, crawled at about eight months and walked at 12 or 13 months. They are utterly individual and it is really important NOT to expect them to do things at the same age.

Janh

I had a brilliant stationary walker. Instead of wheels it just had a big plastic base. The child sits in a fabric seat and can put limited weight on their legs, and the seat can swivel around so they can play with toys on a circular tray that goes around the outside. My son loved it as he could 'sit up' and look all around him. It was expensive but worth it.

Paula1

They will move when they're ready – my best friend's son didn't walk on his own until he was 18 months old and she was beside herself with worry. But when he did, he was off like Linford Christie within days. No toddling for him.

Clare2

It's amazing how much you worry about those early milestones – thinking that if your child crawls at eight, nine, ten or later months is deeply significant, when, in fact, in 99 per cent of cases it's not. It's only when you have a running, jumping three-year-old on your hands and you're scared to death every time she scoots up to the top of the tallest climbing frame that you realize that whether they were early or late crawlers matters not a jot. Still, it's so hard not to be competitive about development (when we all know better, really). There is a real plus side to late crawling, though – safety. Early crawlers have to be watched all the time as they can get into everything. Enjoy the extra few months of peace of mind if your child's a late crawler – who knows, you may even get a chance to read a newspaper while your baby plays happily in one spot on the floor.

Nancy

What equipment do you need to buy?

In my opinion, the only essentials are a cot, a pushchair and a sling. Oh, and a sterilizer, as even if you're breastfeeding, it's good to be able to express and store milk so you can take a break. I found the baby bath useful but not essential and used the top of a fridge-freezer as a changing table. The thing I wish I hadn't wasted money on was cot blankets – I should have just got a sleeping bag plus one or two cellular blankets. Now I have full sets of both and the sleeping bags are much better. You don't need cot bumpers, nappy stackers, baby toiletries, baby towels and all that jazz. But, as with everything in life, if you have unlimited amounts of money, some of those things can be fun and occasionally even useful.

Amber1

I love the baby sleeping bag. Sheets and blankets were never going to work for us. He feels safe and comfy in it, even in unfamiliar surroundings. Also, I could not cope without the Play Nest. He could sit up much earlier than many of his friends so it reminds me of those happy times when I could put him in it and he'd stay there!

Bruntwig

A sleeping bag is essential. From six months our son has gone to sleep cheerfully in beds all over the UK because he was in his familiar bag. As he's got older, his folding booster seat has been invaluable – it's much better than his expensive, impossible highchair.

Clare2

Babywipes! How people managed with just cotton wool is beyond me! It always sticks to their skin when you're trying to get the disgusting, gloopy baby lotion off! And Anywayup cups are the best thing in the world – no more soggy sofas, carpets, car seats or anything.

Lara1

Another vote for babywipes – I shall never stop buying them as they're great for wine spills too. And Anywayup cups (though we've gone through an awful lot of lids and they could do with an inbuilt homing device on them). Dummies are a must – although God knows how I'll get rid of them but they've certainly helped me get some sleep. Disposable nappies are essential – don't know how my mum did it with terries! Intercoms – great invention (and the soaps would lose half their story lines without them). Oh, and those foldable changing mats – invest in one of those.

Berta

It's funny how one person's 'must buy' is another's nightmare waste of money! I can't stand monitors. I used mine for a few days with each child and then figured if they were distressed I would hear them cry. The bath seat was great but stair gates really irritate me. Babywipes I can't live without – no question there.

Crunchie

My favourite products are the Anywayup cup and metanium nappy rash cream. Works instantly and one tube lasts forever.

Debster

A travel stair gate. Quick, adjustable and great for taking to relatives' places, where they think child-friendly means giving them a packet of crisps. Saved endless woes. I've got about three of them – one at my mum's, one across my landing and one for emergency blockings! Also, I couldn't do without my doorstops, the ones that fit over the top of the door. The thought of pinched little fingers makes me shudder.

Emmam

A bath seat is a must. It means I don't have to hold him in the bath and we can both play without worrying. I'm amazed when I find out some people don't use one. The best money I ever spent. I've got a second one now for number two – I've just got to wait for him to sit up so I can start using it!

Bo

The baby sling and then the backpack were two of the best items we bought. We also had my big pram from when I was a child, and I used to take her out in it in the afternoon when I went to feed a shed full of heifers and tie it to the gate. The heifers used to nuzzle the handle and rock my daughter back and forth until she fell asleep – cheap childcare!

Tigger

My vote goes to those triangle-shaped pillows. They're absolutely divine for those uncomfortable hospital beds and at home for getting comfy to breastfeed. They're good for keeping newborns snuggled on the sofa and to put behind babies when they're just learning to sit up.

Madasahatter

I'm adding my vote for the sleeping bag. I made fleece sleeping bags (with short arms and a full-length zip up the front) and they've been wonderful with both my kids. They can't kick them off (both have been athletic sleepers) and have stayed cosy even when camping. Another good piece of kit was a recliner/rocking chair. Number two spent many happy hours in it as a small baby, either sleeping or propped up watching her brother playing. She seemed more comfortable in it than sitting in the car seat, possibly because she was able to lie flatter.

Azzie

I couldn't have lived without bouncy cradles that you can just rock with your foot – and later feed them in. Also the baby bouncer, which gave us the only 20 minutes of peace we had for ages.

Robinw

The wind-up swing was wonderful and the baby monitor is great – it goes on holidays with us as it still bleeps when there's movement even if sound is out of range. A bouncy chair is good for somewhere to leave the baby safely in lie-back position and a stair gate on the kitchen is marvellous, as there's no need for drawer and fridge locks that don't work!

Naddy

Microwave steam sterilizers get my vote. I could sterilize and make up the impending day's feeds in less than twenty minutes. Oh and baby monitors, I live in a really solid house and can't hear the kids upstairs so I still use mine now, even though the children are well beyond the baby stage.

AlJa

The baby swing was our saviour giving us some hands-free 'time off'. My first hated being still for any amount of time – I still find myself rocking and swaying around Asda!

Rosilee

I'd borrow a Moses basket rather than buy one. We were lucky we didn't buy ours because our son was big at birth – it would have lasted about a week. We did have a swinging crib and he slept in that for six months in our room but as soon as we put him in the cot bed in his own room, he slept much better as he had more room. See how big the baby is before you buy anything and then get your partner or a relative to run round like idiots while you're in hospital. We bought the next-size-up baby grows which turned out to be a blessing because he didn't fit into the newborn ones!

Selja

What the experts say
Don't feel you have to buy everything brand new; look out for second-hand items advertised in local papers or on noticeboards in the local baby clinics.
Dr Miriam Stoppard (*Your New Baby*)

Buy a cheap Moses basket or, better still, borrow one. Our little one couldn't sleep in his, as he was too big. It took us over a week to work out that his screaming at night was due to a lack of space around him! A good-quality cot or cot bed is a much better investment.

Fairy

I think a cot bed wins hands down over a cot. We bought ours seven years ago. It has been a cot, a bed for a six year old, and now it's back to being a cot again for our second son. It's the most useful and hard-working piece of kit we own. We used it from the time our first son was four months. Even if your baby ends up sleeping in your bed, you know you can still get your money's worth from it as a bed later.

Frank1

I'd recommend the type of pushchair where your car seat will clip to its chassis. Fantastic invention. I've always loved my changing table too – it has been used constantly for both of mine. A baby bath that sits on or in the big bath or just one of those sponges the baby lies on is useful. Other essentials are sleep suits with the cuffs that fold over (built in scratch mitts) and lots of cloths like cotton muslins or hand towels. Nail scissors for those tiny razor nails – though I used to bite them off as I was too scared to use the scissors! I also loved my Intercom. You don't need a high chair until they are six months but we found one of those low bouncy chairs useful for feeding or just for them to sit in.

Rosebud

Borrow a Moses basket or carrycot – our daughter was in a proper cot at two weeks. We liked having a baby bath and used it for quite a few months, but it would probably have been easier to borrow one as they take up so much space afterwards. Buy the bare minimum of clothes. People we barely know bought us clothes and toys and it was a pity that we didn't get to use some of them very much. Even now, my mother and grandmother-in-law would clothe our daughter completely if they had the chance!

Do buy a carrying sling – when my son wanted to be held I could strap him to me and still get on with jobs. If your pram has a carrycot you can use that and then move straight to a cot so I wouldn't bother with a crib. We never bothered with nappy bags either, we ended up with so many carrier bags from the supermarket that we just used those instead!

BCawthorne

> **Mumsnet tip**
> Keep one of those car window sunshades in each door pocket. You never know which window will need one.

Black-out blinds are essential to stop your baby thinking that 4 am is a good wake-up time. If you're intending to breastfeed then buying or renting an electric breast pump is a good idea. There's one that does both breasts at the same time in about five minutes and is quite painless.

PP

Take up offers of loans – especially for things that you'll only use for short periods like cribs. I agree you shouldn't buy clothes for at least six months – the wardrobe in the nursery is better stocked than mine! Talking of wardrobes if you have space buy an adult one with shelves so that toys can be put away in them as well.

Always buy a new car seat – it's not worth the risk of buying one second-hand. The best thing is to go somewhere that will let you try it in the car before you buy. We found that there were only a few seats which fitted our car and this affected which travel system we bought. The carrycot is great for naps and can be used until the baby is three or four months old. The car seat attachment to a pushchair chassis is fab for quick shopping trips.

Duck

I found that the top of a chest of drawers was fine as a changing table. The sterilizer was invaluable even though I breastfed. You'll be surprised how useful muslin cloths and bibs are, so have lots of those. I'd also recommend a clip-on arch to stretch over the carrycot/cot. Spend lots of time reading catalogues and then just buy the bare essentials – you can add to it later when you discover what you need, rather than buying stuff that you never use.

Alison222

What baby products do you wish you'd never bought?

You actually need a remarkably small amount of stuff for a newborn baby: somewhere for them to sleep, a car seat, a few clothes (you'll be given loads) and that's about it. If you are going to do a lot of walking then you'll want a pram or pushchair but you really need to think about it carefully. I know so many people who regret their first choice. Everything else is for added convenience and it is very difficult to know what will make your life easier until you have had the baby. My advice to any expectant mums out there would be to hold off on too much pre-birth expenditure. You *can* still go to the shops afterwards.

Molly1

What the experts say
It's advisable to go shopping in the last couple of months before your baby's born, while you're still unfettered and feel reasonably energetic.

Miriam Stoppard (*New Baby Care Book*)

One thing I should not have bought is a travel system. The car seat was great for a while, but soon my son was too big for it. The pram/pushchair was just too heavy – there was no way that I could push the pushchair and hold an umbrella at the same time – we got about four months use out of it. What a waste of money! We now have a buggy, which is a lot lighter and easier to use.

Smalline

We spent a lot of cash on a 2-in-1 travel system and it was money down the drain. The pram was a nightmare. It was just so cumbersome. We couldn't get it into any local shops and it filled up the boot of the car completely. We ended up buying a small buggy, which has been used and abused now for 18 months. Other bad buys were baby oil – it brought my son out in a rash – and a big tub of nappy cream – why did I ever think I'd need that much?

Emmam

What the experts say
Preparation for the birth: have all the baby essentials in stock: cotton wool, baby oil, nappies, nappy and moisturizing creams, baby wipes, soft sponges, bath brush, bath oil and baby shampoo.

Gina Ford (*The New Contented Little Baby Book*)

We bought every baby toiletry going: baby oil, lotion, bath, shampoo. Our baby turns out to have eczema and we haven't been able to use any of it.

A wooden swinging crib, which had been bought by my brother for his daughter and which she wouldn't sleep in, was donated to us and our son wouldn't sleep in it, either. Very pretty but a complete waste of money and space. Our most expensive mistake has been our old-fashioned pram. It's heavy and cumbersome, fills the boot and is very difficult to manoeuvre around town. We use a small buggy most of the time now.

Alexsmum

> **Mumsnet tip**
> Rather than spending lots of money on creams for your baby's skin, use olive oil to massage her after the bath. It's a great way of bonding, it calms her down for bed, and it really works for dry skin.

I agree on the 3-in-1 travel system. Although the car seat attachment was indispensable, the carry cot was virtually never used and the pushchair was far too cumbersome to take anywhere, although it was nice for local walks. Our worst buy ever, though, has to be the bottle/food warmer, which we used before we had a microwave. Not only did it take ages to heat the bottles but also, if you leave it too long, the bottle gets far too hot. As for food, it was an absolute joke to suggest that it was ever going to warm anything up to a reasonable temperature. I would definitely say just get a microwave at the outset. The Play Nest was also a disaster – the overhead thing continually collapsed and our son never liked it.

Croppy

We bought a bottle warmer for my first child, which was a complete waste of time. My husband found an old thermos cup and we put boiling water in this to heat up bottles. We thought we were so clever. Child number two comes along and we discover she doesn't care how warm her top-up milk is. She just wants it!

My three year old still plays with the Play Nest ring. She will sleep in it, use it as a trampoline, hat, toy keeper. I was impressed enough to by a second one for number two.

I also hate my rocking chair – also a waste of money. We had to stop it from rocking to avoid little fingers getting caught and then subsequently large holes being knocked into walls.

Carolann

I will step forward and throw my Play Nest and my baby bouncer on the pyre. Both rubbish! My daughter used to lie crying inconsolably in the Play Nest. So we'd move her to the baby bouncer where she would cry at bit more, but this time spinning around very slowly.

Caznay

I bought an expensive rocking chair, which I thought was a complete waste of money as my daughter screamed every time she was put in it. However, the next two babies loved it and spent many happy hours in it. That such young babies can have such strong likes and dislikes was a big surprise to me.

I hate toys that need batteries! Lots of people where we live have battery-powered trikes for their small children. At weekends you hear the noise of the engines as they're all trundling round their back gardens storing up future heart disease, or whatever you get from not taking any exercise.

Javarose

I thought the baby bouncer was a real pain – I remember trying to get it in and out and killing my back in the process, but I thought the play nest was fab. When they were about to sit up but still a bit wobbly it was just the job. Admittedly it has a short life – three months and they're out of it – but a good three months. I would throw my hideously-expensive playpen onto the pyre. It took up the whole living room, looked ugly and my two hated to be put in it – not surprising really, it's basically a cage! Oh, and the Moses basket, which remains practically untouched by baby hands (one horrific night only).

Berta

Mumsnet fact
Parents spend nearly £1,000 on baby goods before the birth of their first child.   *Having a Baby*

The playpen was a waste of a Christmas present. My baby screams blue murder when I put him in it, so now I just plop him in his cot if I need a few uninterrupted minutes. It is, however, useful for hanging damp towels and laundry on, but rather an expensive drying rack.

Pj

The playpen was a total waste of space. My children also despised it with a passion. Once, feeling rather housebound, I decided to dismantle and reassemble the said playpen in the front garden, the rather misguided idea being that I would garden while the babe played contentedly. Instead, we gave the neighbours a wonderful floor show: 20 minutes of me fumbling with playpen, two minutes of gardening, ten minutes of baby howling and 20 minutes of me dismantling the playpen and retreating back inside, defeated. The same goes for the door bouncer. Both my children fought valiantly with me as I struggled to put them in the blessed thing, then they spent all of five minutes hanging, looking puzzled and defiant before screaming blue murder. After two or three attempts, each child would go bonkers at just seeing the box. Happily, neither of these items live with us anymore!

Sylvev

For me, the biggest waste of money was a cold-water sterilizer. The bottles all pong and you have to wash them out after use. It is far easier to boil them in a massive pan. I bought it for when we went on holiday in a caravan and used it once. I also bought a lovely big wooden toy box, but now I realize that as it has a lift-up lid it could give my daughter a very nasty crack on the head. I have to stick up for the Play Nest, though. We ended up getting one because my daughter loved the childminder's so much. She could be propped up in it and her toys didn't disappear – for a while. Once she was crawling, though, it had to go as she kept landing on her head when trying to escape.

Kate71

I'd plump for getting rid of those electronic stimulation toys. I'm sorry, but I'm not convinced that children need everything they touch or, in some cases, breathe on, to play a mindlessly happy electronic tune! They can learn to sort shapes, pull things and even walk without these annoying, loud lumps of plastic. I have, of course, fallen for their promises of sensory stimulation on a few occasions and now I am regretting every single purchase and would happily burn each one. Give 'em a pan and a wooden spoon if noise is what they want to make.

Mumsnet fact
In the last five years spending on children's clothes has increased by 34 per cent in real terms to £6 billion.   Mintel International

I wouldn't bother with changing tables as the floor is much easier to change a baby on (if you don't have any mobility difficulties yourself). And they can't roll off it, either. I bought a rocking crib mainly because I thought they looked nice and it was in a sale. In my case the crib wasn't used all that much as she was in my bed for most of that time, so I'm glad I didn't pay a fortune for it! As a first-time mum I felt a bit of pressure to be buying all the latest stuff but don't be conned into thinking you need everything going!

Lizzer

Yes, all those flashing light/music-playing gadgets are dreadful why do they all play the same annoying tunes? I am sick to death of 'Twinkle, Twinkle, Little Star'! My son has hours of fun putting the pegs in and out of the basket and throwing them down the step into the kitchen – I wish I had known that before wasting my money on toys that are never used.

Plus useless items of clothing to avoid: dungarees without poppers down the legs, sleepsuits that don't have poppers all the way down the front, but only a few poppers across the shoulders and legs – it's bad enough dressing a newborn without these! Do you put the clothes over the baby's head or insert the baby into the clothes bum first, and baby's little arms kept on getting stuck – nightmare! These went straight to the charity shop after one wear.

Donna1

Those changing tables with a baby bath underneath are a nightmare to try to fill, empty and clean. And that's before you've put the baby in! It used to take an hour to bath my newborn. Number two just went straight in the normal bath with a couple of inches of water – much easier. Also, I never used baby lotion or baby oil – we've had rotting bottles on the shelves for years. I also paid for a bike trailer, which is hardly used. It looked like a good idea In the catalogue but it was so cumbersome I kept hitting things with it.

Rosebud

I'll vote against baby baths too. They're awful things that totally wreck your back – as if it wasn't already under enough strain! Number two went in the big bath with his older brother and loved being swished around in the deep, warm water. I also hate those electronic toys. Unfortunately, my husband is Gadget King of the Universe and has to be persuaded at every turn that they really don't need another thing that bleeps and does the exploring for them!

Lara1

My worst buy was a changing bag with integral mat. It was big, bulky, overpriced and a complete waste of space. It had the opposite of the Tardis effect – too big on the outside, not enough room on the inside. We now travel fairly lightly in comparison to the early days when we took the whole nursery out with us. Now I use a small zip-up bag with a side pocket on the inside to stop my son pinching my specs.

Late30smom

Our worst buy was definitely cot blankets and extra sheets as we ended up putting him in a sleeping bag almost straight away.

Amber1

For me, the worst buy was a stupid cot melody and light-show thing. The whirring of the mechanism is so noisy that you have to put the 'music' on really loud to hear it. I cannot see how anyone is supposed to sleep with it on – and it just eats up batteries.

Bo

I've also got a cot music thing and I agree, the whirring mechanism is far too loud. The so-called light reflection doesn't reach the ceiling or reflect off any-where. It was a complete and utter waste of money. And so I told a lady who was about to buy one in John Lewis!

Maisy1

My worst buy was a half-price cotton cot blanket. It looked great until it became 'blankie'. I refuse to buy another one as washing it is a military operation. And the night he was sick on it is still too traumatic for me to recall... he would not let go, it stank, so did the bedroom, and the hall, and the house. Beware what becomes a 'blankie'. I've got all the baby oil stuff as well. I thought once I'd had the baby, other women would let me into the age-old secrets of what the hell these things are for. What are you supposed to do with them? Incidentally, I apply strict Stalinist rules to toys that talk – they all meet a sticky end.

Snowy

And one product which you're not quite sure about...

The Sangenic nappy bin gets my vote for a product I wish I'd never bought. We have under-floor heating and 28 warm nappies stewing in a bin for three days was enough to put you off your lunch.

Pj

I agree – I found it smells, no matter what I do... I much prefer nappy sacks, tied up and placed by the front door so they're ready to go out quickly.

Naddy

My Sangenic is fab on Monday, Tuesday and Wednesday. From then on, it's a pain in the butt. Bin night is Sunday and I have never got the hang of emptying it midweek so we just use nappy sacks from Thursday onwards.

Joanie

Sangenic nappy bin – how I hate that yellow pod! We lost the inner ring with the first disposal. The cutter mechanism never worked properly and I would always have to find scissors...grrr! After the first use, the plastic seemed to take on some hideous stale odour, not poo, but a strange chemical, rotting vegetable sort of stench, which no amount of soaking in bleach would obliterate. I couldn't account for where the stench came from. Was it the scented liner that went off after a while? In the end I just stopped using it and now it sits redundant, a constant reminder of a waste of money (plus the cost of all the refill cartridges).

Molly1

My Sangenic, from 1998, stank to high heaven (it did not help that my husband threw away the yellow circle thingy when changing the cartridge refill). I had another one bought for me when I had my second son last year, and that also smells. Nappy sacks are better!

Wornout

I disagree on the nappy sacks versus the Sangenic. Living in a tall, thin house with 50 stairs between the basement and the top floor, we found it useful to have one at the top of the house. The bin with the nappy sacks in at the bottom of the house gets far, far smellier than the Sangenic.

Croppy

Another thumbs down for the Sangenic from me, I'm afraid. We ended up putting the nappies in a nappy sack and then into the Sangenic, which kind of defeated the object! And I lost most of the white bits, although you can order free replacements from the website. I have now switched to using cloth nappies and even a bin full of dirty nappies doesn't smell as bad as the Sangenic did! I've been trying to sell ours, but no luck yet.

Annwyl

I bought a Sangenic thinking it would save me a lot of time (why I thought that, I'm not really sure) but all I did was take it out of the box, and that was it. I didn't use it once and it somehow ended up wasting away in the back garden – I couldn't even give it away!

Starshine79

My mother suggested I bought one of those 'nappy Tardis' type contraptions, and judging by the line-up at our local NCT second-hand sales, no one else likes them either! Nappy bags are best, and the really dirty ones just get flung out of the window (in the bag) ready for me to pick up and put in the dustbin when I go out. Trouble is, I nearly knocked out our postman one morning. He now always glances up at my son's window as he's passing... just in case!

Huncamunca

I can't understand why everyone's so down on the Sangenic. We couldn't have done without it for our two – we would've been completely swallowed up by smelly nappies (remember the upset tummies?). And no, I've never lost the white bit in the middle and it does a good job of concealing the smell.

Berta

The only time I ever used my Sangenic was when we were in a tall thin town house with the bathroom on the second floor – it was really useful for about six months but then spent three years just wasting space.

Javarose

I'll support the Sangenic! I thought it was great and didn't have any problems. I loathe nappy bags. That sickly smell literally makes me want to vomit!

Baabaa

We love the Sangenic so much we even took it on holiday and were amazed and thrilled to discover we weren't the only ones!

Pp

I'll vote for the Sangenic! I haven't actually used it yet, but it is just the right height for a footstool. It sits in the living room, still in its box, with a cushion on top. Perfect for those swollen ankles in late pregnancy!

Slug

7

Relationships

Introduction

No matter how many ups and downs you went through before, a new baby is likely to put your relationship to its greatest test to date. Small and cute they may (or may not) be, the fact is another person has entered the family. The dynamic has changed. And the question is: can your relationship handle it? As author of *Baby Shock*, Elizabeth Martyn, puts it: 'If you don't want your relationship to change, don't have children.'

Before the birth, you were doubtless two carefree individuals, with little more to worry about than yourselves and each other. But you are no longer the number one player in each others' lives. Never before has the term 'three's a crowd' felt so apt – time together as a couple is a rarity and nights out a dim and distant memory. So how do you nurture your love life when most of the time spent with the other half is engaged in keeping score about who does what with the baby? Almost as important, how do you ensure that the scores come out roughly equal and your partner does his fair share?

Even your bedroom is no longer your own. In Mumsnet's Life After Birth survey 62 per cent of mothers agreed that their sex life was worse after children. In the weeks following childbirth, pretty much everything is stacked up in favour of a good night's sleep over a night of passion – the idea of it taking up even a few minutes of precious sleeping time can seem absurd. Why on earth should you want to commit the act that might even possibly result in you falling pregnant again?

So your relationship with your partner is a whole new ball game but don't think you can necessarily turn to those outside the family unit for sympathy and support. Your relationships with them will have taken a new course as well. You may well feel alienated from friends without kids because they just can't empathize with your new life and yet you don't feel close enough to sit down and discuss your sexual shortcomings with new friends made at the baby clinic.

What's more, before you know it, you find yourself sympathizing with the Les Dawson view of mother-in-laws. How can you stop what seemed like polite concern from your in-laws pre-baby seeming like meddling once their grandchild is involved?

This may all seem a tad depressing but what the next chapter shows is that, along with excitement, your new arrival can precipitate a whole gamut of emotions. Love, pride, unparalleled joy certainly, but perhaps also anger, jealousy and resentment towards those you love. It doesn't hurt to be prepared.

(In the interest of good relationships with family and friends, all nicknames have been removed from this chapter!)

Fathers – how can you get them involved ?

My husband sheepishly confessed that he is jealous of me because I plainly love and am obsessed by our four-month-old son. He's really worried, poor love, because he isn't and finds both him and baby talk pretty boring. This is despite strenuous efforts on his part (he's changing, feeding, bathing, cuddling and smiling at our son as much as he can). I've tried to tell him that this isn't uncommon with a first baby and he needs to be patient and keep doing what he's doing.

Anon

My little boy is nine-and-a-half-months-old and my husband admits he's besotted for the first time since he was born. Now that our son is becoming a little 'person' instead of a little baby, their relationship has blossomed. My husband has always shared the care and been a constant support, but admits he found nothing inspiring about newborns. I don't mind at all... he got there in the end.

Anon

My partner grew to love our daughter more and more, but certainly prefers her company now she is a bit older. He has always loved her deeply, but admitted that he found the early days frustrating and limiting as she was breastfed and I was a stay-at-home mum and tended to do everything for her. She's always been a real mummy's girl too and made it clear that she preferred me, which must have been really hard on him.

I think going away and leaving your partner with the baby helps him to learn how to do the everyday things, but you can't force a bond/love between them, it will come naturally.

Anon

I have to admit that when my daughter first arrived I was at a bit of a loss. I loved her in an abstract sort of way but this little person had suddenly burst into my life and I had no way of knowing what I felt.

Since then, I've begun to realize that I love her and would miss her if she was not there, but I don't think I have bonded anywhere near as much as my wife has.

Our daughter smiles and giggles at us and you can see the love in her mother's eyes when it happens. I just think it is nice and she is cute but I don't have the same overwhelming feeling that some people told me I would.

Anon

> **Mumsnet fact**
> Following the birth of their child, 80 per cent of fathers in a recent study said they felt worried, 60 per cent said they had felt lonely; 12 per cent had felt depressed and 6 per cent said they felt jealous.
>   Jan Parker and Jan Stimpson (*Raising Happy Children*)

I was lucky in that my husband was besotted with our son right from the word go. However, he admits that when our son was tiny he sometimes felt very excluded and useless because I was breastfeeding and therefore was able to calm and look after him in a way that he couldn't. He says he sometimes felt like a bit of a spare part. This amazed me because to me he was totally necessary. I don't know how I would have managed without his care and support.

Anon

My husband bonded with our son straight away. He delivered him, put his first clothes on and gave him his first bath, although he felt uncertain at times (as if I knew how to do everything naturally). He felt a little left out with feeding, but it helped that he did everything first, like bath and solids. He was at work all day so when our son was newborn, he did prefer to be with me and up until a few months ago would only go to sleep with me. Now my husband has a little shadow that follows him everywhere every minute he is home.

Anon

My husband has an extremely close relationship with our son and spent two years being his primary carer when he was at nursery and while I worked. However, this relationship only grew after my son could walk and talk. Before that my husband had minimal interest in him. He admits that he doesn't like babies because he feels he can't contribute, and the baby can't give anything back. I can see this up to a point. I take the attitude, better later than never!

Anon

My husband said that he felt totally useless when the children were very little. I took care of their needs to his exclusion, I suppose. It's very easy to do. You have to force yourself not to step in when food is flying all over the place and you could get it done in half the time. My advice is: don't let your man play the too-tired-to-play-dad card. Nip out to visit someone at tea or bath time and force him to take the responsibility. If anyone asks in his hearing, say how much your son loves his dad and how they have special 'men only' time together – it's amazing what flattery will do.

Anon

> **Mumsnet tip**
> If you can, leave your partner to look after the kids alone for a day every now and again and resist the temptation to leave a list of instructions. It's good for everyone to realize you're not the only one who can run things, and should promote bonding and understanding all round (on a good day!).

Maybe we need to step back and let the dads do it sometimes – and keep our mouths shut if they don't do it to our high standards. Over the weekend, I noticed that I criticized my husband frequently, so I made a real effort to bite my tongue. I often find myself asking stupid questions such as 'did you brush his teeth?' after he'd done the bath.

I think it's all about communication and making compromises right from the start and perhaps that does mean even at antenatal stage. I think more men would be willing to get involved if their partners allowed them. We shouldn't assume that they don't want to be involved and so not even bother to ask them.

Anon

In the early weeks, it is essential that dads get enough time with their babies on their own so they can develop their own childcare skills and build their confidence as parents. Most mums get at least two to six months to do this. What is very common is mums looking over the shoulders of their partners to check they're 'doing it right' and criticizing when they get it wrong. This kind of discouragement just puts men off doing it again. It establishes that 'mum's way is best' but there are real differences between the way that mothers and fathers interact with babies and fathers need to be left with the kids to develop their own skills and style.

I'm sure that when all fathers get two weeks off after a birth, it will become much more acceptable and normal for dads to be more involved from the beginning.

What the experts say
We have to be prepared to relinquish more of the motherhood preserve if we are to bring out the best of fatherhood, and, more importantly, we have to allow them to father in their own way, by learning from their own mistakes rather than expecting them to do everything as we would.

Kate Figes (*Life After Birth*)

Perhaps a lot of mothers have taken on the responsibility for childcare so completely that there is no room for the men. Consequently, fathers can only see themselves as 'helpers', rather than real parents. Unless mothers are prepared to give up some of their status (and time with the kids) and force men into a position of taking responsibility for some aspects of childcare, it's just not going to happen.

I would suggest that if anyone wants to get their man more involved, they have to completely leave the kids with them for at least a whole day (with no checking up on them), and do this as many times as possible – it's only when you do this as a dad that you can really get into the rhythm of life with a child.

Anon

I don't deny that my husband loves our son tremendously and does a lot for him and I do try to let him get on with things when he says he'll do them. However, to take bathtime as an example, I know from experience that if I didn't ask, 'Have you cleaned his teeth?' when they emerge from the bathroom, the teeth wouldn't get cleaned. If I didn't surreptitiously enquire whether the E45 had been plastered on his dry skin, it wouldn't be done. It's not that my husband is lazy, he is either incredibly forgetful or too busy thinking of other things.

Anon

Mumsnet fact
Over 80 per cent of British fathers are working full-time, averaging a gruelling 46-hour week. Elizabeth Martyn (*Baby Shock*)

For me, the key turning point was having a whole day alone each week with our first daughter when she was three months old. Magic! I understood the rhythm and I got onto the wavelength. That simple experience changed everything – no way was I going to lose out on this. Now our daughter is four and we have another child of three months. It is odd to have a second who feels so distant compared to the first – I have not yet had the chance to invest the same time in number two. Just doing bathtime and nappies is not the same as doing a whole day. When breastfeeding stops and my wife goes back to work, I will have my chance and I will take it.

Anon

The trouble is, you can agree it all on day one, but then baby comes along... We used to have the fairest split – alternate cooking, share the housework, each do own ironing. But now that I'm at home with baby, I do all our daughter's laundry, shopping, most of the bathing and all the feeding. When I go back to work next month, he will be able to claim not to know how to sterilize bottles, cook purées, buy nappies or anything else. It's time for more negotiations but this time it will be much harder for me to step back and bite my lip, even though the last time he did our baby's laundry he put the woollens in on a hot cotton cycle.

Anon

Is it possible to share the load equally after a baby?

I think it's common for women to get landed with running the house in a really old-fashioned way once kids arrive. What makes me explode is when my husband says something like, 'What is he having for lunch?' and I'm yelling, 'I don't know. When did I get voted lunch organizer? Why don't you find him some lunch?'

When I want to do something that means leaving my husband with our son I always 'ask permission', but he doesn't. I think this is considered pretty normal, but drives me batty – I work three days a week from home but wanted to spend the extra time with my son, not be a 1950s housewife.

Anon

I snipe at my partner all the time about domestic organization – I resent being put in control of all the drudgery (it feels like I'm failing at a job I never applied for), but if he takes any initiative I hate the 'challenge' to my order. It's true that you divide down the gender stereotype line and it's a real shock to discover you're living a cliché.

Anon

I'm sure that some survey recently showed that men who do their share of the housework and childcare generally get more sex. Sounds right to me: I know I feel more loving and likely to be in the mood when my partner has done something wonderful.

Anon

I cured my husband of the 'you've had a day off while I've been working hard' thing by going on a business trip when our son was about nine months old. I had to leave early on a Sunday, so my husband had our son for a whole day, then had to do the nursery run both ends of the day on Monday and Tuesday. When I got back he said, 'I can see why you don't get anything else done on the days you're home. You can't even go to the loo in peace, can you?' He's never made the mistake again of thinking that being at home with the children isn't a 'real' job.

Anon

What the experts say

Men have to get used to the idea of their partner in her new role of mother and homemaker, and must learn to value her contribution just as much as they valued her salary before.

Elizabeth Martyn (*Baby Shock*)

We have a nine-month-old baby. We both work full-time, yet I handle all of the responsibilities with our daughter. He loves her to pieces – but spends about ten minutes with her then has to watch the news while I do everything around the house – which I just bought.

Anon

After an absolutely horrendous start, I finally got breastfeeding established. I insisted on my husband sleeping in a different room for the first six weeks or so as the baby was up at all times and sometimes I would be trying to feed him for three hours at a time. Aside from wanting my husband to be able to sleep, I also just wanted to be able to put the lights on and listen to music in the bedroom. A lot of people were horrified that he was sleeping in another room at this stage, saying that he should be doing his share. However, I saw absolutely no point in both of us being tired and the fact that he was relatively well-rested meant that when he came in from work, I could rest for a bit and likewise, at weekends I could catch up.

As soon as I returned to work, though, my husband did what he could at night so he would deliver the baby for a feed and put him back in the cot. This may not be a popular view, but I do think that generally, if a man is working long hours during the week and his partner is at home, it is unfair to expect him to take half the burden of being up in the night with the baby.

Anon

My husband promised me all the way through my pregnancy that he would share the night feeding once the baby came along. True to his word he has done so religiously. Every Friday and Saturday night (when he did not have to get up for work the next day) he did his bit during the night. It helped our relationship enormously and also helped the relationship between my husband and my son. Every Friday he would try to get home early then take him off my hands. They would bathe together, then he would feed him, change him and put him to bed, often sitting in the nursery for hours at a time just watching him. I think we both feel that we have contributed to his precious time as a baby and my husband feels that he has not missed out.

Anon

My husband tried to do the Friday and Saturday night feeds when our little boy was under three months old. I would express milk for him. However, it never worked particularly well. I would have to wake him as he never heard our baby crying and then I would find it very difficult to sleep again until our baby went back to sleep. Plus, my husband would moan all day on Saturday and Sunday about how tired he was and keep having to go and have naps.

Anon

Mumsnet fact
Only 17 per cent of new fathers regularly get up to comfort a crying baby, and about the same number never stir from their slumbers at all.

Mother and Baby

In the very early weeks my husband would do the first night feed and I would do the last or vice versa. When it went down to just one feed a night, I usually did it. I could manage to creep around the room quietly, with minimal light, and feed my son and get him back to bed. When my husband did it we would all be awake. He would need the main light on and generally cause a lot of bother. I got fed up with it and it was easier to do it myself.

Anon

I'm actually quite worried my daughter will grow up with the idea that daddies are for play time only and mums do all the housework, pay the bills, and do all the general babycare and discipline. Well, my dream would be to leave my husband with our daughter for a whole weekend (fridge empty) to sort everything for himself. I might do it one day (I'm just afraid of finding her with the same nappy I left her in!).

Anon

What the experts say
In this day and age parents can be nothing but equal, and parenting and childrearing must be equally shared. It should really be viewed as a contract: you're equally responsible for your child's conception so you should take equal responsibility for rearing him or her. It is just not good enough for a woman to be expected to take on the role of nursemaid, childminder and babysitter, confined to the house with its limited horizons and interests, while the father leaves early in the morning and doesn't return home before the baby is asleep.

Dr Miriam Stoppard (*New Baby Care Book*)

It's a lot easier for me to expect my husband to do his fair share now we're both working full-time, and he's very good at looking after our daughter. But I don't think that's something I should feel 'grateful' for. He does all his own ironing, and if I do any for him I expect to get thanked, just as he would if a friend did something for him. However, there's still room for improvement: I'm always thinking ahead, but my husband doesn't so much (though is getting better – he's now trained to buy more of everyday things if they are on offer in the supermarket).

Anon

This issue of being seen to be 'grateful' is difficult and no doubt controversial to many but I am the first to admit that I am grateful that my husband works hard, is in a very good job, and that his salary enables me to stay at home. I am sure my husband would love to spend more time with his son but, quite bluntly, his earning capacity is far greater than mine.

Anon

My husband, while being a lovely man and a good dad, is completely unable to dress our son in anything that I would let him leave the house in. He's a big 15-month-old and on Saturday morning my husband brought him downstairs in a T-shirt for a six to nine-month-old and some 12–18-month-old's dungarees that came up to his knees, like knickerbockers. He commented that the trousers didn't look right! Another day he dressed him in a forest green and red striped velour winter jumper and summer apple-green cotton dungarees and was very proud of himself because they were both green. I have to give precise instructions about what clothes to put him in.

Anon

What the experts say

If women quickly assume the lion's share of childcare and domestic responsi-bility, they set standards by which they expect things to be done and find it hard to allow men to be fathers in their own way… When she criticises him for not doing things in the way that she would like them done, he takes umbrage, feels inadequate and is even more likely to abandon tasks.

Kate Figes (*Life After Birth*)

When we go away I always end up having to find the suitcases, pack all of my stuff and everything for the kids: travel cots, buggy, all toiletries for all of us, all guide books, currency, passports, and all his undies and socks. He'll always have some small job that he must just do. The only thing he has to pack is his own clothes. But guess who gets blamed if anything gets forgotten?

Anon

I've got a three-month-old baby and I would say that I am pretty laid-back about things on the whole. I imagined, when I got married and had children, that in this modern age of equality my other half and I would split all the childcare and household responsibilities between us. So why does it not work out that way?

Three weeks ago after a lot of 'verbal encouragement' he attempted some ironing. Thirty minutes and two shirts later he stopped for a rest. He will attempt some tasks, it is just that it is usually half-hearted and half-done.

Then he gives me the 'look' – the one to remind me that he has had a hard day at work and then he comes home to a nagging wife. So it is usually quicker and more efficient if I do it myself. I know this is the worst thing I could possibly do.

Anon

Well, my solution to all of this is that neither of us do any housework! Well, nothing major. I work full-time and he works sporadically as an actor. We have two kids and our only solution (or I would cry) has been to have a cleaner, a gardener, a dishwasher, creased clothes and to use internet supermarkets. Oh, and a nanny for the kids!

Anon

Feeling isolated after children – what can you do about it?

I think isolation is a very common problem for new mums. I find it even more difficult as I am new to my area so all of my new friends are work colleagues and they are not around during the day. I try to get out of the house every day even if it is just a walk to the local shop. I'm glad that I had my baby in the spring, not the winter as that must be very hard.

Anon

I live 200 miles away from family and many miles away from (once close, but mainly childless) college friends. I'm settled where I live now and have made friends through mother and toddler groups. But the friendships never seem to be more than superficial. Everyone where I live was born and bred here, have family close at hand and friends that they've known forever. I'd really love to find a friend with whom I could form a mutually supportive friendship, so it wouldn't be all one way. At the moment, if I need a babysitter, I have to ask one of these friends. They have family coming out of their ears, so I can't return the favour.

Anon

I've got friends at work who are both married and single, but they have no kids. So the weeks when I'm at home with my son I go to TumbleTots, and Mums and Tots two days a week, but have yet to make a firm friend. There's lots of friendly chat and although I don't feel like such an outsider or the 'new' mum any more, it would be so nice to have someone to go around the shops or to have a coffee with.

I went shopping yesterday with my husband – it was nice to spend time on our own as it very rarely happens these days – but I found myself feeling very envious of all the friends I saw out pushing their buggies together.

Anon

We moved to this area eighteen months ago and I have really worked hard at making friends, going to everything and getting involved in things. It has paid off in that I am not too lonely. My advice is to persevere, go to Mums and Tots, library story times, playgroups, local play areas, even doctor's waiting rooms. Become a recognizable face at things and people will eventually talk to you.

Anon

The NCT actually makes up coffee groups of five or six people so you can meet in your own homes. Everyone joins for the same reason – they want to meet new friends. Speak to the post-natal coordinator (Bumps and Babes organizer) for your area. Tell her you want to meet new friends and ask what goes on in your area. Find out who has kids the same age as yours and join the committee! It's great fun but do persevere.

Anon

I met several of my closest friends through the NCT. I went to the local NCT tea afternoon, which was specifically for new members or those new to the area. As we were all there because we were new and lonely, the atmosphere was open and friendly – we all wanted to meet new friends. Our local branch organize these new members' events every quarter. I remember coming home after the first after-noon (having been in the area for about 18 months without having made any good friends) thinking: 'Yes, I feel that I've made progress.'

Anon

I have found very different friends from the ones I had (and still have) when I was young, free and single, but that does not mean they are inferior. Sharing the frustrations and delights (not too mention the hard graft) of motherhood does create a bond that I can't imagine will ever be broken.

Anon

Be open-minded and don't automatically assume that you need to meet someone just like you. One of the closest friendships I have made in the last few months is with a girl 14 years younger than myself – there are many differences between us: she completed her family at 28 – I had my first baby at 42. Her eldest is at school, she has one toddler at home while my son is ten months. She is fiercely ambitious, has several part-time jobs and is looking forward to resuming her career, while I like to consider myself 'retired' from the workforce now. She is fit, active and trendy – I am frumpy and lumpy! I haven't a clue what she is talking about when she mentions the latest music and bands but we have become firm friends and are always happy to help each other out with childminding, coffee and wine. I like to think we can bring different experiences and opinions to the friendship.

Anon

When I was on maternity leave, I didn't make any new friends with women who had new babies and a lot of the time I felt out of my depth with the whole 'new mum' experience. Having a friend with a baby the same age at the same time would have helped enormously.

I suggest trying different baby and toddler clubs and the library. Try going at about the same time on the same day of the week if you can. You never know, one day some other mother will also let her guard down a bit and chat – the hard thing is starting off the process.

Anon

I felt very isolated on becoming a mother with my first baby 11 years ago and with my second baby, who's now almost eight months. My answer on both occasions was to decide to return to work. It is, for me, simply about contributing financially to the household and keeping a sense of self, though I appreciate that it is not for everyone.

Anon

I decided my baby son would have to fit his life around mine – at least some of the time. No on-the-dot nap times, changing times or feeding times at home. A lot of it was done on the run, as and when. It's amazing how many places you can take a baby: markets, cafés, shops, musical events – and many classes and sports activities have crèche facilities. Just decide what you want to do, then work out how you can do it with your baby. Okay, not everything is possible, or you may try something once and it may be too much hassle. Just don't feel that every minute of your life has to revolve around your baby's routine. I think it's an easy trap to fall into and often ends in tears.

Anon

I felt isolated initially too. It is a strange transition from independent working person to parent. I have gone back to work part-time and loved it but I know that this may not be an option for everyone. However, before I went back to work I went to library groups, swimming groups, YMCA groups, mother and baby groups and church-organized groups. You name it, I tried it. After a few times, I was able to work out whether they were 'me' or not.

Anon

One of my tricks was to join a gym. Believe me, I'd never been to a gym in my life until now. They run different classes through the week (step, body-conditioning) and for three of them they run a crèche, so I got chatting to mum's from there and now after the class we have a coffee together in the leisure centre. This usually takes up the entire morning. There are all sorts of different women there, I'm a bit fitter and I get a break from my little one for an hour.

Anon

If you want to meet people without your baby there's an organization called the National Women's Register. It's basically a discussion group but not high-powered. I've belonged to groups for over 15 years and have made some great friends. Some have lunch groups, book groups and so on.

Anon

I think everyone feels a bit lonely after a baby, even if they live in a big city. I was at home with my lovely baby for ten months and loved it, but my husband was rarely home before 8.30 pm and the days seemed long and lonely at times. I had to really make the effort to call old friends and make new ones. But I found most people pretty easy to get to know as you instantly have something in common. You really have to plan to meet up with one other person every day, or every other day. One of the hardest things to cope with post-baby is a lack of structure to your week, but if you have organized things to do, it helps keep the week going.

Anon

I somehow thought my post-natal groups would be full of people just like me, I'd make wonderful new friends and our children would all be friends for life. Well, I did make two good friends and very glad of them I am. But I also met about 25 people I would not choose to spend time with, for various reasons and it was clear the feeling was mutual. You feel so desperate to fit in when you're a new mum, all of it is such a shock to the system that you always assume it's your fault if you don't get on with others.

Anon

I spent a long time trying to fit in with some mothers with whom I had nothing in common except my baby. I got no joy from it – I could not believe how competitive some people were over their baby's progress and education. I gave up when one mother actually sneered at me after I had told her my plans for my daughter's care and education and walked off in disgust. I have never regretted it. There are some wonderful non-judgemental parents around who live and let live – just look at Mumsnet – it just takes a while to find them sometimes!

Anon

I spent ages yearning for a 'soul-mate' friend when mine were babies and wasted too much time trying to fit into groups where the other mums obviously thought I was 'different'. I don't actually think it works just to meet lots of mums or try to bump into people in the park – you can exhaust yourself and end up feeling a failure.

I use to dream of a network of drop-in centres for the absolutely desperate times (usually mid-evening when my kids didn't sleep much and my husband worked late), just a warm room somewhere with coffee and a human being there to say hello to. I thought about starting a 'Pyjama club' for all us isolated mums meeting 4 pm to 7 pm in each others' houses. But I never met anyone else who admitted they needed it!

Anon

Mothers – how does your relationship with them alter after children and what can you do if they interfere?

My mother isn't even a grandmother yet and already she is interfering! She told me that I'd better not pick a name that she can't spell (my husband's foreign) and she's already criticized the pushchair we have chosen (without even seeing it). I didn't ask her round to look at our nursery preparations because I knew it would result in a huge row. I feel like picking a really unusual name just to spite her – but I know that whatever we choose will be wrong.

Anon

My relationship with my mother has really deteriorated since having children. There is a power struggle going on and she takes every opportunity to question my decisions. It feels like there is a competition going on but I don't know why. It could be connected with the fact that my brother was a very difficult child who caused lots of problems – perhaps she's trying to 're-live' bringing him up through my children.

Anon

What the experts say

...women feel demoralized or over-anxious about their ability to mother well because their mothers constantly interfere, questioning their capabilities.

Kate Figes (*Life After Birth*)

I have spent hours trying to figure out my mother since I had a baby. We were never the closest mother and daughter in the world but we had a fairly good relationship. She was very supportive during my pregnancy but seems to have undergone a personality change since my son was born. She adores my baby (her only grandchild) and practically lives for him. She completely takes over and sabotages my best efforts by feeding him chocolate, giving him a bottle in the middle of the night, and so on. We need to stand up to our mothers. We are mothers now and our children need to know we are in control otherwise they may be confused.

At some point we all have to tell our parents to back off (or some such words) and take the responsibility of doing so even if it hurts and someone gets the sulks for a while. It's worth trying the 'you'll always be my mother, and the children's grandmother, but the buck stops with me, not you' talk. Don't let her get away with the 'I only want to help' routine. It's a classic that parents pull on their kids and it's meant to keep you quiet out of guilt.

My father has got it sussed – he waits until I mention a need, like new shoes, then pops a cheque in the post. What a gem!

Anon

> **Mumsnet fact**
> In 1951, 39 per cent of new mothers were living with relatives and nearly
> 50 per cent of all new mothers were being helped by their own mothers.
> But in 1985, only 25 per cent of new mothers were receiving help from
> their mothers and nearly two-thirds cited their husband as their main
> source of support. Kate Figes (*Life After Birth*)

My mum looked after my son when I went back to work full-time, and also when
we went on holidays. I know that I've got an absolute gem of a mum. At first I
found it really hard to accept that she did things different with him than I did, like
she slept in bed with him every night (not just if he woke up in the morning like
we did), gave him treats all the time and various other things. He has always
realized that things he does with grandma are different and special, and has
never expected the same things with us – he just seemed to know without
anything being said to him. He is now in full-time nursery, so only gets to see his
grandma at weekends and he is so excited to see her, it is an absolute joy for her.

Anon

Are we influenced by our mothers when we become mothers? Perhaps some
mothers are the opposite of role models? I only understand how difficult it is to
be a mother now that I am one. I always assumed I would be perfectly in control
and have an almost effortlessly good relationship with all my children. It isn't like
that at all. And I often feel that compared to my own mum I am making a poor job
of bringing up my children.

Anon

I have always said that I have become the person I am despite my parents and
not because of them and strive to be a better mother through that. It frightens me
when I recognize things that I do that my mother used to do (she blamed a lot of
her behaviour on PMT/hormones and unfortunately I am now battling with a similar problem but I won't give in!). She always used to criticize me, usually without
thinking, which made it worse as it was clear that was what she really thought!

What the experts say
Many people find their understanding and respect for their parents increases
dramatically. For others it is a disturbing time, when old wounds are opened
and memories revisited.

Jan Parker and Jan Stimpson (*Raising Happy Children*)

Since my daughter was born, I have actually thought a lot more about the
emotional abuse my mother inflicted on me, and I am so angered by it I can

hardly bear to talk to her sometimes. But in a strange way, I think it has actually made me a better parent. I am determined that my little girl will grow up knowing how amazing and wonderful she is, and how much she is loved.

Anon

No matter how meddling the mother, at least it's attention – I don't have one. When my son brings back yet another picture from school, or the toddler increases his vocabulary to two whole words, they can only rely on me (and my husband) to praise them. Friends are interested in a way, but they are hardly waiting with baited breath to hear how the potty training is going. Sometimes I would give a lot to have a mum or a dad pop round to get their regular fix of our family progress.

I think it's important that all the adults in our children's lives present a united front. It's worth outlining to your mother your general view on important issues like eating, sleeping and smacking. Then, if they ever overstep the mark in a big way, find a method of tactfully reminding them. As for the little things, let them go, especially if she is doing them when she has your children and you are not around – all free baby-sitting is to be encouraged.

Anon

I think our mothers come from a generation that believed the way to bring up children was to criticize them all the time in case you 'spoilt' them. Our generation, of course, is more enlightened about the psychological effects of constant criticism. Maybe some parents refuse to move with the times because they need to justify their parenting 'style'. Maybe they are jealous of our freedom and not having to conform as much as they felt they had to. Whatever, none of this makes them any easier to deal with.

Anon

In defence of our mothers I agree that styles have changed. Positive parenting is much more in vogue these days and bringing up children brings back all your childhood memories – good and bad. The problem is if you've grown up being criticized (which seems to have been common in our parents' day) you've learnt to be critical yourself and first in line is often your own parents and the way they brought you up.

Anon

In-laws – a help or a hindrance?

We hardly ever see my mother-in-law even though she lives close to us. She hardly ever phones or comes to our house. Basically, she expects us to visit her if we wish to see her. I'm tired of this tedious relationship and last night my husband and I had a fight over his mother. He knows what she's like but he doesn't want to discuss it, and I (stupidly) vented my frustrations about her again. I think it hurts him to even think about her.

Anon

When my son was first born we lived five minutes' walk from my mother-in-law. She would pop over all the time, even if my baby was sleeping during the day and I was napping (she could tell I was trying to catch up as the curtains would be closed) but she would be knocking on the front door, never worrying that she might wake the baby. If I didn't answer she would walk home and then start ringing me on the phone. I would sometimes feel she was stalking me. She caused endless rows between myself and my partner. Guess what? We have moved and now live much further away from her.

Anon

What the experts say
Your brother-in-law and his wife, whom you never much cared for before, are suddenly critically important as your baby's uncle and aunt. You want your baby to know them, be friends with their children, to feel loved and protected by them.
Vicki Iovine (*The Best Friend's Guide to…Surviving the First Year of Motherhood*)

My mother-in-law has always disliked me. We're always invited round for Sunday lunch and I dread it. It's like being on your best behaviour for school. She gets at me with snide little comments. I heartily sympathize with anyone who has an over-bearing mother-in-law. My husband and I always end up rowing about her.

Anon

I have a lovely mother-in-law but I don't think she has ever popped round to my house to see her grandchildren, though I do take them round to her house at least once a week. She is very respectful of our privacy.

Anon

I always end up visiting my daughter's grandmother on her father's side (we're not together) rather than her coming here (a round trip of over 100 miles). It really winds me up sometimes but I grin and bear it and think that I'm doing the best for my daughter. Some people tell me I'm crazy for putting up with it, but I have tried to build a good relationship with her for the sake of everyone involved and I actually feel better for putting in the hard work and effort.

Anon

What the experts say
You find yourself on a completely different footing with the in-laws as soon as you have a baby. Suddenly you're closer than you were before, exposed to all of the intimacies and irritations of another family network, which were previously hidden from view. You are no longer an outsider because you have given birth to their new grandchild, but you are not entirely accepted as an insider either.

Kate Figes (*Life After Birth*)

My mother-in-law is one of those who thinks that no one can be as good for her sons as she is. You know, that disapproving look at me that says, 'Are you feeding him enough?' while saying to my husband: 'You're looking pale and thin.'

Anon

I've had a rocky relationship with my mother-in-law over the years, my chief gripe being that she appears not to be that interested in her grandchildren (mainly because she cannot relate to children when they're playing). Things get better as they get older and I realize the problem is that she does not know how to play or imagine herself in a child's position.

Anon

Mumsnet fact
After studying sheep and goats, Cambridge scientists claimed that a man is more likely to fall in love with women who look like his mother.

The *Observer*

My partner's mother is a very nice woman and very generous. She puts a tremendous amount of time and effort into her grandchildren and absolutely adores them.

So here is my gripe. Every time she sees my nine-month-old daughter, she oohs and aahs over how pudgy she is, she says: 'Look at you, you fat little girl!' and when she picks her up: 'What are they feeding you?'

When we took our daughter to the doctors last week, she said she was in the 90th centile for height, and only 20th centile for weight. I told my partner's mother this and she said: 'See? I told you she was pudgy!' I had to explain to her that that meant that 80 per cent of the children her age weigh more than she does!

Anon

There are many things my mother-in-law does that drive me mad. But I grin and bear it, ignore it and try not to let it get to me. You should do what you have to do to ensure that your own family unit is strong, happy, supporting and loving.

Anon

> **Mumsnet tip**
> Be nice to your in-laws. They would just love to have your little brat for the weekend – and your little brat will still be a little angel to them no matter how badly they've actually behaved.

I guess part of my reluctance to leave my daughter with the in-laws is because they have a very different outlook on childcare to my own. I'm into routines and cooking healthy meals (I'm probably a completely OTT first-time mother) whereas they just go with the flow.

Anon

You have two families during your life – the one you are born into and the one you make for yourself. The first one you cannot choose, the second one you can.

All quite true, but no one mentions the family you inherit when you make a family for yourself, like your children's grandparents.

Anon

I have to say that as the mother of a son, I absolutely dread him getting married, having kids and me being regarded as the hideous mother-in-law by his partner and not seeing the baby very much. I think that we give our own mums the benefit of the doubt: she cleans up and we think, 'how helpful' but when our mother-in-law does it, we think, 'hmm, so she thinks I don't know how to clean my own house, eh?' When our mum croons over the baby, we think, 'aah, nice to see how much she loves him' whereas with the mother-in-law, we think, 'so, she thinks she's a better mum than me.'

Believe me, I'm no saint and I've had my share of frustrations but do try to think the best even when I'm simmering. After all, that might be me one day!

Anon

Whenever I get a bit exasperated with my mother-in-law, I just think what a dreadful mother-in-law I'm bound to be (if my current behaviour's anything to go by – all possessive and dismissive of all other efforts to take care of my boy) and it makes me smile. I imagine myself in 30 years' time terrorizing some poor woman and making a better fish pie – oh, and buying cheap toys – I can't wait!

Anon

Can you keep up friendships with childless friends after having a baby?

There is a widening gulf between me and someone who has been one of my best friends for ten years. It's partly to do with changes in my priorities since having kids and with her being a single working woman. I feel like I hardly have time for myself, my daughter or my husband and that friends in the same situation are easier to be with.

Anon

What the experts say

Few of us understand just how much motherhood changes our relationships with old friends until it is upon us, drawing us away from the childless ones and closer to those with children.

Kate Figes (*Life After Birth*)

I should be going out tonight with a friend who has no children, but my little one's not settling well at night at the moment and I need to have a few nights to get her back into a routine. I know that's going to sound so lame to someone who hasn't been there. I find that when I do get any free time I want to do something with my husband to try and keep that relationship alive. I guess it's a case of finding out who your friends are. If they really are your nearest and dearest, you should be able to say that life has changed and you just can't go out as much as you used to – but they're very welcome to pop round with a bottle of wine and help with bath time. Let them see the chaos close up and they might understand more.

Anon

I think the problem is that you change so much when you have children and they become such a big part of your life that inevitably it's difficult to stay as close to friends who can't empathize with those changes.

Anon

I'm 20, married and have a little boy of 13 months. We find that our friends just don't bother with us! They seem to think that because we have a child, we no longer want to go out. It's quite upsetting when we find out that everyone's gone out and they haven't bothered to phone us. Obviously, we don't go out very often but sometimes we need to have a night off and see our friends.

Anon

I can remember this happening with a couple of my friends when they had a baby. You ask them to go out a few times, they say 'no' and then you kind of assume they won't want to come. The worst was when we organized a trip away as a group and just assumed they wouldn't be able to make it – they were very upset. Now we're on the receiving end with kids of our own and sometimes feel a bit left out (though frankly we have to admit that most of the time we just can't take the pace anymore). One solution we've found is to be a bit more proactive – we're never going to be able to nip out to the pub on a whim, so we ring round in advance and do the organizing ourselves. Or meet everyone for Sunday lunch – that way we don't have to get a babysitter and don't have to get drunk and end up going to bed too late and regretting it at six the next morning!

Anon

What the experts say
I'd be willing to place money on the fact that we've all lost one friend to parenthood.
Penny Wilson (*Wipe: Survival Tactics for Parents with Attitude*)

I rarely go out in the evenings any more. One solution is to meet a pre-baby friend when she takes a day off work. Then we go for a few drinks at lunchtime and I can take my son with me. It's quieter on a weekday. We don't get as much peace as we would on our own but it is a good compromise.

Anon

My sister had two small children and at the time I had none. I was always pleased to see them but not crazy about them. I felt a definite friction between my sister and myself about it. She would often interrupt a conversation by saying: 'Oh look at...' because she thought he was doing something incredibly cute, and it used to bug me because I did not find it remotely endearing! It lead me to make a conscious effort never to expect others to find my children appealing. And of course now that I have two this is not as easy as I thought it would be, but I do try to restrict my displays of glowing pride to grandparents, who think the same way anyway!

Anon

What the experts say
Keep in mind that other people, especially people who haven't got children of their own, will greatly appreciate brief and superficial answers to the question, so how is the baby?
Vicki Iovine (*Best Friend's Guide to...Surviving the First Year of Motherhood*)

Some single friends may seem less comfortable with you. This may be partly because you share less in common and partly because some of them, consciously or unconsciously, are envious of your new family.

Eisenberg, Murkoff and Hathaway (*What to Expect the First Year*)

Some mothers (perhaps dads too) expect others to have as much of an interest in their children as they do. I am very late to motherhood and most of my friends had children well before I did and, quite honestly, I was often bored or annoyed that when I went round for an evening the children would be up late and we couldn't have any adult time. Now I am a mum myself and I am acutely aware of the need not to bore other people with my child.

Anon

I discovered that my old pre-kids friends are still around now my kids are older (six and three) and I can see them again and pretend not to be a mum!

Anon

Sex life after babies – is there such a thing?

As much as I love my husband, I just don't fancy sex any more. I just can't seem to get through to him that by the end of a day running around after three children, I am just too tired. It is as if having sex with him has become another chore that I have to do before I can finally go to sleep at night.

Anon

I just don't feel the same about sex anymore. The demands of a baby are so intense, tiring, all-consuming and physical that often sex just feels like another demand on me. I really want to lie in bed with a book and be quiet and self-contained, and then sleep and sleep – during sex I actually think, 'I could be asleep by now!'. I feel bad about this, and don't think it's fair on my husband, but I am so off sex it's not true. I would love to know if this total lack of libido will ever pass.

Anon

> **Mumsnet fact**
> More than 50 per cent of couples have not returned to their pre-pregnancy levels of sexual activity one year after the birth of their child.
> Kate Figes (*Life After Birth*)

My partner and I have not had sex since the birth of our daughter nearly four months ago, and I'm worried that this will affect our relationship. I feel so unattractive at the moment as I put on nearly four stone while I was pregnant and am not losing any weight. I feel that my self-esteem and confidence is being affected and this has a knock-on effect on my libido.

Anon

After the birth of my second child, I really had to force myself to have sex again. I was too tired and scared of the physical pain that it caused me, but I felt I should make the effort, even though I didn't want to do it out of desire. A few months down the line it is getting better. As well as less pain, there's even a hint of desire, so I'm glad I have pushed myself.

Anon

I worried a lot about sex just after I'd given birth, and I came to dread it. When we did start again properly (when the baby was six months old), I remembered what I liked about it. The baby was on three meals a day and my periods had just returned, so I figure that my body was telling me it was okay to start again. I've told my husband that next time there's going to be no sex for the first six months after the birth. That way he won't feel rejected (hopefully) and I won't feel under so much pressure.

Anon

I ended up with a forceps delivery, had an episiotomy and tore too. I was incredibly sore and my stitches were pulled very tight. We didn't try to have sex until five months afterwards and it hurt me so much that we didn't try again for another two months. Even at seven months, I found it an uncomfortable process rather than something pleasurable.

The doctor suggested internal massage to help the scar tissue breakdown. I reckoned sex was probably similar and did find that eventually things got more comfortable to the point where it even became enjoyable again!

I would recommend a few glasses of wine to help your muscles relax. There is nothing less likely to put you in the mood than anticipating something painful.

Anon

Sex was very painful after my first child and it was putting a strain on our relationship. I don't think my husband realized just how much it hurt. I went to the doctor after about six months and she checked to make sure that it was just the stitches. She said the scar would need time to heal, but if the pain didn't stop I could have surgery to remove the scar tissue. Once I realized that it was just the scar tissue I did relax a bit and everything was fine.

Anon

My mum told me to have sex as soon as I could after the birth. Despite an episiotomy but with the help of alcohol, I managed it exactly two weeks to the day after the birth (although I've since found out that some doctors advise waiting until after the six week check). It was pretty much lie back and think of England but within a couple of weeks things were back to normal. I think just getting the first time out of the way is the biggest step.

Anon

I think my lack of interest in sex after birth is due to an altered body image. With engorged, leaking breasts, sore nipples, stretch marks, an exhausted saggy body and a collicky baby either screaming or sucking 24/7 I find it hard to morph into love-sex goddess between breastfeeds.

Anon

What the experts say

Some women cannot enjoy genital sex so long as they are breastfeeding. They feel their bodies are dedicated to their babies and raised prolactin levels during lactation may enhance these feelings.

Sheila Kitzinger (*The Year After Childbirth*)

After the birth of our first son our sex life was pretty good – less frequent perhaps but of greater quality. It's only since having child number two (who sleeps less soundly) that our sex life has gone downhill. When we do, it's highly enjoyable, it's just that I've somewhat lost the will to get started. I wonder also whether, psychologically, it has something to do with the fact that I just can't face taking the risk (however slight) of falling pregnant again.

Anon

My main problem is that I get so much affection from my kids (and give them so much back) that I really don't need any more from my partner!

My tip is to go away for a night – if at all possible. Sex is so much more feasible if you're not worried about being woken up at the crack of dawn or not trying to squeeze it into the kids' afternoon nap time!

Anon

I love all the physical contact that goes with being a mum and frequently get hold of my children just for a cuddle. So by the time my partner gets round to his turn, it's not that I can't stand to be pawed any more, it's more that I feel I've already had my share for the day. He'd be horrified if he knew how much I try to avoid sex at the moment, but I'm just not interested. I didn't use to be like this at all! I've wondered if it's because I don't want to get pregnant again, but I know that isn't the real reason. I really think it may be that I have so much cuddling during the day that I don't need the physical affection that badly. When we do make love it's great, but he has to do all the running.

Anon

What the experts say

As your baby grows, sex drive may increase but opportunities for sex may still be few and far between... A sense of humour is important, as is considering ways to negotiate these huge shifts in your relationship. Having no sex can be habit-forming and you may need to act to break the pattern.

Jan Parker and Jan Stimpson (*Raising Happy Children*)

I didn't make love for at least three months after our daughter was born. I was very conscious of our change in sex life but found that when I had the courage to discuss it, my partner totally understood. I needed to explain that I still found him attractive and loved him, but sometimes sleep seemed even more attractive. I've found that a really good 'mood enhancer' is a night out together, on our own, laughing again and drinking a little too much. Although we can't do this as often as we'd like, it really does help your mood.

Anon

Relaxation is perhaps the key. It's worth trying candles, a warm bath and a bottle of your favourite red wine. It usually works for me.

Anon

Try to get some time on your own during the weekends because while you are bound to be exhausted and right off it by bedtime, you might manage a little afternoon delight!

Anon

I think the only solution is to pay a babysitter or get a relative to take your baby out for a couple of hours on a weekend afternoon. Do make sure you leave explicit instructions for the babysitter not to return even if it's pouring and tell them about all the local indoor play areas just in case.

Anon

> **Mumsnet fact**
> More than half the people who work more than 48 hours a week don't feel like sex when they get home.
> Chartered Institute of Personnel and Development

You need to try and stop making excuses. We waited three months as I had suffered a bad tear, which was quite painful. But when we started again, we both said, 'Why did we leave it so long?' Now our love life is, if anything, better than before our baby was born as we have much more reason to love one another.

Anon

Don't dwell too much on how long it's been. The time goes so quickly when you've just had a new baby. Try and work up to it gradually, getting close again without having sex. Hugs and kisses sometimes get lost along the way, cuddling up in bed together and just talking can bring back that closeness. I found that the first time we (eventually) got round to making love after I had my son, the earth didn't exactly move! But it was a step in the right direction.

Anon

My advice is just to go for it! I know it's a nightmare when you're so tired that you feel sick, but suddenly you realize it's been months and I do think there's no substitute for sex (though not necessarily penetrative sex) for making you feel close. My suggestion, for what it's worth, is if one of you shows the slightest interest – have a go. It's amazing how the tiredness fades and you remember how much you enjoy it when you get started. Oh, and you sleep well afterwards too and it's great for relieving tension.

Anon

8

Childcare and
going back to work

Introduction

Before you had your baby you probably knew you'd be in for some sleepless nights, you no doubt had an inkling that your body would never be quite the same again and you may even have suspected that your relationship would come under a bit of strain. What you might not have bargained for is just how terrible you feel about leaving your baby and going back to work.

Finding someone to entrust your precious little one to can be the most prickly of parental decisions and regular scare stories in the media about cruel nannies and neglectful nurseries don't help. But most of us do find one or more people to care for our babies – seven out of ten first-time mothers return to work within one year. How do they go about choosing childcare? Should you plump for the safety in numbers of a nursery or the intimacy of a childminder? And what's the best way of settling your baby in once you've made your choice? A dash in and out approach or a gradual, stealthy retreat – either way it can be painful.

Should you be lucky enough to have the dosh, what about a maternity nurse to help you find your feet early on? Are they godsends who allow you to enjoy your first precious few months while coercing your contented offspring into a faultless eating and sleeping regime or will they interfere, wreck your attempts to breastfeed and leave you feeling hopelessly inadequate?

However traumatic and difficult it may be to find someone to look after your baby – and according to a recent Mori poll three out of four parents say they cannot find enough affordable childcare – going to work has advantages. At least you can go to the toilet and eat lunch in peace (depending on where you work, of course). But even with the best childcare in the world, working mothers often feel guilty, worry that their absence is harmful to their babies and just downright miss them. How can you manage the guilt and how can you manage your life if you are working full-time and a parent?

And what about when your baby falls sick and can't go to nursery – how do you tell your employers and how do you cope with the workplace resentment that many parents seem to feel?

If you can afford it, is working part-time a better option and how do you go about persuading your employers to let you (and to let you alone on your days at home)?

Of course, if finances allow, you could always opt to stay home and have what may be the toughest job of them all. The next chapter has the answers to all these questions and more that you might have about choosing childcare and going back to work in the first year of your baby's life.

Maternity nurses – are they a good idea?

I had a maternity nurse for four weeks after my son was born and have mixed feelings about them. It is very hard having someone living with you at such an amazing time of your life when you just want to experience your new family unit, and It didn't help that I didn't get on with mine at all. She picked at a lot of things I did and gave my son formula milk when I wanted to breastfeed only. As a result, I spent a huge amount of time on the phone to my mother for reassurance that I wasn't going mad.

The way I coped was to get my husband to speak to her about anything I couldn't face bringing up (I was very emotional) and a couple of times I actually lost it with her myself. I tried to remember that it must be a very hard job moving from place to place, where your boss is always a very tired and tearful new mother.

> **Mumsnet fact**
> Maternity nurses in the UK earn an average of £450 plus per week (even more for twins). Daily maternity nurses can earn up to £75 per day. (2002 figures)   www.bestbear.co.uk

BUT, BUT, BUT, there were some big pluses – I managed to sleep a lot when she was here, which was great for getting over a C-section and by the time she left, my son knew the difference between night and day. So I would have another maternity nurse next time (although clearly not the same one) and I would be much clearer about what it was that I wanted help with.

It's a good idea to interview with someone else whose judgement you trust, to think out all possible questions you want to ask beforehand and to make it absolutely clear how you wish things to go when she is with you. If she doesn't like it, then find someone else. It's better to find that out beforehand.

Tinkerbell

I think this must be horses for courses. I would hate someone coming in and sorting my baby out into a routine and so on – sounds like they're programming the video (which I can't do, so maybe that's not a good analogy!). I think it would be utterly pointless to have one who annoyed you, or did things you didn't want her to do. Help with winding, settling and taking the baby for walks is very useful, yes, but that's what dads and grandmothers are for, not maternity nurses. Of course, if there is no other adult around, I can see a need.

Tiktok

It depends on the individual maternity nurse as to how much non-baby help they're prepared to give. Mine has taken over all the washing, takes my three-year-old to the park with my twin babies, picks him up from nursery, makes me lots of snacks and cups of tea and even meals sometimes. I was very against having help the first time round but with twins I think it's essential. The babies sleep in her room so I only get up to feed them during the night. She also takes them out for a long walk twice a day, which gives me time to rest or to spend time with my older son.

I would recommend it highly, as long as you stay in control. You don't want to feel vulnerable when she goes so don't let her do everything. I encouraged mine to leave me on my own for the odd afternoon or night so I could feel confident that I would be okay when she finished. I had bad labours with both my babies so it was lovely to have someone who allowed me some rest so I would not be up all night. They are expensive though. An alternative is a night nurse, which is cheaper.

Lauraw

I had a maternity nurse for two months to help with my twins. The second month she just did nights. They were very premature and I'd had a C-section so we needed some help. It's not the easiest relationship because you're so hormonal and instinctively you want to do everything for newborns yourself. But our nurse was very supportive with breastfeeding and saw it as her role to look after me as much as the babies. She helped to get them into a good routine and they subsequently have always been good sleepers. She also taught me lots of tricks of the trade – so I was much more competent when she left than I would have been otherwise. As I was breast-feeding I still got up in the night but she did all the settling afterwards (she slept in their room) so I got a lot more sleep than I otherwise would. It was quite nice to have the second month where she was still around for the nights, but I flew solo in the days, as it meant it wasn't too terrifying when she left. Of course, it all cost and arm and a leg (I can't even bring myself to add it all up!).

What the experts say
As well as providing welcome help with the baby, maternity nurses are invaluable teachers.

Dr Miriam Stoppard (*Your New Baby*)

If I hadn't had twins, I wouldn't have had a maternity nurse, because I like the idea of bedding down with my baby for a couple of months with no one else getting between us. Of course, if you've got other kids as well, I think a night nanny for a couple of months would be a great luxury, but choose carefully – having someone living with you when your hormones are up the spout can be quite testing and if you have some specific ideas about the way you want your baby looked after (like whether they have a dummy or not, your feeding preferences and sleep routines) spell them out how during the interview – I've had friends who had difficult experiences because the maternity nurse just took over and didn't take enough account of their views.

Berta

Even with just one baby (and especially the first) I think it's fantastic to have someone to help with the baby. A maternity nurse is, surely, experienced with breastfeeding and can help with that if any problems arise. I would have loved to have been able to hand the baby over after the feed so that someone else could nurse them through the inevitable 45–60 minutes winding session that always followed feeds with my two in the early days. I found that so tiring, and it was a huge relief when my mum or someone was around to take over. If they're feeding every two and a half to three and half hours, then if someone else settles the baby and you only have to do the actual feeding, you may stand a chance of getting a couple of hours sleep between feeds.

Also, it must be reassuring to have someone experienced on hand to bounce ideas off – like whether the baby is hungry or sleepy or whether there is anything else that can be done to help with this particular problem or not. I think it would have greatly reduced my stress levels.

Plus, I find it very difficult to sleep if the baby is in the house because the slightest whimper wakes me like a shot. Someone to take the baby out for a walk would have really helped me relax. While I'm feeding they could bring me food and drinks, tidy a little and maybe even defrost the dinner! Woohoo! I'm getting excited here... Maybe next baby... (and pigs might fly!).

Amber1

How much maternity leave do you need?

I think the newborn stage flies by and is gone just as you are getting to grips with it. I always advise pregnant friends to wallow in the early days because it is never the same again and the emotional rollercoaster combined with the physical demands need to be counterbalanced with enjoyment of the baby. I do think that physically and emotionally you need time to adjust but I am not sure I could say how long it takes exactly.

You probably won't know yourself how you feel about going back to work until after the baby has been born and your life has settled down a bit (does it ever?). Whatever you do, make the decision that is right for you. I went on maternity leave at the first opportunity because I was having so many problems with colleagues and my pregnancy, but I was not desperate to return to work when my paid maternity leave ran out (although we needed the money). However, within a couple of months I was climbing the walls and started looking for employment. Some friends who'd planned to return to work after their babies were born found it an enormous struggle and one in particular returned to work only to leave again a few weeks later because she hadn't been ready for it. Others thought they'd want to stay at home but quickly found they weren't cut out for it. It depends on the individual and it does not always turn out as you'd expect.

Winnie

With my first baby I went to great lengths to stress to my employer that having a baby would interfere as little as possible with my job. After taking six weeks off, I made myself available via a networked PC. Looking back, I think I must have been mad to bother as it was all fairly pointless and caused me a lot of stress and upset.

I returned to work after 14 weeks and I felt it was too soon. My baby was born two weeks late and I found it quite traumatic leaving him at 12 weeks. It was made worse by the fact that he was sleeping very poorly at that stage too. Also, as I wanted him to be solely breastfed until he was six months, I had to use a breast pump extensively at work, which was not fun

Inevitably, if you are a valued employee, people will forget how long you had off quite quickly and I think it's better to have a longer break and return at a time when you can focus on your job properly and be happy with your decision to leave your baby during the day. Next time, I will definitely take six months.

Ringer

I had six months' maternity leave and that was just right as I was getting a bit bored with the monotony of the house by then and my son was ready to socialize! But at 16 weeks, he was not sleeping through the night and I would have missed him too much.

Lil

I only took two weeks off because I felt fine. If I had been ill, of course, I would have taken longer. But if a woman feels okay, why not? Physical and mental fitness will vary from person to person.

Jbr

Leaving aside what the baby needs, it takes most women time to recover physically and emotionally from a birth. And if you choose to breastfeed, it takes time to get this established. So, just from the mother's point of view, going back to work too soon is not desirable.

Even if you do struggle into work, still sore and befuddled from lack of sleep, what sort of professional image are you going to put across? Isn't it better to wait until you can hit the ground running?

Frank1

What the experts say

I worry when mums return to full-time work in those early months after birth. I do not believe any newly delivered mother is physically fit for this.

Dr Christopher Green (*Babies!*)

Why do people have children if they're only going to shunt them on to someone else? I know that people have financial pressures to return to work (and I know a lot of mothers choose to take on part-time work to get a break from full-time parenting) but making the most of the time allowed would seem the best option to me. I was very nearly in a position where I would have to go back to a 40-hour week when my daughter was ten weeks old. When pregnant, I didn't think this would prove too much of a problem but as soon as she was born I saw a major problem and thankfully I didn't have to do it.

Lizzer

The reasons for women returning to work are varied, but each to their own. I know one woman who had her baby after finishing a day's work on the Friday and was back at her office on the following Monday. She is married to an extremely wealthy guy and doesn't need the money. She works long hours, travels extensively and has two kids, who are looked after mainly by her mum and sisters. She is happy, her kids are lovely and I think it's up to her at the end of the day.

Evesmum

People have no idea what's in store when they have their first baby. I was set to go on maternity leave when I was 38 weeks pregnant but ended up having to leave work (for bed rest) at 34 weeks. I was in hospital at 35 weeks and induced at 36 weeks. So I ended up having a baby one and half weeks before I was due to go on maternity leave.

I went back to full-time work when my baby was three months old. This was not nearly enough time off for me, but due to financial constraints I had to go back.

Chelle

I took my full 16 weeks maternity leave with my first son (having worked up to my due date) and six months with my second. The first time round I thought I would breeze back to work and was really taken by surprise at how hard it was to leave him – with lots of doubts and howling. The next time around I thought going back would be easier because my second son was older when I went back and we still had the same nanny from my first son. But I was totally floored again!

Lara1

I only had 14 weeks off, which I had to start early because of illness. It was a shock when they changed my baby's due date at the last moment. If he hadn't been born early I would have had to have left him at 6 weeks. As it was I had to leave him at nine weeks, which was hard. Fortunately, they had tissues and sympathy all ready at work. I am now expecting my second child. I think I'm going to miss out on the full maternity leave entitlement by one week so I'm thinking about leaving and then finding another job. Though I love where I work, I know I need more time with my baby.

Peachey

After my first son was born I had to go back to work as soon as my paid maternity leave stopped when he was about four and a half months. I wasn't happy about this but we couldn't afford to live on one wage. I gave up work altogether after having my second son.

Some people need to work for their own sense of self worth and sanity. I've heard of people craving to get back to work within a few weeks of the birth. Others, like me, are happy to stay at home and find other things to do.

Whatever you decide, it must be your choice. But don't feel guilty if you do decide to go back sooner rather than later because you will probably be happier in yourself and more able to be a happy, caring mother to your baby. Bear in mind that babies often become more clingy at around seven months so leaving them with someone else at this stage could be much more difficult.

PamT

I went back to work for four days a week when my daughter was four and a half months old and although, ideally, I would have preferred only three days, I felt good going back. Whether or not you're ready to go back will depend on how well your baby is sleeping by then. I was lucky and my daughter was just starting to sleep through the night by the time I went back.

Rkayne

My son is now six months old and, while I have days where I feel I would enjoy being at work, most of the time the idea of going back and leaving him is hard. I know that my employers would not welcome me going part-time, so that would mean my son would be in childcare for long hours as I have to be in by 8 am and the journey takes an hour. I also know that the job would bring lots of stress as we are over-worked and under-staffed, and have to work at home each night. I can't see how I could do all that then come home, do all the housework, look after my son and still be up and out the door to work on time every morning.

Carrieboo

> **Mumsnet tip**
> You don't know how you will feel about maternity leave until after you've had your baby and been at home for a few months so try to delay the decision if at all possible.

Your employer may want to know when you plan to return to work but they do not necessarily have the right to know. If you are returning to work at the end of Ordinary Maternity Leave or Additional Maternity Leave then you can just turn up on the day, but if you find that you want to return sooner then you need to give three weeks' notice. The law is written this way because you cannot possibly know how you're going to feel about returning to work until the time comes.

Lois

I went back to work full-time when my daughter was four months old as I was not entitled to any more paid time off. I found the hours and pressure very difficult to deal with, given the amount of sleep I was getting. My daughter would wake at 5.30 am, which meant that once I had fed her and put her back to sleep it was not worth my while going back to bed. I seemed to spend all day at work and all evening preparing for the next day. I also feel that because I went back to work early I did not get the chance to meet other mothers and form friendships when I would have had the energy to do so.

Minks

Those first months are the toughest time – not only are you establishing feeding and sleeping routines, but you're also adapting to the whole change in your own identity. It affects everyone differently. I think it's important not to judge your experience of motherhood by those early months as things change so quickly after that. Very soon it is not only about feeds, naps and nappy changing, but about smiles, laughs, sitting up, playing and before you know it, they are crawling, talking and walking.

If you are lucky to have options, don't feel pressured to go back too soon; return when you think you are ready and only for as many hours as you want to.

Mollipops

Child-minder or nursery – what's best?

I decided on a nursery rather than a child-minder for a number of reasons. Having more kids around means my son has a wider social circle and having more staff around means he doesn't get attached to any one person. A friend used to be a child-minder and the little boy she looked after was so fond of her, he cried when he had to go home and in the holidays – something I couldn't cope with! It's nice to know your child enjoys life when you're not around, but not to that extent. I also felt the range of activities was better at nursery, loads of toys I could never afford, and also (heaven forbid) you'd never have the worry of your child being mistreated by someone. The downside is that they pick up every cold, cough and conjunctivitis going – mine's even had hand, foot and mouth.

Peta

My son went to a child-minder from three months to 12 months. Unfortunately, she often had to cancel a day's child-minding because one of her daughters' children were sick and she had to look after them instead. When my son was 12 months, one of her daughters had a fourth child and so she left to go and look after her grandchildren for six months. We had to find somewhere else for our son. Though I thought the 'home-away-from-home' system would be better for a young child, my son was very upset when he had to leave the original child-minder and I wondered if the same thing could happen again and again.

I decided to look at nurseries to try and give my son some sort of stability and continuity of care. It was very hard to leave him for the first two weeks but the carers would phone me several times during the day to let me know how he was settling in. Since then he has never looked back and can't wait to get there each morning.

There have been no changes in staff (except for the comings and goings of students). For babies under six months there is one carer per baby, so this is a lot better than when my son was at the child-minder's.

Chelle

Both my children have been at nursery since they were babies. My initial concerns about sending my son were quickly dispelled when I saw how well he settled and how many cuddles he got from the staff. My daughter went at six months and loves nursery – she has never been upset about going – in fact, if things start getting a bit boring at the weekend with mummy and daddy, she has been known to demand to be taken to nursery! (Not so good for parental morale.) So much depends on the individual nursery, the staff and on the character of the child.

Azzie

Like all working parents we ummed and aahed over the child-minder/nursery dilemma for ages. We finally opted for a very good local nursery, which my son went to full-time from five months. We had a friend who had had a very distressing experience with a child-minder – basically she was called by social services at work and advised to collect her daughter as a neighbour had reported the child-minder for cruelty. This particular child-minder had a daughter of her own of similar age, and was getting angry because my friend's daughter was developing more quickly and so was being really hostile to her.

As a result, we felt that we didn't want to rely solely on one person whom we didn't really know and who wouldn't have anyone to check on them during the day when we were out. Somehow we felt the collective responsibility of nursery was somehow preferable.

We have been very lucky: the nursery is excellent and has very loose routines for the babies and an excellent curriculum for the toddlers. My son has positively thrived there. But as I said, it depends: you really have to trust your instincts, both about the quality of any care, and also your child's reaction to it.

Motherofone

I'd endorse the benefits of 'collective accountability' of a good nursery rather than the one-to-one relationship with a child-minder. I was unlucky with mine, she turned out to be a grasping, manipulative bully – something that social services checks may not pick up. We withdrew him immediately she started insisting that I gave up breastfeeding because it was preventing her from bonding with him.

Our son went to a small nursery full-time at eight months which has a low turnover among its largely mature and 100 per cent qualified staff. We looked at other local nurseries and were concerned about the variability of the care and in particular the cramped conditions for babies in some of them. Until the age of two, our son was one of only four in the Baby Room and he loved it there. Now he's one of only eight in the Toddler Room. I think size does matter!

Clare2

I tried to find a child-minder when I was pregnant but couldn't find one who would take a young baby. I went to see all the local child-minders and wasn't impressed by any. Then I went to the local nurseries. What a difference – professional, excellent facilities (such as child-sized toilets and sinks and a large enclosed garden) and when I couldn't think what questions to ask, they gave me the information anyway. Each child had a nominated carer and a book in which you were told what they'd eaten and when they'd slept. My daughter sometimes cried when I picked her up – embarrassing but at least I didn't feel guilty over leaving her.

I must put my tick in the nursery box. I feel happier knowing my son does not have to rely on one carer every day and, most importantly, the carers are qualified. It is frustrating not being able to leave my son there when he is ill, but then it works both ways – he is less likely to catch illnesses himself.

I like the fact that the nursery gives me a daily written report. The downside is that the waiting lists are frustrating and it is painfully expensive.

I like to think back to when we were hunter-gatherers, as that seems to explain how we've evolved mentally. If you think about childcare then, it was always done as a 'collective' with all the kids running around together while the mothers looked after them *en masse*. I guess a nursery is pretty much like that, so they can't be so bad!

Lil

A few tips to help you choose a nursery: drop in rather than schedule an appointment – you get a better idea of how they operate. Check that each child is assigned a key worker who is personally responsible for their welfare and progress, and find out what mechanisms they have for letting you know what he or she has been up to. The only downside we have found is at times of sickness when they can't attend – a nanny or child-minder would probably still have them. Also, there is no flexibility on time – you have to be there to collect them.

When our daughter was a baby she really was given individual care and there was not a rigid timetable for the under twos. They have always allowed the little ones to feed and sleep when they have wanted to and often when I went to collect her when she was a baby she was cuddled up in her keyworker's arms really content. I guess we have been really lucky with our choice of nursery.

Viv

If you do decide to use a nursery there are a few things you need to bear in mind. Most nurseries ask you to sign a contract where you have to give three months' notice for any change in nursery days. Check this contract carefully. I had to remove my children from a nursery which had persistently failed to provide enough staff to cover the rooms. After drawing this to their attention a number of times, I gave them two months' notice and left. At the same time, another seven children were removed from the nursery for exactly the same reason (inadequate staffing had resulted in a number of minor accidents). Both my friend and I were taken to court over the extra months' nursery fees, even though the children had not attended nursery and they were failing to adhere to government rules and regulations. As a result of this I found out some fairly worrying facts:

1. You cannot find out whether a nursery has had any social services complaints upheld against them, or even if they are being investigated unless the nursery chooses to tell you.

2. You cannot get a copy of any inspection reports unless the nursery chooses to show them to you.

3. Failing to conform to social services regulations does not constitute a reasonable reason to break the contract with the nursery, as most contracts only stipulate that they will be open at certain times to receive your child.

The complaint we raised against the nursery was upheld by social services (the baby room had seven babies and one member of staff at the time of the inspection), but my friend lost the case as this was not sufficient reason to break the contract. I won mine on a technicality.

One thing to bear in mind is that any nursery that provides three- to five-year-old cover should probably have an OFSTED inspection – you can check the reports on the internet. I wished I had done it with the old nursery as I would probably have left immediately.

Mumsnet fact
Children put in daycare when very young will perform better in school, have more friends and be more creative than their peers, but only if they are cared for by trained and well-qualified staff.

Daycare Trust

When choosing a nursery look at the ratio of qualified to unqualified staff. As we all know, one of the major criteria for dealing with young children is experience! Make sure you drop in to check it out – lunchtime is a good time. Are the children being entertained while waiting for lunch, or screaming their heads off while too few harassed staff try to feed the forty thousand? The final point I'd make is to keep checking. Our eldest daughter had been happily attending the nursery for two years and so it was very difficult for us to admit (to ourselves) that things weren't quite right. You owe it to your children and your own peace of mind, to keep constant checks on the nursery. It's amazing how fast things can go downhill.

Scooby2

I am in the process of taking my son out of his nursery as things have gone from bad to worse. The cleaner did not return after Christmas and the place is just filthy. The nursery staff have to fit cleaning around looking after the children and, as each room is overcrowded, the cleaning is not getting done. The licence on the notice board quite clearly states that it should have no more than nine children in a room and in most of the rooms there are 14 kids. Not surprisingly, the staff turnover is very high. My son has had a few bouts of sickness recently and I am sure it is because the place is not clean. I only have to give a month's notice so I am paying the money up front and he is not returning. And this is one of the best and most expensive nurseries in Edinburgh!

I called the Local Authority to get them to spot check the place and they phoned the nursery to tell them they were going to have an investigation in two weeks time. So guess what? The nursery is very, very busy just now repainting, cleaning carpets and rearranging all the staff.

Mima

I have been a registered child-minder for 15 years. I am very anti-nursery for under twos. I believe a baby is better off in a home environment for the first two years. Most child-minders can only have one baby under a year old and a total of three children under five. The benefit of a child-minder is that children have the same constant care from one person and lunch is prepared for them when they need it, be it 12 pm or 2pm. It is a home from home environment.

I know a lot of people prefer the relative 'safety' of a nursery and also find it easier to hand their child over to a nursery as it is more impersonal. Also, the parent does not have to get too involved in the nursery, which can lessen parents' guilt about handing over their child. Some parents resent the affection child-minders show to the children – they feel that the relationship can get too close.

I am lucky that the parents of the children I look after are delighted that their child struggles away from them to come to my arms in the morning and barely waves goodbye – they know the child is secure, happy and contented. What more could they want?

One simple piece of advice is to look for a child-minder who is a member of the NCMA. If they are, they are generally more committed because it costs a lot of money just for the membership. They are also nearly always trained.

Alibubbles

What the experts say
Under twos seem to flourish best in a one-to-one relationship with not more than two or three carers, including you.
Sheila Kitzinger (*The Year After Childbirth*)

To fulfil a very young child's needs, each child needs to be looked after by one, or at the very most two key carers throughout the day.
Jan Parker and Jan Stimpson (*Raising Happy Children*)

I wouldn't want my child to 'bond' with just one carer. The thought of relying just on one person to look after my child worries me. That person could be having an off day, plus there's no one to monitor what the children do with the child-minder and there aren't the same facilities as in a nursery. There are also more children of the same age, which must be preferable for the child. The nursery nannies are also not in their own home or distracted by their own children, so they can concentrate on your children and not on the housework!

Lil

I think that it does depend on the nursery. My daughter's is fairly flexible about meal and sleep times – at the nursery they wait till she wakes up to give her lunch. She sleeps whenever she wants to – in fact, they wouldn't all be able to sleep at the same time because there aren't enough cots. Her keyworker is fantastic and has taught her loads of things that I wouldn't have the time or knowledge to do. And even as babies they go on trips to the park and they go swimming each week.

Pamela1

My child-minder is extremely flexible – my husband works shifts, so I let her know the hours I need her to take my son on a monthly basis. She charges by the hour, not a fixed day rate as nurseries charge. Also, when my son is off sick or we are on holiday I only pay her 50 per cent of the usual fee. She will keep him longer if I am late with absolutely no problem.

She takes him to baby gym one day a week and toddler group another. If the weather is good they will often go out for a walk or go to the park. In the summer they will go for a picnic. Although his day follows a very similar routine, I like the fact that there is some spontaneity for him and that he might do something different if there is an event on or the weather is good.

She will take him if he is sick as long as she has no other child that day. She is happy to take him with colds and coughs, even with diarrhoea. The only time she will not take him is if he is vomiting or has a contagious illness, such as hand, foot and mouth.

I like the fact that my son has another adult that he trusts and loves, and who plays an important part in his day when we can't be there. We have never had any conflicts and we have very similar views anyway.

I did look into nurseries and found them very costly, not very flexible and the staff seemed to change a lot. I save over £100 a month by using a child-minder instead of a nursery.

Emmam

> **Mumsnet fact**
> There are 82,000 childminders in the UK with 16,000 new ones registering each year. The *Guardian*

I have visited many child-minders over the years (we have gone through the choosing process five or six times) and I did find that some child-minders had a bit of a 'pack-them-in' attitude (as I suppose some nurseries do). But it seems more of an act of faith to give a young child over to a very busy child-minder, even if she comes highly recommended, than to a nursery.

My experiences with child-minders have been really positive on the whole, hence my continued reliance on them. But I have never put my child with a child-minder who has anything near their full legal quota of children. Most child-minders I have known, seem, in any case, to stop far short of this.

There is something you have to bear in mind when you find that wonderful child-minder: she may stop child-minding. This has happened to me twice. Finding another can be temporarily traumatic for all concerned. At least with a nursery you are more assured of some continuity, even if some of the staff leave.

Frank1

We have ended up using a combination of child-minder and nursery, which seems to give us the best of both worlds. This originally came about due to the horrendous waiting lists at the local nurseries. I put my son's name down when I was six months pregnant and finally got a place when he turned one. During the first year he went to a child-minder. Now he and his brother go to the child-minder two days a week and the nursery for the other three.

The nursery is superb for socializing and doing all the messy stuff and activities. However, my child-minder is much more flexible about times and sickness. And obviously with her they get more of the sort of 'at home, one-to-one' (well, two) care that they'd have got if I was at home.

The great thing is that we have a fall-back if one or other can't provide the childcare, so when my child-minder goes on holiday the nursery often finds extra slots for us. When the nursery won't take the children due to illness the child-minder steps in.

One of the drawbacks I've found with a child-minder is that I have to be very careful about criticizing any care she gives. It's a much more personal relationship. The only drawback I've found with the nursery is the rule about not being able to take the children there if they are sick. Obviously this can cause chaos in a busy household!

Hmonty

> **Mumsnet tip**
> See a number of nurseries when making a choice. I hated one which two of my best friends had chosen; they in turn didn't like the one my son goes to. So use your gut feeling – recommendations are nice, but at the end of the day it's your choice.

I spent a lot of time going to see nurseries and child minders when deciding where my son would go and I have to say that the standard of care varied hugely. Some nurseries had such a high turnover of staff (always one of my first questions) that I just knew they couldn't be happy places for infants to be, whereas others seemed much more established and the workers were very caring and attentive. Likewise, there were some child-minders I wouldn't have left a pet with, let alone my precious baby.

It does seem very important for small children to form some kind of bond with a few key carers to give them a stable base and make them feel secure. A good nursery should be able to do this, although possibly not with quite the same degree of penetration as a child-minder. It is not so much the number of children that the carer is looking after but the regularity with which that carer is responsible for the infant, like nappy changes and feeding.

Molly1

I would be loath to say which childcare is best for which age group. I really do think that it differs from baby to baby and nursery to nursery. I wouldn't leave my cat at some nurseries I have looked at, and the same goes for some child-minders (both registered and unregistered). I'm not sure I agree that child-minders are always more flexible. Babies still have to fit into their timetable (however flexible that may or may not be) and if there are three children under five, some things, such as meal times etc, have to be fairly rigid simply in order to get through it!

Batters

Starting nursery – settling in tips for you and your baby

My baby started at nursery at six months. The week before he started full-time I took him in on three occasions. The first time I stayed with him in the babies' room for an hour. The second time I left him in the room for an hour while I went to another part of the nursery. The third occasion I went shopping for two hours, with my mobile phone! He has settled well, eats well, naps well and has fun with an array of toys. He has made closer attachments with a couple of the staff but seems fine with most of them.

For about the last month he has been very tearful when left in the morning though he has always calmed down by the time I've left his food in the kitchen and am about to leave the building, and he's fine when I pick him up in the evening. I feel confident that the staff care for him well, enjoy his company and will contact me if there is any problem. They also are very understanding and helpful if I'm feeling anxious during the day and call to see how he is.

I avoid visiting him during the day, as much to avoid upsetting myself as him. I find that once I'm involved at work the time passes quickly and it's soon time for us to be reunited.

Wol

When my daughter started nursery they suggested short sessions for a short while then full days and it worked fine. The problem is not so much the baby as the mother. I went home and cried the first time I left her, but she really enjoyed it. There are lots of other children at nursery, more toys to play with and probably more attention that you can give at home with shopping, cleaning and cooking to do. It's tough to leave them – but it's harder for you than for the baby.

Robinw

Two of my children went to nursery, one at nine and the other at six months and both settled quickly. However, my partner and I never adjusted to not caring for our babies ourselves. We have recently reassessed our priorities and have taken our baby out of nursery while I take a sabbatical from work. So mixed reviews from me – your baby will be fine but be prepared for a period of adjustment.

Sarac

My daughter started nursery at four months for three full days a week. I cried for the first two weeks but the nursery was brilliant and encouraged me to ring whenever I wanted to for reassurance. I did this two or three times a day in the first week – apparently this is perfectly normal. I think that if you stay around at the nursery your baby will get used to your being there and it will be a greater wrench when you do leave.

I left her for a couple of hours at a time for a few weeks and she was perfectly happy. The one thing that really helped me was the nursery keeping a diary of what she had done, how much milk she had had and even how many dirty nappies! This made me feel reassured that I wasn't missing out on what she was doing. She is now three and still going to the same nursery and loves every minute of it.

Viv

Mumsnet tip
Get someone else to do the stressful drop off at nursery (partner/friend) and you do the fetching.

My first child went to nursery three days a week from six months. I think a phased approach is likely to be more painful than taking the plunge immediately and just going for it. We started off with a trial session for an hour in the week before he started. I was encouraged to disappear for that time and arrived back to reports that he'd spent the whole session bouncing on his bottom going 'da da da da da' – he hardly noticed I'd gone. I'd spent the whole session wandering aimlessly round town with my eyes full of tears! He started properly at nursery the week before I went back to work and I set about things like getting my hair done and thoroughly cleaning the house, which gave me time to get used to the whole idea before getting immersed in professional work.

I wouldn't go in during the day to feed him. While it might be a nice thing to do to start with, by nine months, your child may not want to let you go away again – my son was more reluctant to let me go in the mornings at that age, but he always settled happily within ten minutes after I'd gone (this is just a painful phase).

Helento

My daughter started nursery five days a week at just under six months old. I spent a week settling her in – the first day I went in for two hours with her and stayed the whole time, then gradually lengthened it until the final day when I left her for nearly the whole day. She settled in fine and there were no problems. The nursery gave me lots of advice on what to do and sent me away in order to make sure she got used to it! She's now 13 months old and still loves nursery.

Pamela

I went back to work part-time when my son was four and a half months old. It was very hard, particularly when my relationship with his child-minder broke down. Sending our son to nursery was the best thing I ever did and transformed me from a really hesitant and miserable working mum into one who still misses her child but knows that he is very happy and settled. I'd agree with settling them in gradually, for you if not for them! I worked up over a period of ten days from coming in and sitting with him for an hour or so, to leaving him for a couple of half days. He settled very quickly indeed – and with one lot of childcare arrangements breaking down, I was hyper-alert to any problems.

I used to feed my son at lunchtimes and we both found it hard to say goodbye, even though he was otherwise happy so maybe it would have been better if I had taken expressed milk in and left him for the whole day rather than go in to feed.

In the right kind of nursery, a child benefits from the knowledge that there are other people out there who love him too. He gets messy play in an environment where the floor is designed to take upturned tins of paint, he sits down at a table with other children to eat, chat and read, he will have visits from friendly police dogs, adoring sixth-formers on placement and Father Christmas. All this helps to balance out the feelings of loss and loneliness that you feel when you hand them over.

Clare2

Going back to work – did you feel guilty?

I've just come back from a wedding and spent a large portion of my time talking to other mums, some working, some not, some who wish they were, some who wish they weren't – all wracked with guilt of some sort or another – funnily enough, not many of the men were having the same conversation!

Kr

After my baby was born I wasn't sure whether to go back to work or not. But for me, staying at home was just too boring. That's not to say I don't adore my daughter or like spending time with her, but when you're at home you've also got to do the housework and all that. So I decided to return to my job. It still means I've got to do some housework but it's not such a feature and after an intellectually challenging day it's sometimes quite lovely to bleach the loo and have it all sparkly and clean.

Working is something that keeps me sane. When I was debating about whether to go back to work (would it make me a terrible mother?) a friend was very honest with me about all the organization and effort it took to work and be a mother, but she also asked me what kind of example I wanted to set my daughter: did I want to encourage her to do well at school, perhaps university and then tell her it's all over when she decides to have a baby? Why do men not feel (and get made to feel) like they're bad husbands or fathers for working long hours and travelling? Why is it always the mothers?

Miriam

I am a mum of three and have tried all the options since starting out with kids five years ago. Full-time work, part-time and home full-time. I am currently home full-time. All of the options have drawbacks and problems. I certainly felt guilt about working. Now, I often feel guilty that I am just processing the kids and not really giving them the attention they need as it's crowd-control half the time. I think that if you do work, however family unfriendly the environment, you should stick up for what your family needs from you. I regret every late night and weekend I worked when my first one was small. I think that if you are adamant about your needs you will often find there is more flexibility than you hoped for, even if it means your career being put on the back burner for a while.

Buster

I am guilt-free but it has been a long and difficult road to get there. After my daughter was born I went back to work full-time but after 18 months I realized I was the one losing out while my daughter had loads of fun with her grandparents. Then I tried part-time work but had a demanding job that I tried to shoe-horn into three days resulting in lots of stress.

Three years ago, I gave up totally when my son was born and stayed at home for two and a half years. It was fine, but I began to realize that he was too dependent on me and his clinginess was making me ratty.

So, off he went to nursery and blossomed. So I tried working from home. That was grim. There was no definition between work and children, and I frequently found someone important was trying to talk to me on the phone while I was frying fish fingers for screaming kids. Hideous! I got cross with the children too often and suffered from cabin fever.

So I took a long look at our lives. I did need to work. I had children later in life and after 20-odd years of a career I didn't feel I wanted to let it go. So I made a SWOT list (strengths, weaknesses, opportunities and threats) and worked out that I needed a part-time job with clearly defined goals that did not roll over from day to day (so no worrying about the job when I am with the children).

And here I am. My family says I am nicer, calmer and I am infinitely happier. My children accept that mum works too, but most of the week I am around and glad to be home. We have more fun than when I was simply processing the kids: feeding, washing, ferrying around. Yes, I have given up any hope of going back to my 'big career'. But I have two lovely children and am really content for the first time.

Jb

I went back to work full-time when my little boy was 13 weeks old. At first, I struggled through lack of sleep and not being 'with-it' and eventually realized that, despite my efforts to be superwoman, my work was suffering as well as me. I've cut down to four days' work a week and it is so much better. Now I have an extra day at home with my son when we do 'special' things together – and maybe catch up on the ironing and cleaning if he has a nap.

My husband doesn't help a lot – he's a workaholic and determined not to change, sadly. He often doesn't see our son, who's in bed by the time he gets home, so I insist on my husband helping him dress in the morning. I'm hoping he'll change his attitude once he's older and playing footie but at the moment he wants to be a ballet dancer so there's no camaraderie yet.

I realize now that work is less of a priority than my boy's welfare but I'm sure being at nursery is good for him. He has kids his own age to play with, learns from them, is not shy or self-conscious and hopefully the transition to school will be easier for him too. So think positive, all you guilt-ridden mums!

Peta

I don't regret going back to work full-time for one moment. I am determined that my kids will have a better childhood than I had. I don't want to be scrimping and saving just to be able to put food on the table and clothes on our backs like my mother had to.

Ailsa

Why guilt? My children are eight and four, and still with the same child-minder we chose all those years ago. My kids love her just as much as they love me – and they have a loving extended family to boot. I don't have the least problem with that because they don't love me any less just because they love someone else. She goes to speech days, coffee afternoons, looks after them when they are sick – and demands them overnight if she thinks we need a break. Children she minded 15 years ago pop in during the holidays to 'help out' and to play with the little ones. She's far better at child care than my mum (love you, mum!) – just as helpful, non-judgmental, very experienced and I pay her, so I don't feel I'm putting on her if I'm late. At least in the time I have with my children we can all chill out and have fun – the child-minder does the intellectual stuff during the week.

Diane

What the experts say
Perhaps 'good' mothers have to find the generosity in their hearts to understand that their children are separate individuals who are entitled to as much love and variety of stimuli from different types of people as possible, rather than selfishly keep the child to themselves by not working.

Kate Figes (*Life After Birth*)

My daughter has been going to a child-minder on a part-time basis since she was four months old. Yes, I feel guilty about the time my daughter spends there but she has a lot of fun as there are three other children. I have been fortunate enough to witness the first roll, crawl, steps and words. A lot of people comment on how sociable my daughter is, and she is generally very happy. I do try to do as much as I can on my days off with her but without the help of the child-minder and the other children that she mixes with, I am quite sure she wouldn't be where she is now. At the end of the day, she knows that I am her mum (something I used to worry terribly about) and she also has a lot of valuable time with her dad as well.

Dolphin

I can't see how spending time with a good child-minder can be 'bad'. My mother wouldn't send me to nursery or playgroup – she wanted me at home. In hindsight, I can now see I was a shy and introverted kid, and I think it would have been better for me to go out and spend time with other kids. My first day at primary school came as a huge shock – I remember it vividly.

Mothers are so often made to feel like aliens if they dare to admit that time out from their child can be beneficial to both. I have certainly noticed a difference in my one year old just from attending a twice-weekly playgroup. He is much more adventurous now and is perfectly happy to wander away and be around other people while we are there. Kids are so receptive – I'm sure they get bored with seeing the same old face all of the time. Input from others is invaluable.

Late30smom

People really think that men are somehow 'natural' providers and women 'natural' carers. If it hurts children for their mothers to work, it hurts for their fathers to work also. What's the difference? Why should women who work feel guilty? I am suspicious of anyone who wants to keep women out of the work force. I sometimes think the whole working mother equals bad mother thing was invented by a man frightened of the competition!

I don't know where the idea that being a mum means one thing and being a father means another comes from. Everyone should be a balanced individual, with bits of everything. I heard someone on the radio the other day say that children under five need 'mothering' not 'fathering'! As if there's any difference. Except for breastfeeding, there isn't really.

Jbr

I don't feel guilty about working. I might feel annoyed or put upon, or over-worked, or sorry when I can't do something I want to with the kids. But not guilty. My eldest child is nearly 13, so perhaps I have a longer perspective on this than when she was 13 months. I have the clearest memories of things when she was tiny and she has very happy memories of her first child-minder and nanny.

What I find really encouraging, though, is that she is proud of what I do and takes it absolutely for granted that I work. She sees that I am an interesting person in my own right (even to a 13-year-old). We talk a lot more about things in general than I ever did with my mother, who stayed at home and was the 'perfect' mother of her generation. Now I find it difficult to talk to my mother about anything outside the family. I think I'll probably have a very different relationship with my own daughter.

Copper

What the experts say

Women work outside the home for many reasons. It may be the only way which they can keep some control over their lives, and look forward to a future beyond child-raising.

Sheila Kitzinger (*The Year After Childbirth*)

Though many have tried, no-one has yet shown that children of good, working mothers are damaged or disadvantaged in any way.

Dr Christopher Green (*Toddler Taming*)

Other than the fact that I think guilt is pointless, I also think that there is nothing wrong with women going to work. Women have worked for hundreds of years and it is only in the last century that it became popular for women to stay at home. This was largely due to economic factors: such as that for the first time middle-class men earned enough to provide for their families so it was seen as an indicator that a husband didn't earn enough if his wife continued to work. If you feel confident about your childcare and want to work, have to work or enjoy working – why feel guilty? The human race has thrived since its inception with women working, so I don't think that we're all going to spiral into decline now!

Molly1

It is funny how everyone assumes you feel guilty if you are working but it can happen the other way round (when you are at home). Because I spend so much time with my child I worry that I am not fresh for him and that I lose my temper and am generally irritable. I think he wouldn't encounter this if he was at a nursery and that his life would be more exciting if he was going somewhere every day and seeing lots of different people. I try to have an active social life for him but some days he just stays in with me and watches me trawl through the housework with perhaps a walk to the park. Why is it assumed that this is 'better' for your child?

I do agree that putting very young babies into nursery is perhaps not a good idea and that you miss out on them because they are only babies for a short time. However, certainly by the time they are toddling around they don't need to spend all day with you. In any case in this modern society that simply means social isolation for both of you. In the past, kids would have had more contact with extended family.

On the other hand, my friend who works full-time says that her boy actually gets too much stimulation at nursery and as a consequence is bored very quickly when he is not there. So who can say which is 'better' – I think it depends on what you do with your child, whether it is in the evenings, weekends or in between the washing up.

Eulalia

> **Mumsnet fact**
> In the 1950s fathers spent an average of 11 minutes a day caring for their pre-school children. Now it's 44 minutes a day.
>
> Professor Jonathon Gershuny

It is tricky for working mothers. Even if women go out to work, often the domestic responsibilities are not evenly shared. There seems to be an element of guilt because mothers usually assume prime responsibility for their children.

If there is guilt it is worth investigating why. There are plenty of studies to show that children *are* adversely affected by being separated from their mothers at too young an age. Mothers may not feel particularly fulfilled at home but, more importantly perhaps, many households simply need the extra money a second income brings.

I don't want to impart more guilt but I do believe all the factors need to be considered – not just by the mother, but by the whole family. I do not agree or disagree with working mothers. I'm just very thankful I was able to remain at home for both my daughters while they were little and so saw their first steps, heard their first words and witnessed their early development.

Kate

Those of us who decide to stay at home can feel guilty too. Especially when we find the mothering task too much to handle for the full seven days and opt for a few hours' break a week by using a child-minder. The guilt comes when everyone expects you to be out at work on that day, as if it is shameful for a stay-at-home mother to need help.

Bj

The truth of it is that it's okay to go back to work, and it's okay not to. If you are feeling guilty, you have unfinished business somewhere about your decision. If you can get it cleared up, you can feel free to do what you have decided to (your choice that you made for your circumstances) and focus on the really important things like not forgetting his lunchbox and finding some form of protein that she is prepared to eat.

Woffles

Guilt is a big bag of burden that the midwives deliver along with the placenta. No one warned me about this at all. I feel guilty every time the kids get a cold and every time they don't like their meals. It's ridiculous when you look at it. As for feeling guilty over working – absolutely! Every time I go to work, I feel bad; every time the phone rings, I feel bad. I deal with it by understanding that as a single parent I simply don't have a choice and I work very hard to make sure that the children understand this and that if the world were different, I would not be working at all. The best tip given to me about guilt was from my mother. When I was talking about angst over having to work and what a terrible mother I was, she sighed and said, 'Look Lou, do what you feel to be right at the time. No matter what happens, the children will reach 16 and say that whatever route you took was the wrong one so you may as well do what you feel. Hopefully when they get to 18 plus they will suddenly realize what it was all about.'

Loola

Going part-time – how can you persuade your employer and is it a good idea?

I went back to work part-time and frankly, I don't know how I would have coped otherwise. It's meant that I can 'keep my hand in' with the job yet still have time for the house and children for two days a week and at weekends. Even so, I have to be strict about hours and feel guilty leaving on time when everybody else is doing overtime (I work in a 'long hours' culture).

As I understand it, an employer is obliged to give reasonable consideration to a request to work part-time so if you can stand a proportional cut in salary, it's worth asking. All I can add is that you need to be strict about your working hours, get as much help about the house as you can and make your time with the family as constructive as possible. Whatever you do, don't beat yourself up about it – after all, by carrying on, you are bringing valuable income into the family to improve the quality of life in the long run, if not immediately.

Helento

Part-time generally means you work 100 per cent of the time you are at work, and the administration gets done at home, so your employer gets far more for his money than with a full-timer – and there's no time for chats round the coffee machine either! It also means that you can generally work round the usual set of child-related problems, such as health visitor appointments and dentist visits, without having to take time off.

Provided you are prepared to be a bit flexible (and this does depend on your childcare arrangements) most meetings can be organized, so they are convenient for both parties.

My husband says he likes employing part-time mums because they are, in general, far more committed workers when at work and far more organized (you have to be able to fit four days work into three!).

Scooby2

One of the reasons I wanted to go back to work part-time is that I made some really good friends through having my baby and felt that my daughter and I were missing out on their company. Most of the mums I knew did not go back to work or worked part-time. It was very hard to hear about the great music, swimming or gym classes they had been to while I was at work. I also missed out on their support. It's just not the same trying to meet up at weekends, as this is family time or time when I can catch up with pre-baby friends.

My selling points to my employer for letting me return part-time were that my partner would do nursery pick-ups and drop-offs on my work days so that I could work longer hours, that I would try to fit in extra days during busy times (month ends) and that I would take phone calls and emails at home when necessary.

I suggested a trial period, starting off with four days then going down to three. For some reason it was unheard of in my department to work part-time – but then I was the first woman in the office to have a baby.

I have a team working for me and do find it quite hard to reconcile the fact that they work longer hours than me and that I often leave before them. However, I know that I still get my work done and I try not to let it bother me.

Not only has my salary gone down by a fifth but I've also had to contribute a fifth of the cost of healthcare benefit and a fifth of my company car benefit. I hadn't really thought about those elements, I must admit!

Pamela1

> **Mumsnet tip**
> If you are moving from a full- to a part-time job make sure you set really clear boundaries between when you are willing to take calls at home and when you are unavailable. Otherwise you'll find yourself tied to the phone on your days off.

One cautionary note from my experience of working part-time is about saying you'll take emails and calls at home in order to make it seem more workable for your employer. You will almost certainly take a pay cut and only get paid pro rata for the days you work in the office, but it can really take over your days off if you're not careful and you may end up resenting the infringement on your time with your child.

The other thing I'd say is that it will be up to you to ensure that you stay in the loop with regard to meetings that take place when you aren't there, especially if you are breaking new ground by being part-time. They will be unused to dealing with that situation and may find it hard to ensure you are fully informed.

Nonetheless, I worked three days a week between my first and second child and found it provided me with the right balance.

Emmagee

I have a deal at work whereby I fit five days work into four and then supposedly have Friday at home with my son. I always seem to be needed on Friday and so end up working a fair amount. I also feel I can't move far from the phone on that day. So my Fridays have become a horrendous juggling act on top of the four hard, long days I have already done that week.

Also, the fact that I am not supposed to be in contact on Fridays means that I feel I have to be available at all other times. So I end up on the phone at the weekends, in the evening, whenever there is a spare moment. The result is that I never feel I am not working.

> **Mumsnet tip**
> Don't try and be superwoman and get all the shopping and chores done on your day off so you and your husband can have a job-free weekend. Your day just ends up more stressful than any in the office!

Working part-time is great as long as everyone understands that you are just that, part-time. So don't feel guilty about the apparently great deal you have and make yourself too available. You run the risk of working as hard as before for less money and everyone will suffer, most of all you.

Sari

After I had my baby, I made it clear that I was only returning to work on the basis of a four-day week. I did so because our hours are a minimum of 7 am to 6 pm which, including commuting, would have meant our son being in childcare for a minimum of 60 hours a week (and obviously would have involved two forms of childcare, given that it would be unreasonable to expect a nanny to work these hours). My request was met with a pretty hostile response but I got my way on the understanding that on Fridays, I would be contactable and would come in if it was absolutely necessary.

Twenty months down the line and, although I wouldn't swap my day at home for anything, I still don't especially enjoy Fridays. I am the only woman in my team and I get a lot of resentment from my male colleagues. I am often too paranoid to leave the house on Fridays in case work calls me and if I do go to the shops, I get panicky at any hold ups. I stay logged on to the internet all day long so I can receive messages and any delay of more than around 20 minutes in answering them leads to more snide remarks from my colleagues. This is despite the fact that I am paid around 30 per cent less than when I was full-time!

> **Mumsnet fact**
> Nearly nine out of ten big employers think family-friendly employment policies will become more important to employers in the next five years. The Daycare Trust

I find the attitude totally perplexing. Given that my productivity is now the same as it was previously (due to vastly fewer lunches and no gossiping) and I am paid considerably less, my employer is getting a good deal. Especially as I inevitably do at least two hours work on a Friday. It just goes to show how entrenched these sorts of attitudes are.

It is vital to outline clear boundaries from the outset, otherwise you will find yourself being paid less and working just as hard while being subject to an intolerable amount of pressure on your day off.

It is really important not to lose sight of what you are trying to achieve by working one or two days less a week in the office – namely a relaxed time with your child and the opportunity to go out and about. If you begin by assuring your colleagues that you will be available on this day you will quickly find yourself chained to your PC and phone, and panicking about leaving the house for any length of time.

Ringer

I think you have to look quite closely at your working week before deciding on going part-time. Is it full of meetings and briefings held at very short notice? Do you have definite busy and quiet periods? If this is the case, it may be more workable to suggest four days off a month, as opposed to a four-day week. That way the days off can be arranged around work commitments, so you are more likely to be there when you are needed. This, of course, means you are dancing to the tune of the company, and makes it difficult to take your baby to regular playgroups. However, if your company is reluctant to agree to a four-day week, they may agree to this.

Frank1

> **Mumsnet fact**
> Eighty-one per cent of the UK's big employers have part-time or flexible working; 76 per cent job sharing and 52 per cent home-working.
> The Daycare Trust

I worked for an investment bank which had no official policy about part-time working. It was up to each person to negotiate with their manager (and also depended on whether they liked you and wanted you to stay). I negotiated a six-hour day without a lunch break. My son was in nursery for the two days that I worked 9 am to 3 pm and my parents had him for the other three days when I worked from 11 am to 5 pm. He gradually increased his nursery days to three a week and then five, so I worked from 9 am to 3 pm every day. My salary and all other monetary benefits were scaled down by one seventh.

It always worked extremely well for me as I'm the kind of person who would have worried that I'd forgotten something if I only worked for part of a week. I think that part-time workers have this kind of guilt complex so it makes them work harder than anyone else just to prove that they're not taking the piss.

Paula1

I work part-time and get a very good deal. I work three days a week from 8 am to 4.30 pm so I am always home for bath-time. I love it. It's the best of both worlds.

Tillysmummy

I live in Hong Kong where it is quite unusual for anyone to request or want to work part-time. I asked for a four-day week and was lucky that my employers agreed.

I originally planned to take one whole day off each week, but I have settled into a routine of taking two afternoons. This works best for me at the moment because I am only ever out of the office for an afternoon and it is less obvious to others and less inconvenient if they are trying to set up meetings.

I do have to be very flexible though but as I have a full-time nanny this is easier for me than if my baby were at nursery. Also, I find I do work late the afternoons that I am in the office, as I need to catch up and, also, it helps build my relationship with my colleagues. I know I do five days work in four and often have to read emails or catch up on reading at home. My arrangement is that I take four-fifths of my salary, but I've decided that it is worth it.

Sjs

Full-time work and parenting – how do you cope?

I have two children and work full-time. Though I have a very supportive husband and family, it's a struggle. I arrive at work at 8.30 am on the dot and I leave on the dot of 5 pm. I used to feel guilty about this but these are my contracted hours. I figure if they're not paying me to be there then I'd rather be with my family. I always take my lunch break as this is the only time in the week that I get to myself.

The bare minimum of housework is done (don't look under my bed or behind the doors... it's scary) and the family are now heavily into the crumpled look as I don't do ironing. We live on ready-made meals and as for the garden...!

At the moment, we juggle childcare between a child-minder and a nursery. Both are brilliant but it's really not working. Ferrying the children to and fro and working out what to do when they are sick just adds extra stress. I think we'll have to look at getting a full-time nanny.

What the experts say

Earning and mothering merely involves a gigantic, years-long compromise, and the almost total destruction of your free time. It takes a lot of managing and a lot of sacrifice. It is not a selfish option, except very rarely indeed. But nobody is going to feel very sorry for you.

Libby Purves (*How Not to be a Perfect Mother*)

I try to spend as much time as possible with the kids but have to admit that by the time I get back from work I just have time to bath them and get them in to bed (trains permitting) and I'm grouchy as hell due to tiredness. After they're in bed my husband and I eat and then I do whatever needs to be done (tidying, washing, preparing clothes for next day, paying bills) before collapsing in bed at about 9 pm. The weekends are better. I have a lie-in on Saturday (till about 8 am!) and my husband gets Sunday, and we try and make sure that we do family things together. We don't go out during the week (no time and certainly no energy) and at the weekend we only go to places where we can take the kids as I feel so guilty about being away from them the rest of the week that I can't stand being away from them at the weekends, too.

I don't think my children suffer – they are happy, bright and sociable. My husband has to help more, but that's no bad thing. I'm the one who suffers. I hate being away from the children so much and at the same time feel that I'm not giving my job the attention I used to. Consequently, my career is suffering and I feel guilty all the time. It's the worst of both worlds really. I'm hoping that eventually working from home or part-time will save my sanity.

Hmonty

Since being back at work I feel much more confident and am also a happier mother which, in turn, makes my time with my son a lot more productive.

When I was at home, I felt quite one-dimensional in that I could only communicate with other people if the conversation was about babies and nappies. I also missed the social aspect of being at work, the contact with the outside world.

My son has the best time at nursery. They are incredibly good and have loads of activities that I simply could not provide at home, for example, a huge 'soft room' full of padded blocks that the kids can jump around on.

I do miss certain things like taking him to swimming classes (for some reason these only take place on weekdays), but it certainly helps knowing that my son is having a great time while I am at work.

If work is something you have to do then the best thing is for you to lessen the guilt as much as possible and try to think of all the positive things that working full-time brings.

Debster

I was able to shift my working day from 9 am–5.15 pm to 8 am–4.15 pm. This has helped a lot. My husband takes our son to the child-minder's in the morning and I collect him. Being able to finish at 4.15 pm has made a big difference as we can get to the shops before they shut, get a load of washing on or just play for a good long time before I have to think about dinner. I do feel less stretched.

I still work full-time, but it doesn't feel like it. The morning is quiet and relaxed and then when 4.15 comes around and I leave, others are still working, so I feel part-time. Having that extra hour in the afternoon really makes a difference.

Emmam

I have a son of just over three years and a daughter of seven months. I returned to work full-time when my daughter was six months. I had to return to work for financial reasons and never have time for myself but I feel that providing a positive future for the family is very rewarding. At the end of the day, it is these early years that are the hardest – once the children are at school you may as well work as they will be out of the house all day anyway. Some of the things that make my life easier are having the childcare in my home so I don't have to race around with two children and 17 bags of things each day, an extremely supportive husband, a supportive mum who lives less than five miles away and the thought of long-term financial security. We are really the first generation to juggle our lives like this on such a scale – we are paving the way for our daughters to have more freedom of choice, so be proud of what you are doing!

Stocksie

I work four long days a week for a company with a long-hours culture. My journey to work is at least an hour each way. I have returned to work after my second child and this time has been easier. Last time I constantly battled with feeling guilty about not being home and not giving 120 per cent at work. This time I have stuck (more or less) to my hours (I get to work at around 9.30 am and leave at 5 to 5.30 pm). Once in a while, just to catch up, I get to work by 6.30 am. My husband works for himself, which helps enormously as we share the childcare.

We have a nanny, a cleaner and a gardener, which seems a real luxury but it means on Fridays and at the weekends we have quality time together. I would hate to give up work, although on dark, rainy days when I'm trying to get home I do question my sanity.

Pc

I work full-time and my partner works ridiculously long hours. I am just so tired all the time. I feel I never give anything 100 per cent anymore because I am too tired to do it. I leave the house before 7 am (daughter in tow) and go to nursery. I drop her off at 7.30 am and get to work by 7.45. I work straight through until 4 pm (when I always feel like I am sneaking off as I used to be here until 5 pm) as I have since made arrangements to finish early. I don't get home until 5.30 pm on a good night. My partner is not normally home from work until after 9 pm, by which time I've had to do everything for me and my daughter all by myself and I am exhausted.

My career is important to me but so is my family. Why is it that my partner feels none of the guilt that I carry with me everyday?

Amandag

Mumsnet fact
Only five per cent of employers provide workplace nurseries.
The *Evening Standard*

In my case, something had to give, so I left my job and got one five minutes from home, where overtime is not expected on a regular basis.

Javarose

My motto in life is 'work to live' not the other way round. It's amazing how little money you can struggle by with if you put your mind to it.

I'd only work if I enjoyed it – if it made me feel miserable I'd not hesitate to give it up – kids only have one childhood, you can always get back into working later on. This applies to men as well as women, of course! I am not suggesting that women should give up their careers. I just don't think it is always necessary for both parents to work full-time.

Eulalia

I think the two most important aspects to combining full-time work with parenting are maintaining your quality of life and being organized. It is vital to have any sort of domestic help that you can afford. I would put this as a priority ahead of things such as eating out. You simply have to be able to relax sometime and I think that an untidy home can potentially make you feel as though you aren't in control of your life and that just gets you down.

> **Mumsnet tip**
> A slow cooker is a good investment if you're out at work all day. You just put something on in the morning and in the evening all you have to do is cook the rice, pasta or tatties.
>   Tigger

I enjoy sitting down to a home-cooked meal every night with a glass of wine. It's good for your health, your relationship and your general wellbeing. My husband and I both work 11-hour days, minimum. I manage to cook proper meals via a combination of supermarket shopping over the internet but, more importantly, cooking in bulk. I keep large batches of frozen home-made Thai curry paste, various stocks, pie fillings, and so on, which can be turned into a meal in around 15 minutes. I have a cook-up every two months or so which never seems a chore and at any one time I have around 40 meals in the freezer. I fill in with stir-fries, risottos and pasta the rest of the time.

I am a big fan of combining a career with motherhood. Sure, it's tough (unbelievably so sometimes) but it's also very rewarding. Remember, you only have one life and you need to fulfill your potential. If this is best achieved by staying at home with your kids that's great, but if not, persevere. All children want is a happy family, however this is achieved.

When you're older, and your children have left home, hopefully you will reap the benefits of all your hard work.

Ringer

If you can afford it, I strongly recommend getting a cleaner who will iron or, failing that, sending clothes out to an ironing agency. I do all my grocery shopping and as much other shopping as possible over the internet or through catalogues.

If you are really pressed, it might be worth taking a half-day off with your partner to look at ways that you could organize things better. I know it may seem like a waste of precious holiday time but if it frees up weekends and makes life less stressful in the long run it is worth it.

Molly1

I am now back at work full-time after having my second baby. I have an incredibly supportive husband and family but I am still finding it very hard to balance everything and maintain a semblance of sanity.

Though I doubt anyone has lain on their deathbed lamenting not spending more time at the office, I'd also be willing to bet that there are a few women who didn't fulfill their ambitions as they would have done if they hadn't had children.

I just think that it is a shame that we work in such a long-hours culture. If a woman wants a career, at some point she has to decide to sacrifice home and family life and work very long hours.

Ultimately, it is important that *everyone* in the family is happy and for me that means working as well as bringing up my children. As long as they are happy and well-adjusted, I guess I will feel okay about working full-time. It is just very tiring!

Micg

> **Mumsnet fact**
> Forty per cent of parents admit that their working lives would be impossible without the childcare provided by their parents.
>
> The *Guardian*

There are five years or so before the state lays claim to your child when they start school. So whatever decision you and your partner come to regarding full-time work outside the home, you may still be able to rethink your life or change the decision as you go. Do what's right for you at the time – and, of course, what you can afford to do.

Frank1

A friend remarked that I was lucky that my husband worked from home and that my job didn't entail horrendous hours. What she failed to see was that it was a lifestyle choice that we had made and that there are certain sacrifices that go with it, such as less money. Luck was definitely not involved here, merely a question of working out our priorities and making sure that we did everything we could to stick to them. For us, this has meant fewer holidays and not having a flash car but it has given us more quality time together and a less stressful lifestyle.

Pamela1

At the weekend, I found some of my old exercise books from when I was about ten. One piece of writing was about my family: 'I have two brothers... my dad is an accountant', then came the classic piece, 'my mum used to be an occupational therapist, but she isn't anything anymore!'

As a new 'full-time mum' I found this very amusing as only the previous day my daughter had asked 'Mummy, why aren't you a dentist?' Will she one day soon write a story about how her mum used to be a marketing manager but isn't anything anymore?

Emmagee

I have been working full-time since my daughter was four months old and I have not regretted it. It is nice to have a lunch break! I do envy people with part-time jobs or who work from home – probably my ideal solution would be a job share with my husband. However I am lucky that my husband is a full-time dad so I know that my son has always had the best care.

For any psychoanalysts out there who think I am a bit weird legging it back to work so quickly, I blame my upbringing (lame excuse). I was brought up by my aunt and Nan while my mother worked away and visited occasionally (father unknown at that time). So a working mum has always seemed normal to me. What is important is love, stability, reliability and consistency from whichever carer you choose.

> **Mumsnet fact**
> Babies with two working parents by the age of nine months do 10 per cent less well in tests at the age of three than those with a parent at home. Those with one parent working full-time and the other working more than 30 hours a week had the lowest scores. But
> parents were urged not to panic: 'There are effects but they are not huge, your child's life will not be ruined.' said one of the team.
>
> Columbia University

Two things have always been very important to me and would be essential if I were to start job hunting. First is flexi-time so I can have time off without eating into holiday time and so I can be there for those important moments like health visitor checks (my mum was never there for them). Second, a flexible start time to enable me to take my daughter to school. That way we get some time together every day. Finally, each weekend always includes a 'girls' day'. This gives my husband a break and can be as simple as hanging out with a friend for the afternoon or an outing.

As long as you have confidence in your child's carer, working full-time just means you have to make the most of the even shorter time you have together (though without being fixated on spending 'quality time' doing stuff).

Madmaz

Is working full-time harmful to your child?

I have had many conversations with friends who work full-time and at times I truly wonder what the benefits of staying at home are for my child. It seems that babies get more attention at nursery than at home as the carers are there purely for the babies' benefit rather than having to run their own lives as well. My own daughter is very self-contained and well-used to entertaining herself while I get on with doing things around our home. Remember that a lot of stay-at-home mums are simply making the best of a situation where they may not be able to get a job, or having a job may not be financially viable after childcare is paid for.

Enid

What the experts say

It's much better for a child to be at a good nursery than to be at home with a parent who is lonely and miserable and who resents staying at home all day.

Dr Spock and Stephen Parker (*Dr Spock's Baby & Child Care*)

Our belief, based on a lot of work with new parents, is that one single adult needs to be the primary carer in the first 12 months of life... We believe this person should be the mother, unless there are compelling reasons otherwise.

Steve and Sharon Biddulph (*Love, Laughter and Parenting*)

When I've paid my childcare and travel each month I contribute a grand total of £350 to the family coffers and when I'm having a tough time at work and all of the best-laid childcare plans are collapsing around me I have to wonder whether a totally stressed out and exhausted mother is what my daughter needs at the end of the day. I really feel now that when we have our next child I will stop work for a while and give myself totally to the children. You can always decide to work again. Okay, so you may not make Chief Exec but we don't all need that.

Emmagee

I think that leaving children in a nursery from 8 am to 6 pm is selfish and cruel. Go ahead and put your own lives before your babies' but please don't pretend it's good for the child. It's not. Why even have a child if you are going to leave it to someone else to bring up?

And if I hear the 'but we need to work to live' argument one more time... Do not expect me to believe that you need two salaries to just get by. For one thing a good chunk would be swallowed up by childcare costs. Downsize your spending habits and work out what's more important in life – A: spend, spend, spend or B: your baby. If the answer is A then fair enough – to each their own.

ASF

If you read, talk and listen to other mothers you will realize that the reason why many women work is only partly financial. Some of us do it because we need an identity outside the home, some of us do it because we know we would not make great stay-at-home-mums and that our children truly benefit from spending time elsewhere, some of us do it for money, and some of us do it for a combination of all three. And indeed many households (especially London ones) do need two salaries to get by, my own being an example – even after taking childcare costs into consideration, it makes a huge difference. And I'm not talking four overseas holidays a year, lunching out every day and buying designer clothes. I mean a reasonable standard of everyday living, the odd day trip and looking out for sale stuff! Still, at least I don't have to worry about the journey home – I go by broomstick!

Batters

I work because I have to, there is no choice in the matter. But even if we were financially stable to the point where I could stay at home I still wouldn't because the kids drive me up the wall. My priority is making sure I have got enough money to get to work and put a meal on the table. This is real life, whether they watch too much TV, whether breastfeeding is the best option, whether I am a bad mother for going to work are not even worth debating. I do what I have to do to get by, as do most people. Should we not have children because we are poor?

Lisalop

I agree that nursery is not the best place for babies under one year. Although we might not like to hear it, there is something quite sad about only watching a child through a web camera instead of having physical contact with it during the day. I put my daughter in day care at four months – at the time I was a personnel manager of a large confectionery company and very ambitious. However, I now regret those missed early years and feel envious of my younger sister, who is experiencing the highs and lows of motherhood with a young toddler first-hand instead of through a web camera or a nanny's report.

Paigesmum

What the experts say

Childcare is not necessarily a second-best option. When it's good it offers a child an enriched social environment, stimulation, and friendship with other children and adults.

Sheila Kitzinger (*The Year After Childbirth*)

I think most parents genuinely want the best for their children in whatever circumstances they find themselves in. Just because you are in full-time paid employment does not mean that you shouldn't want, have or love your children.

If people who worked full-time didn't have children the human population would have died out long ago!

Molly1

Over the years, I have been variously a working mum, a stay-at-home mum and a mum who works from home. I have experience of using nurseries and a nanny, whether I was working at the time or not. Never before have I encountered anyone criticizing me for making any of these choices.

What I have encountered is other women anxiously trying to do the very best for their children while balancing family finances and their own sanity. This is against a background of never-ending press reports and research showing that whatever a mother decides it is bound to be wrong according to some expert or pressure group.

Women already have enough to deal with – unequal pay, reduced career prospects, lack of status and a shortage of quality childcare – without having to suffer criticism about their choices. In many cases (due to the above problems) the choices on offer are not really what a woman wants anyway.

Smokey

The fact is that all mothers try and make the best decisions we can for our families as a whole. What is important to me is finding the environment that will make our daughter a happy, secure and fulfilled child. I believe that I am really lucky to have days at home with her when I can contribute more to her happiness because I have been to work on other days and feel refreshed and ready to make pirate ships out of old cereal boxes. I'm not saying this is right for everyone but it is right for my family and that, at the end of the day, is what is important.

Viv

I used to work in a very demanding environment with long hours and lots of after-work socializing, which was tiring. However, I have found that being at home all day with a young baby is much more difficult (my partner agrees!).

I feel that being a parent is the most important thing anyone really does in their lives. For me, being at home to bring up my child is absolutely the best use of my time and it's time I wouldn't be able to get back if I returned to work too soon. I do sometimes miss the fun and challenge of work but I couldn't bring myself to leave my nine-month-old.

Josie

> **Mumsnet fact**
> The longer young children spend in childcare away from their parents, the more likely they are to show aggressive behaviour when they reach nursery school.   Birkbeck University Study

I too think that bringing up another individual is the most important thing anyone can do. For 18 years that person looks to you for guidance. How you respond and give that guidance stays with them for the rest of their lives. Do it well and you will enjoy a fabulous relationship with a son and daughter and probably with their family also. Do it half-heartedly or in a state of exhaustion and neither job is done well or will properly fulfil you.

Maryanne

Whether or not the mother works has very little to do with whether or not she brings up her children 'well'. It is all about the quality of the relationship. I admire parents who have achieved a happy and well-rounded family irrespective of whether they happen to have worked. My mother was a politician and I loved having such a positive role model as a child (and yes, we are extremely close).

Unfortunately, career women face constant digs about the fact that their work is somehow impinging on their ability to be a good mother. I personally have never seen any evidence of this at all.

I would never criticize a woman who elects to stay at home. All I ask is that women who decide to pursue a career and a family are left alone to do so rather than encountering suggestions that their career is somehow affecting their ability as a mother. What a terrible place the world would be if motherhood and work were mutually exclusive.

Ringer

I think that whether you go back to work or stay at home, if it's done for the good of all your family then they will sense this and you will not lose out on their love.

If you return to work because you find the company of your colleagues more stimulating than your children and want to 'fulfil' yourself, then your children will know it – maybe not today, maybe not tomorrow, but soon and for the rest of their lives. Conversely, if you stay at home because it's a more pleasant life than going out to work, even though some extra income would take the pressure off, your whole family will know this too.

But if the family is well-off enough financially and you know you can make them happiest by staying at home, then this is obviously the right thing to do – and if you need extra income, going out to work is obviously right as well. Mothers who go out to work bring their children up, just the same as mothers who stay at home, it's just different, that's all.

A mother who is a positive role model is very important too. I think that after children are at school, one ought to make a push to earn some money, just so that they (and you) can see that Mum can do that too.

I don't apologize for sounding like a martyr to the family – I think that it is right to consider what's best for everyone before you decide what you want yourself while your children are babies and toddlers. After that, you can hopefully manage a bit of both!

Javarose

I have encouraged my sons to watch TV at times and banished my eldest child to a nursery part-time. Before that, I had a nanny two days a week. I have a mother's help at the moment so that I can take a break from the youngest to do some housework. I regularly have a babysitter in to do the bonding activity known as bath and bed. I don't have a paid job or a volunteer job or any sort of a work outside of the home at all! Here's the worst bit: I think I'm a better mother now than when I only had one child and was staying at home doing everything myself. It's interesting, though, that we're all ('we' being my husband, myself and two boys) much happier this way. That's where this sort of bad parenting will get you, I guess.

JJ

9
Travel

Introduction

It seems only moments since a trip to the park with your precious newborn was a major expedition. But now you're thinking of venturing further afield. You've finally worked out that you can afford it, have time for it and you know you deserve it, so what kind of holiday works best? Camping, hotel or self-catering? Which is the best option with a baby in tow?

If you've never been on holiday with a baby before, be warned: it's still a holiday, but not as you knew it. You may get a change of scene, but unless you're blessed with a remarkably adaptable baby (or 24-hour childcare) you're quite likely to come home at least as exhausted, if not more so, than when you set off. As seriously dedicated holiday-makers we found the realization that holidays with a baby can be anything but, an unexpected shock of seismic proportions.

But there's nothing quite so portable as a small baby. You don't have to pay for them, they're not that fussy about entertainment and they don't take up much space. Well, they may not take up space but the mountain of equipment required to keep them fed, watered and sterilized could potentially fill a jumbo jet. So what do you really need to take with you to ensure a happy, healthy baby and to spare yourself a nervous breakdown on holiday?

Having pared it down to the bare essentials – four suitcases for the baby, a small holdall for the rest of you – how do you survive the journey? Should you opt for car, train or plane and once ensconced in your confined space with your infant traveller, how do you pass the seemingly endless hours before arrival?

All being well, you will eventually reach your destination – surely now the holiday really begins? But if you've opted for that long-haul destination there's the small matter of jet-lag waiting for you when you get there (and on your return). Are you really destined to do all your sightseeing and sunbathing at dawn, or are there ways to minimize the effects of the time difference? And what about the one holiday preoccupation that never changes – the weather. If you're blessed with sunshine, how do you keep your baby safe and comfortable in the heat?

Even if you've stayed closer to home with no jet-lag (and perhaps no sunshine either) there's the issue of food. Unless you're exclusively breast-feeding, travelling with a baby throws up (sometimes literally) all sorts of questions about hygiene and availability. Will jars and formula be readily available and sterilizing possible at your chosen holiday haven?

No amount of advice and preparation can guarantee you a relaxing holiday with a baby, but your best (perhaps only) hope is to listen and learn from other intrepid travellers who've been there, done that and bought the – now somewhat milk-stained – T-shirt.

What sort of holiday works best with a baby?

I think the key to a successful holiday with a baby is decent childcare. We tried all the options – taking the grandparents, going to a resort with childcare on site and taking our own nanny. Of the three the latter was definitely the most successful with a young baby. We found with grandparents that it was a bit awkward – they, after all, thought they were on holiday too and they'd forgotten what holidays with babies were like. They were quite happy for us all to hang out together but not too keen on mum and dad having an afternoon on the beach alone. Our experience of resort holidays with nannies on site is very mixed and it depends entirely on the quality of the nannies and the staff ratios.

> **Mumsnet tip**
> If you're travelling with a partner, decide before you go how much time off from the baby you're going to give each other. Even if it's just taking turns getting up in the morning or allowing each other an hour off to read on alternate days. It saves all those competitive tiredness arguments and stops you resenting having to play with the baby!

At one well-known holiday operation they had one nanny to seven babies in the baby room and our assigned nanny had arrived the week before, hoping to be working in the kitchen – she had no relevant experience and was completely out of her depth. Needless to say, my child spent almost no time in the nursery. By far the best option for us was taking our nanny and staying in a self-catering apartment. Obviously, it's not cheap – though if you are driving rather than flying the extra cost of another passenger is minimal. Also, you need to explain before you go what you expect your nanny to do and remind her that it's your precious two weeks' holiday – she's working. The upside is that the children have childcare they know, and hopefully like, and she can do all the things she does at home – like preparing meals and doing some laundry. Also, you have ready-made babysitting.

Berta

Consider going by train or putting the car on the train. When our youngest was a baby we were both so exhausted by lack of sleep that driving long distances was probably dangerous. On a train you can take it in turns to amuse the child, there are toilets (of a sort) and you can eat. We put the baby's car seat on the table in the middle so she could see out and arrived more refreshed than if we'd driven. Another suggestion would be to make sure you find a room with an en-suite bathroom big enough to take a cot – it means you can read (oh, how exciting) at night, but still be close by for nocturnal feeding and comforting if necessary.

Babsy

What the experts say

A train journey in any country is a cultural adventure in itself and it remains probably the easiest way of travelling with children.

Helen Truskowska (*Take the Kids Travelling*)

Families should not be encouraged to travel on trains. They fill a whole car so they're not wasting petrol and they'd reach their destination in half the time. Besides which they wouldn't irritate the hell out of other people on the way there.

Penny Wilson (*Wipe: Survival tactics for Parents with Attitude*)

We took our daughter away in a caravan at 12 weeks and it worked out really well. It's like a home from home, you can do what you like when you like and you can cut down on cooking by going out for meals or getting barbecuing. We stayed at the same site as other family members so there were plenty of babysitters.

Lollypop

Self-cater, and don't go with friends who have a baby the same age because your routines are bound to be different. Ahead of you lie numerous holidays where plastic, chlorinated water and pizzas will figure prominently. If you want to see the Prado, Neuschwanstein, the Louvre or Prague by night – whatever – do it now, with your baby in a backpack or sling.

Clare2

We camped in France with a six-month-old and it worked really well. Next time, though, I would go with a company that provided a ready-built tent as it was hard work setting it up while looking after the baby. We've found camping easy and relaxing with a baby (we bathed him in a washing-up bowl!). If you go by ferry, always book a cabin, even for a day crossing. It doesn't cost much extra but gives you some space.

Lindy

If money's an issue, house swaps make for an affordable and potentially easy way of taking a holiday. If you can match up with another family with children of a similar age, it means you know they'll have all the gear like high chairs and cots.

Suew

What the experts say

Without great determination and lowish expectations of pleasure, attempting adult pastimes with small children in tow can seem to be barely worth the trouble.

Libby Purves (*How Not to be a Perfect Mother*)

The perfect holiday is staying in the best hotel you can afford and getting the largest space you can afford, preferably a suite, so the child has a separate space at night. I would rather do this for a shorter length of time than self-cater. Driving is no problem as long as you have frequent overnight stays that are also in luxury hotels. Having the room cleaned, beds made, room service – that's my idea of a holiday. Even two nights away like this recharges your batteries totally.

Cam

I'm definitely a luxury hotel kinda gal (self-catering just doesn't seem like a holiday!) but rooms have to have a kettle, a mini bar (for storing milk and food) and ideally be close to a lift (we once had to drag baby, buggy and four bags up what felt like fifteen flights of stairs). Room service is also good, then you can still eat in your room but you don't have to cook it yourself. Even better are some places where they have a microwave in the lobby or vending machine area (particularly in the US). It was great for our two-bottle travel sterilizer. Throw in the fact that your partner can take the baby while you have a facial in the beauty salon and your holiday is perfect!

> **Mumsnet tip**
> If possible, try and choose a country known for its love of children – we had great times with our daughter in Ireland and Italy where everyone seemed to adore babies and we were welcomed into every restaurant with open arms.

Travelling by car was harder than I anticipated – I'd recommend holidays within a two-hour drive, or face the fact that travelling takes up the whole of one day and you must stop a lot. If you drive for too long the baby will get bored if she is stuck in the back on her own so one of you really needs to sit back there with her. And if you want to fly, go somewhere you can get to from your local airport. The whole airport and flight thing is traumatic enough without a three-hour drive before you start.

Philippa

A luxury hotel would be lovely but I'm sure a lot of people with a new baby (and the stretched finances that follow) can't afford this. I would recommend self-catering. This gives you the freedom to fit around the baby. If you're breast-feeding, go on holiday before you stop or start weaning. There's nothing more portable than a breastfed baby. In fact, I think in a lot of ways the younger the baby is the easier it is – so don't put it off!

Bozza

What do you really need to take with you (and what might just help)?

Don't take anything you can buy when you get there and, if possible, get hold of travel-size baby essentials (shampoo, baby bath, nappy cream). We found a UV sun-suit a godsend – it protects them from the sun for longer and it's also okay in water.

Dixie

Take your car seat with you rather than relying on hiring one along with the hire-car. That way you can be sure baby will be comfortable right up to the steps of the plane (and with any luck will continue to sleep after the drive to the airport). You will also have something to use in your hotel room. If your baby is too small for an umbrella buggy, just take a baby sling (and the car seat).

Lkm

A small, blow-up paddling pool is great to keep by the pool or on the beach. It stops them straying too far. If they're crawling, take some long trousers so they don't get hot, sore knees from the ground. Take a couple of legionnaire's hats (one for the wet, one for dry), Calpol in sachets, a hooded towelling dressing gown for when they get out of the pool and a favourite blanket or toy.

Rosebud

I suggest taking a buggy sun-shade that unclips from its holder plus a tea towel and a couple of clothes pegs. The parasol alone won't shade a child completely and it's easier to construct something than have two parasols. Peg the tea towel to the bonnet of the buggy to shade the head and angle the parasol to cover the feet.

> **Mumsnet tip**
> Pack a non-slip bath mat for inside the bath. I've needed one everywhere from hotels to my in-laws and it's always on my list now.

Apart from that, I'd pack a sun hat with an elastic strap to keep it on, a backpack for mobility, child-friendly mosquito repellent, one of those plug-in mosquito-repellents to protect the room from biting insects and something soothing in case anyone does get bitten. Some familiar, small bath toys are good for playing with in the pool, but it's usually worth getting a cheap bucket and spade out there and leaving it behind, rather than taking up precious space.

Malmomum

Buy a sun cream that sprays on – it means you don't have to rub it into sandy skin or grumpy and impatient babies. Take big beach towels and plenty of nappy pins, so you can attach the towels to the curtains and make black-out blinds in the hotel room so you have more chance of a decent night's sleep. Take the minimum of clothes for the baby – you can always rinse them out and dry them quickly.

Bee

UV sun-suits and beach shoes are good if it's going to be hot or the beach is pebbly, and a wide-brimmed hat, if your baby will wear one. Take talcum powder, even if you don't normally use it – it's great for getting sand off small people's bodies without causing a riot. And we definitely made use of disposable swim nappies under the sun-suit.

Clare2

If you don't want to splash out on a UV sun-suit, a tube of high factor sun-tan lotion and some light T-shirts that you don't mind getting ingrained with sand can work just as well. If your baby is doing lots of walking, beach shoes are useful, particularly around pools as they are non-slip – otherwise wait until next year for those. Take any medicines you've ever given your child, then you can be sure that you won't need them!

Molly1

> **Mumsnet tip**
> Sun tan wipes – if you can find them – are very light and very handy.

A seat swimming ring, a sun canopy, a pushchair, a drink beaker and a baby blender. We used the pushchair as a high chair to feed him and a bed if he fell asleep when we were out in the evenings. We also took a small cot blanket in case it got chilly.

Eulalia

Take reusable swim nappies – you can't always guarantee to be able to buy the disposable ones. My swimming instructor said to put a tight-fitting swimming costume over the top of the swim nappy so if there are any accidents, it doesn't get into the pool or sea when you move them around! I'd also take some rehydration sachets in case of tummy bugs (you can get them on prescription).

Bundle

> **Mumsnet tip**
> Take a baby's towelling dressing gown to the beach or pool. That way the baby's warm and dry and you have time to get yourself ready.

Take a baby carrier (the ones that are like a backpack) even if you have to beg or borrow one – pushchairs on beaches are a nightmare. We got our backpack when our first child was seven months and used it nearly constantly for six years after we had two more kids. They're great for hiking, beaches, airports and the zoo as well as they are up high and the child can see everything.

Maryz

Only take things that you need in a specific brand. I take enough soap powder for three washes and lots of nappies (I like a particular brand), plus sun tan lotion that I know and trust. I buy things like shampoo and beach toys when there. Pack a small first-aid kit with things you might need quickly, like plasters, Calpol sachets and a thermometer. There are always doctors and chemists if you need anything more serious. Take a light, umbrella-folding buggy and a light cloth you can use as a sun-shade. Try to bring one or two very big suitcases rather than lots of little ones. It's much easier to keep track of your luggage and to get from plane to car to hotel.

SofiiaAmes

What the experts say
Make a mental review of a typical day at home, from your child's wake-up time to her bedtime, all the clothes and other items you use. If you keep a running list, so much the better. Start making lists several weeks before you pack in case you need to buy something.

(*Fodor's FYI: Travel with Baby*)

There is a balance between bringing everything your children might use or want, and packing what they will actually need.

Helen Truskowska (*Take the Kids Travelling*)

I only pack two days' worth of napples (in case of delays), one pack of baby wipes and a hand-towel which doubles as something to lie on for nappy changing. I tend to buy everything else there. I also make sure I find out if there's a washing machine before I start packing every item of clothing we own. I always find my son has tons of stuff when I get to my destination and I've forgotten my swimsuit. One thing I've learned is to only take three toys. The first time we went away I packed everything but the kitchen sink and my son wasn't interested.

Selja

We always take a portable highchair – we've got a new inflatable one that packs away small – a wipe-clean bib and at least two sippy cups (you're bound to lose one) and Tupperware containers to take fruit and other food to the beach. Don't be ashamed to over-pack – maybe you *can* do washing when you're away but who wants to? As long as it all fits in the car, plane or hire car, who cares? Don't pack all the baby's things in one bag and make sure you have enough nappies and other essentials like changes of clothes in your hand luggage so you could last at least until the shops open, in case one of your bags goes missing en route (it happened to us and it was a nightmare).

Biza

We take a pop-up sun tent. We found it invaluable as it gave our 11-month-old somewhere to sleep and play in the shade. A harness and reins – not for walking, but for winding around the back of chairs to 'strap' him in. We didn't find any high chairs in Greece, and most of the chairs were not a suitable base for the portable high chair that we had.

The backpack baby carrier was also useful – not all of the beaches and paths were suitable for a buggy and certainly not for the umbrella style one we'd taken. We thought longingly about the fancy ATP (all-terrain pushchair) we'd left behind, thinking it would be too bulky – it wouldn't have been. The backpack carrier meant we could go to some of the nicer beaches off the beaten track.

JanZ

> **Mumsnet tip**
> A packet of balloons means you always have (almost instant) entertain-ment on hand, and they don't take up any room in your case.

I take a collapsible tent whenever we go away. My son recognizes it, so he doesn't feel so out of place. He loves sitting inside it and crawling in and out and I can throw all his toys inside when I'm on a tidying binge.

Lorien

I found the sun cabana thing a nightmare, by the time we'd got it up and secure my son was tired and didn't want to be out in the sun at all (he was only five months). Then, trying to get baby plus equipment back in the car while my husband wrestled with the sun cabana 'easi-fold' mechanism – hah!

Lindy

Our sun cabana has been great. It's designed to filter out the sun's harmful rays so we tend to encourage the kids to sit inside for their picnics and to get them out of the midday sun. They can then curl up for a nap and take a rest from the sun and sea breezes. We also keep all our belongings in it, including the ice-box as it helps keep it cool. All that combined with high-factor sun cream means that we haven't yet shelled out for expensive UV clothing.

Lill

> **Mumsnet tip**
> I've always found a bottle of bubbles very handy to take on holiday. They don't take up much room and are good for entertaining indoors and out.

A useful strategy (for the journeys as well as the stay itself) is to have a bag with mostly old favourite toys but also a couple of new ones, and bring them out one at a time, always putting the previous one back. This kept us going on a four-train journey to France. Also, if you think you'll be swimming a lot, get more than one washable swim nappy – they're horrible and clammy to put on when still damp.

Wmf

We don't take much in the way of toys when we go away, just a couple of books and some small favourite things. Our son didn't seem to miss his toys as we were out and about so much and you can always buy a cheap bucket and spade locally.

Demented

In terms of entertainment, when we went away our baby was only six months so we survived on very little. We took stacking cups as they pack away easily and are great for the bath and on the beach, plus wooden spoons and things from home that pack easily into luggage. We had a bag of crisps that came everywhere with us – he scrunched and bashed the bag (he didn't know it was crisps!) – a small inflatable ball that he liked to watch rolling about and some new jingly-jangly things to hang from the cot and pram. I've never done it but I know I could take the remote control from home and mine would be happy all holiday!

Maisy1

Long car journeys – how do you survive them?

We drove from Edinburgh to Brittany (in two days) with my daughter who is 11 months old. She started the trip by throwing up after 30 minutes – and she's never sick – because I gave her too much lunch in the hope it would make her sleep! Apart from that, it wasn't too bad. Lots of different snacks helped, plus she likes noisy or tearable toys so we took lots of different rattles, musical instruments, bits of paper and small cardboard boxes. She loved drinking out of one of those sports bottles of water, especially if we drank from them first. Also useful are a muslin to play peek-a-boo with and a song tape. I had to sit in the back until she fell asleep, but as I get car sick easily I would nip into the front as soon as she dropped off.

Nusch

Buy a clip-on tray for the car seat. It was possibly the best money I ever spent. It's a small but stable surface for cars and trains. It's great for raisins, and also catches quite a lot of vomit... well, it's better than getting it all over the car seat. If one of you can bear to sit in the back for part of the journey it helps keep the baby more cheerful.

Clare2

Try timing the journey with nap time or do something that wears them out before setting off, like swimming or walking. Take toys but only let them have one at a time and put the ones they're bored with back in the bag. Take non-messy things to eat, little raisins and tapes with ridiculous songs that you can all sing to.

Rosebud

Attach those buggy links so you can keep tabs on the toys. Try to plan for plenty of stops – it's a nuisance when you want to get on but they needn't all be long stops, just 10 or 15 minutes for everyone to stretch their legs or crawl around.

Baabaa

> **Mumsnet fact**
> On average people in Great Britain travel 11000km a year excluding travel abroad. Office for National Statistics – survey 1998–2000

Let your little one sleep whenever she wants to. We stop at all her usual mealtimes and have a good meal and a walk around but usually drive constantly in between these. We always stop at a reasonable time if we're going to stay the night – and go to the most luxurious place we can afford as this gives great restorative powers to all of us.

Cam

Forget sleeping patterns, they will probably go a bit pear-shaped anyway if you are on holiday. Pack more than one of everything you need like drink bottles, so if anything falls or is thrown you have a replacement ready to hand. I also have two or three little treats wrapped up in brightly coloured paper as a back-up for the really difficult times.

Shiv

> **Mumsnet tip**
> Keep an 'essential supplies' bag permanently in the car with things like nappies, wipes, ready-made milk, pre-sterilized disposable bottle, change of clothing, couple of toys and jars of food in it. This takes the last-minute panic out of preparing for outings with the kids, and has saved me countless trips back into the house to fetch something I've forgotten.

If you're breastfeeding and your baby is grizzling or won't sleep it's quite possible to feed on the move. You both need to be pretty proficient at feeding and be comfortable with the idea of feeding in public (especially if you're in a traffic jam or at traffic lights – which we always seemed to be). Just sit in the back and lean over so your breast is in the baby's mouth. It kills your back, but it's worth it for a bit of peace. Obviously, it only works when they're in rear-facing car seats (unless you're a contortionist). A sleeping bag that lets you slot the car seat harness through it is also a good investment if you drive at night – makes it easier to transfer your sleeping child.

Biza

Our son generally goes to sleep about 20 minutes after setting off in the car so we just put him to bed a couple of hours later than usual when we arrive. It doesn't always work, though and sometimes he'll whinge for over an hour before dropping off. We have loads of toys, drinks and snacks, which placate him for a while, but it becomes very irritating (not to mention giving me a stiff neck!) having to keep turning round from the front passenger seat to pick up a thrown beaker. Sitting in the back seat next to your child is easier, but doesn't help if you're navigating! Ultimately, we found that the best option was to set off at the children's bedtime and drive almost non-stop until we reached our destination. One person does all the driving then sleeps for most of the next day, that way the kids are asleep for the whole time.

Donna1

> **Mumsnet tip**
> On long car journeys steer clear of expensive, crowded, service stations.
> Take a slight detour into any decent sized town and head for the leisure
> centre. You might find a soft play area and a pool and you can have lunch
> for half the price.

If you're baby is still at the crawling stage then make sure you've got some
scruffy clothes, for all of you, for those motorway stops. For entertainment, we
found the only thing that worked was to take it in turns to sit in the back and read
stories (exhausting). It's a lot easier once you have two as the eldest one does
the entertaining! We've never found that the baby sleeping during the drive has
caused problems with bedtime, but if you do decide to drive overnight make sure
one of you, or someone else, is around to do the next day-shift. We got home at
daybreak after a 26-hour drive from Switzerland, our son was just waking up
wanting to start his day and it was pretty grim.

Azzie

I recommend frequent stops, plenty of snacks like cubes of cheese and grapes,
and tying the beaker or some toys to the car seat with short lengths of string
(nothing long enough to be dangerous) so you don't have to keep picking them
up. Try and relax and enjoy it, especially if it's a holiday. Your child might cry and
whinge for a bit but that's just the joy of travelling with babies! It's not usually as
bad as you are expecting. Stay calm and relaxed, and remember that babies are
great barometers and will pick up your mood instantly and reflect it right back
at you.

Bluebell

Plane journeys – how do you survive them?

I've done a lot of long-haul flights with babies and tend to check in as late as possible to avoid hanging around. Most airports now have some sort of playroom, where the baby can crawl around before boarding, so ask about that as soon as you arrive. I pack more milk than they'd normally need as it's a good pacifier. Lift-the-flap books, wrist bells, mobile phone, keys, all the usual suspects also tend to do the trick, brought out one at a time, as well as finger food – raisins, bread rolls, yogurts, apple pieces and celery.

I found that people didn't seem to mind babies crawling around as long as the cabin staff weren't trying to sell things or serve food. I'd rather risk germs and use wet wipes if it makes for an easy life.

Angharad

I was very nervous about taking our nine-month-old on a plane as he has never been good at sitting on my lap and was too old for a sky cot. However, after a cuddle on take-off I put him in the footwell to lie down and he slept happily the whole flight! I'm sure it was the vibration through the floor and the darkness that did it.

Lil

If you see any spare seats once everyone has boarded, ask the crew if you can move to get more space. A baby can easily sleep on a spare seat, with a barricade of pillows and blankets to stop them falling. If they're on your lap all night, even asleep, it's impossible for you to sleep too, and makes for very tired arms!

Neverhomealone

What the experts say
Children often make brilliant travel companions, simply because they bring with them none of the baggage – anxieties and fears – which occupy adults on a trip.
Dr Nick Jones (*The Mini Rough Guide to Travel Health*)

Don't leave the house with a small child unless utterly compelled by imminent starvation or the pressing need for other adult company.
Penny Wilson (*Wipe: Survival Tactics for Parents with Attitude*)

Try and fly in and out of small airports, where queuing is not a big deal. Drive to the airport if at all possible. If you're travelling with a partner, ask if you can get three seats even if the baby doesn't get one by right. This makes nappy changing mid-flight in the seat between you much easier than struggling in the toilet.

Lkm

Stick to usual mealtimes as far as you can. Also, feed little and often, and offer cool, boiled water in between because it's easy to become dehydrated when flying. We didn't attempt to use the toilets to change our son and just did it on our laps, which was interesting but easier because both of us could hold him rather than one of us fighting in the small toilet.

Tigerfeet

When your child falls asleep make sure you've got the baby seat belt around him already. Ours fell asleep without the belt on and we had to wake him when there was turbulence, which led to screaming. When we could, we took it in turns to walk up and down the aisle with him.

Fionn

If you're travelling with a partner and one child, take it in turns to look after the baby so you don't both get stressed out. Have an hour on and then an hour off each, or plan it so you can watch a film while the other one looks after the baby and vice versa.

Rosebud

> **Mumsnet tip**
> If you're travelling by plane I find the most useful piece of kit is a pillow. If you put it across your lap your child can sleep much more easily and you can also hand the whole bundle to your partner for a break!

Buy a couple of new small toys or picture books and keep them hidden until you have started flying. Pack more than enough nappies – you never know if you are going to be delayed. When they announce boarding, wait until the end. Boarding early adds at least half an hour to the length of time you have to contain a bored child in a confined space.

Meadow

I found a vibrating teether was a good distraction for mine. Ice-cubes and slices of lemon from the drinks trolley can also be fascinating, plus little packets of raisins, yogurt in tubes and old and new toys at regular intervals.

Be prepared for delays so that they don't catch you out and you're pretty self-sufficient. Look after yourself too with some sandwiches and treats. It's easier to keep your cool if your own blood sugar level and mood is pretty even.

Malmomum

Take a load of sterilized teats and disposable bottle bags with ready-made formula or sachets of powder and a big bottle of sterilized water. Try to get your child used to having bottles at room temperature before you go. Feed them on take-off and landing, but don't start until you are just about to take-off as there's a big delay between leaving the gate and actual take-off, and you could finish the feed before the wheels leave the tarmac.

> **Mumsnet tip**
> On a recent 11-hour flight to the US, I took a piece of string and tied anything my daughter wanted to play with to my wrist. It meant that I didn't have to go scrabbling around on the floor every time she lobbed her toy from the chair.

Avoid the buggy and take a carrier or sling if you can. I got rattles and tied them with ribbon to the straps of the sling so the baby had toys ready to hand and I kept my hands free.

Airlines sometimes provide bibs, nappies, wipes and food but don't rely on this – the chances are it will be a jar for a 12 months plus child and the nappies will be the wrong size. Double and triple check the sky cot is available if you've ordered one as they often forget this. Your baby needs to be under the weight limit for the sky cot (usually 9–10 kg/18–19 lb) and you need bulkhead seats.

If you have a stop-over, get on the net and look at the facilities available in the stop-over airport – some of them are excellent with baby equipment, toys and sometimes a baby bath. Pack as light as possible for yourself, but do include a change of clothes for both of you in case of accidents!

Amber1

For long-haul journeys choose night flights if possible. We stuck to the normal routine on the day of the flight, even putting her to bed for a couple of hours before going to the airport. We took a baby sleeping bag for the sky cot (if you don't use a sleeping bag, take a sheet or baby blanket to line the sky cot because they gave us the adult-sized blanket and pillow). Give them a bottle at take-off and landing to help their ears adjust, and ask for an aisle seat so you can get up and walk around, if necessary.

Tell the airline (before arriving at the airport) that you're travelling with a young baby. They should let you take your buggy right up to the plane door, but ask if you can have it again as soon as you land, i.e. at the door. Baby carriers and slings are handy too in case the buggy doesn't arrive. Even if it does, you can put the baby in the carrier and all the baby gear in the buggy.

On day flights, finger puppets helped us – she had endless hours of 'sorting' them in and out of bags and boxes, and loved it if we put them on our fingers, plus they're really easy to pack! It's amazing what else occupies them as everything is new – a walk round the aircraft, playing with the magazines or the baby pack. Try not to get too stressed if your baby cries, after all there is a limit to what you can do and being stressed doesn't help.

Sjs

What the experts say

There is no evidence from research to show that flying is unsafe for a baby under one year, if they are healthy. When flying, follow the same guidelines to reduce the risk of cot death you would at home:

Sit well away from the smoking area (if there is one). Keep your baby cool. Remove hats and extra clothing. When you check your baby, if he or she is sweating or the tummy feels hot to the touch, take off some clothing. Don't worry if the baby's hands or feet feel cool, this is normal. Make sure your baby takes appropriate feeds, and does not become dehydrated. Go to your doctor if you have specific questions about your baby, e.g. if your baby has a cold, or is not well before the flight.

The Foundation for the Study of Infant Deaths

Jet-lag – how can you lessen the effects?

We took our 12-month-old to Florida and it took a while for her to adapt. She woke at 2.30 am the first morning expecting her bottle. It took us roughly four days to get her to adjust (every day we stretched her bedtime a little more). We coped by taking it in turns to get up with her and by going to bed early. The good news was when we came back we got her to settle on a later wake-up time.

There were other parents who managed to keep their child awake for the entire flight. They found their kids were so exhausted by the time they got to bed on the night they arrived that they slept for 12 hours and adjusted straight away. I didn't feel I could inflict my hysterically-tired one-year-old on the rest of the passengers, but if you can keep them awake for the flight, it's probably the best way to do it.

Jraven

We stuck to routine mealtimes on the plane and once we arrived, we tried to stick to the same mealtimes again. It probably meant that our son had tea twice that day but by keeping the meals light I don't think he was particularly bothered.

Tigerfeet

We went to New York from the UK with our four-month-old son. He slept most of the way and just woke for his feeds. He adjusted slowly to the time difference, but we did end up seeing the city very early most mornings.

Jds

Try to keep them up as late as possible on the first night. I know it's hard with babies but it worked for me.

Leander

One thing to bear in mind is that if your child has bad sleeping habits at home, the chances are they'll have bad sleeping habits away and it may not be due to jet-lag. The first time we went to Australia our son was five months and his sleep was awful, but I don't think that was jet-lag. The second time was much better. The first 12 hours of the flight it was night-time and with the help of some children's sedative our son slept for most of this leg of the journey. For the second 12 hours of the flight (UK daytime) I just let him sleep as much as he wanted to, although he was awake for much of it.

On arrival we went straight into our normal routine as if jet-lag were not an issue. We found that he napped longer than usual (for obvious reasons) but settled fast into the new time zone (faster than we did!). We had about three disturbed nights – by which I mean he woke for about 15 to 20 minutes. By the fourth day he had fully adjusted to Australian time. Exposure to daylight is important in setting body clocks, so try to get outside for a walk or two on the first day.

Amber1

What the experts say
Before your departure date, alter your child's schedule so that it's closer to what it will be on the road. Going west to east? Over a three-day span bump bedtime and wake-up time back a little bit more each day. Do the reverse going east to west.

(Fodor's FYI: Travel with Baby)

I agree about routines. We went to the Far East with a nine-month-old whose regular routine was to nap after lunch. We joined the baby and all had a nap for the first three days for about an hour. You need to set an alarm clock, though, both for naps and for the morning, and drag yourselves up but it makes the process quicker in the end.

Batey

We live in Hong Kong and came back to the UK when our daughter was four months old (it's an eight hour time difference.) She slept most of the (night) flight but woke up at her normal time. I'd made a note of the equivalent UK times for her bottles so that I would give her enough at each feed, and let her sleep when she got tired (a bit more than usual) but tried to steer her as much as possible into a 'normal' routine. I also took her out for walks in the sunshine.

She went to bed at 7 pm as usual the first night but woke up in the middle of the night for a couple of hours. I just got her up at 7 am as normal, and the next day she was fine and back on schedule.

Mumsnet tip
When you're trying to adjust to jet-lag, stick as far as possible to the same schedule as your child. We found that as long as we went to sleep and took naps around the same time as our daughter, we weren't too shattered to enjoy the very early mornings on a deserted Caribbean beach!

When we flew home, our daughter was waking up in the middle of the night screaming at about 1 am. When we tried feeding her, it turned out she was hungry (personally, I always find I'm hungry at odd hours when I have jet-lag.) After being fed, she went straight back to sleep for the rest of night. We'd only just given up a 10.30 pm feed while we were on holiday, so we just went back to waking her for a few days until she was properly back into a routine, and then dropped it again. To be honest, she adjusted better than we did.

Sjs

The regular advice to adults on jet-lag is always to avoid alcohol and caffeine, and drink lots of water on the flight. I don't suppose anyone would dream of giving their baby a coffee, but if breastfeeding, it's worth avoiding stimulants at least for the flight and making sure the baby stays hydrated. It's almost inevitable that you'll have one or two bad nights, but if you're not travelling alone you can always take it in turns to get up. There's also something quite magical about being up and about before everyone else and seeing a place (particularly if it's scenic) early in the morning. Of course it's not quite so magical if you're on your own in a grotty hotel in the middle of the night, but as everyone advises, try and get onto local time and it won't last too long.

Sica

Feeding your baby abroad – how do you manage?

Don't assume there will be a kettle to make up formula. We have twice travelled to European four- and five-star hotels to find there wasn't one. They even find it difficult to source one quickly for you as there's such a strong 'coffee culture' and they often don't use them. We now take a travel kettle. It's also worth calling to check to see whether your room has a fridge or mini bar that you can use to store milk (although these don't always run at as low a temperature as a fridge at home). We use the bathroom sink to wash and rinse bottles (taking our own washing-up liquid, and brushes) and then sterilize them overnight using cold-water sterilizing tablets. We used still, bottled water to make milk, but you're probably okay with tap water if it's boiled first – we used it when we ran out of water and the faffing around was getting to me!

Motherofone

I became very attached to thermos flasks – they keep water warm for bottles, so all you do is pour it into the bottle and add the powder. I found a really neat one in stainless steel, which held enough water for two bottles. So as long as you can find somewhere to heat your water you can store it until needed and you don't have to lug loads of stuff around with you.

Pob

Buy a sterilizing kit. Each sachet contains a sterile bag, which you just hang from the bath or shower, and two sterilizing tablets, which will keep the water and any kit contained within it sterile for 24 hours. These kits take up no room and are very easy to use. We used Evian each time we travelled when our son was under one year and you don't need to boil it. I would recommend taking a couple of the small bottles just in case you arrive at a time when the shops are shut. It's also worth taking a couple of cartons of ready-made formula too, just to save messing around with containers or sachets of powder at tricky times.

Molly1

> **Mumsnet tip**
> Carry formula powder in zip lock bags. It's much lighter and easier to transport flat in your case and if you get stopped, it gives the drugs squad something to look at!

There are some really dinky little disposable travel sterilizing bags that you fill with water and heat in the microwave. In terms of water I use boiled, cooled Evian water (low sodium).

Enid

Evian, Volvic and Vittel are all absolutely fine for babies. Most mums in France and Belgium don't boil water, they just use bottled. In France, they now sell disposable bottles – pre-sterilized. Failing that, restaurants in hotels are usually happy to help – though try to avoid asking at peak meal times!

Pupuce

> **Mumsnet tip**
> I travel armed with cold sterilizing tablets and a one-litre ice-cream tub –
> it's very easy, you can use tap water and it's all done in thirty minutes.
> The tub makes a useful container for bottles, brushes,etc.

We bought a huge plastic bottle of water and cut the top off to use as a container for cold-water sterilizing. I would also definitely take the cartons of formula milk as they're great when you're actually travelling or are just out and about.

I started by boiling tap water and making up bottles – then I had a cup of tea and it tasted foul because of all the minerals. I used bottled water after that but boiled it as it wasn't a brand I knew.

Minky

Last year we went to France and I discovered that nobody knew what SMA was and they have very little in the way of organic baby food.

Chiara

If your baby's weaned you might be surprised by what they'll eat. My daughter still has a thing for olives and olive tapenade after two trips to Italy at six and ten months. She also ate pasta and tomato sauce, bread, fruit, soups – the works. The other big hit and staple when all else failed was avocados and banana – mashed together – both usually very easy to get hold of abroad. The fruit jars in Italy were fine as they were basic fruit purées, though not organic or sugar-free (if that's important to you) but the savoury selection was pretty weird – rabbit, lamb, tripe?! We recently came back from Corsica with baby number two who loved the gourmet French baby food – dauphinoise potatoes and fish stew – all neatly packaged. No wonder he's turning his nose up at English jars now!

Biza

We've been to France and Spain and, as well as local food, we found the baby food jars in the local supermarkets were fine. It was a bit hit and miss with some of the flavours, but our son ate most of them. I also took a couple of packets of baby pasta (nice and lightweight) and made sauces out there from local vegetables.

Tetley

What the experts say
Feeding your child abroad requires meticulous organisation and an obsession with all things clean and sterile.
Dr Nick Jones (*The Mini Rough Guide to Travel Health*)

Our daughter was eight months old when we went to live in an hotel in the US for two months. We didn't take anything with us and we survived. We ordered food for ourselves and she ate whatever we felt was suitable from our plates. She tried everything – pancakes, grits, fruit, pasta, polenta, meat, vegetables, cereal. Basically, if it was good enough for us, it was good enough for her as long as it was within the usual guidelines.
SueW

We travelled to southern Spain when our son was nine and a half months. The only thing we took was the baby blender and travel adaptor. Our son ate the local food, so apart from baby cereal we didn't take any jars or tins.
Eulalia

Mumsnet tip
Always take a very mini blender so you can make anything edible if your baby's a lump-phobic!

We went to Portugal when our son was nine months old and we ate out a lot. We found the jars of food available locally were fine, either smooth fruit purees or varieties like sardines and vegetables (which led to some very interesting nappies). We bought cereal for breakfast and the rest of the day he either had a jar or some chips (not very healthy but we were only there for a week).
Demented

We took our five-month-old to Crete last summer and I was pretty much regarded as a mad woman every time I enquired about jars of food. Greek mothers just don't seem to use them (they're obviously far less lazy than we are). Eventually I tracked some down but that was only after much searching. I ended up cooking stuff myself after a while. If you're heading to Greece, either take jars with you, or don't forget to pack a couple of ice-cube trays to freeze things in.
Grizzler

What the experts say
Babies almost everywhere in the world are fed out of jars and packets, and your baby will not go hungry.
Helen Truskowska (*Take the Kids Travelling*)

One place you don't need to take baby food is the US. Baby food seems to be readily available and really good. It's organic, contains no added sugar and salt and there are lots of great flavours (butternut squash, sweet potato). I even found it in Jamaica. By contrast, in Brittany, the hypermarkets only sold Nestlé stuff and that was full of added sugar and salt. Only in France would they sell a jar of artichokes and anchovies as baby food – you should have seen the look of horror on my eight-month-old's face when she tried it!

Berta

How can you help babies cope with the heat?

I live in a hot climate and suggest trying to follow the same routine the locals follow. Go out in the mornings, stay at home and sleep between 1 pm and 5 pm. In the early evening, take a swim or go to the beach (it's the best time of the day and the sea is warmer) and go out for a meal later. Of course, this depends how upsetting you think a major change in routine would be for your child, but it's nice to be able to go out and eat in the evenings when the temperatures are cooler. Mine always change quite easily to a more British routine of early nights and less sleep during the day when I come home every summer.

Other top tips include taking a fan (it will probably be very useful, especially for siesta time). Take very high-factor sunscreen and don't even think of trying to take home a sun-tanned baby! Take lots of T-shirts for wearing in the pool or sea and don't use vests for babies as their shoulders burn easily. Make sure a hat is worn at all times, even in the sea or pool. Take a sun-shade for the buggy – the big ones that can be tilted backwards and forwards provide more cover. Give plenty of fluids and light meals, and use insect repellent. Sprays are much easier to apply and I always use Citronella – it smells good and it's non-chemical.

Grmum

> **Mumsnet tip**
> Always put sun-tan lotion on your child before you hit the sand. It saves their tears as you try to hold down a wriggling child while massaging in an abrasive sand and sun lotion mix.

I always take a small water spray bottle when I'm out in the heat with me and use it to mist my three children and keep them cool.

Threeangels

We live in Spain and our son copes well with the heat. During the summer he just wears a nappy, even at night, and we use a mosquito net that goes over his cot and pushchair. You might think babies don't sweat, but they do, so lots of fluids and a fan are essential.

Art

I tend to take cold, boiled water everywhere with me either in a sports drink bottle or a light plastic flask. If it's really hot I also put a couple of ice cubes in them (from my ice cube tray made with boiled water).

Jendy

I took my daughter to Greece when she was six months old and my son to Spain when he was five months. Neither place had air conditioning, so we just hired a couple of fans and it was fine. In fact, I think they slept better than normal and on both occasions the temperature was at least 30 degrees. Just make sure you take a sunshade for the pushchair and plenty of sunscreen.

Lou33

> **Mumsnet fact:**
> One severe bout of sunburn in childhood is enough to cause melanoma
> later on in life. The *Evening Standard*

I found our nine-month-old baby was okay in the shade and at night he just slept in his vest. I followed the usual advice about not going out in the middle of the day, plenty of sun-cream and so on. At least before a baby is walking it's easy to strap them in their pushchair on the beach with a sun canopy. I would sit on the balcony with our baby in the shade, a washing-up bowl of water and a few containers and let him play around with that. You can always take a fan and a travel plug for evenings when the air can get very still.

Eulalia

A washing-up bowl on the beach under a sun umbrella worked well for us when it all got too hot, or if your baby's too big, a paddling pool. They stay cool and can splash around without too much danger! A sun cabana or UV tent – left open to catch any breeze going – are useful for baby siestas and prove popular for imaginative play for toddlers later on!

Biza

Fill a pop-up sun tent with fun toys and an immobile baby will be fine. We also use UV sun suits and despite their rather synthetic feel we have never had a problem with over heating or prickly heat in Spain, Portugal or Florida. A blow-up boat filled with water and put in the shade makes a nice cool paddling pool. Hats are essential but we had problems making the boys wear one. It's worth persevering, though. If you keep trying, they get used to it eventually.

Soupdragon

UV sun-suits are fantastic. We only had to put cream on faces, hands and feet when they wore them so there were no burned shoulders at all and they didn't seem to get too hot. Lots of drinks are another essential. I kept forgetting a baby (like my daughter) cannot ask for water or milk and she gulped it down eagerly when offered.

Clary

> **Mumsnet tip**
> Pack an old-fashioned folding fan. A few minutes of wafting during nappy-free play-time cools my nine month old right down – and he loves it!

Our daughter wouldn't wear a hat as a baby but we were given a hat with a strap underneath, which attached with Velcro. It was brilliant and she couldn't remove it, so it's worth trying to track one down.

Sjs

> **Mumsnet tip**
> If you can't find a hat that your child will tolerate try making a bandana style one out of a large cotton hanky. Not great for shading their eyes, but better than nothing and as it's tied on it's harder for them to pull off!

We found the only way to get our very hat-phobic baby to wear one was to distract him with something else and then plonk a very loose oversize cloth hat on his head. If it wasn't tight he didn't seem to mind as much. The problem was that the only large, wide-brimmed hat we could find was pink and frilly so he's going to hate all the holiday photos when he's older!

Sica

Bibliography

Adamson, Nicky. *Is Breast Best?*, Hamlyn, 1990

Brett, Simon. *How to Be a Little Sod*, Orion mass market paperback fiction, 1999

Biddulph, Steve. *The Secret of Happy Children: A Guide for Parents*, HarperCollins, 1999

Biddulph, Steve and Biddulph, Sharon. *Love, Laughter and Parenting: In the Precious Years from Birth to Age Six*, Dorling Kindersley Publishing, 2001

Bradford, Nikki and Williams, Jean. *What They Don't Tell You About Being a Mother and Looking After Babies: The Definitive Guide to the First Two Years*, HarperCollins, 1997

Eisenberg, A.; Murkoff, H.E; Hathaway, S.E. *What to Expect the First Year*, Simon & Schuster, 1993

Ferber, Dr Richard. *Solve Your Child's Sleep Problems*, Dorling Kindersley, 1986

Figes, Kate. *Life After Birth*, Penguin Books, 2000

Fodor's. Fodor's FYI: *Travel with Baby: Experts Share Their Secrets*, Fodor, 2001

Ford, Gina. *The Contented Little Baby Book: The Secret to Calm and Confident Parenting from One of the World's Top Maternity Nurses*, Vermilion, 1999
The New Contented Little Baby Book, Vermilion, 2002

Gookin, Sandra Hardin; Gookin, Dan; Shaw, Mary Jo. *Parenting for Dummies*, Hungry Minds Inc, 2002

Gordon, Dr Yehudi. *Birth and Beyond: The Definitive Guide to Your Pregnancy, Your Birth, Your Family: from Minus 9 to Plus 9 Months*, Vermilion, 2002

Green, Dr Christopher. *Babies!: A Parent's Guide to Enjoying Baby's First Year*, Simon & Schuster, 2002
Toddler Taming: The Guide to Your Child from One to Four, Doubleday Australia, 2000

Hames, Penny. *NCT: Help Your Baby to Sleep*, HarperCollins, 2002

Herman, Deborah. *The Complete Idiot's Guide to Motherhood*, Alpha Books, 1999

Hilton, T. & Messenger M., Graham, P. (Ed). *The Great Ormond Street New Baby and Child Care Book: The Essential Guide for Parents of Children Aged 0-5*, Vermilion, 1997

Hogg, Tracy. *Secrets of the Baby Whisperer: How to Calm, Connect and Communicate with Your Baby*, Vermilion, 2001

Iovine, Vicki. *The Best Friends' Guide to Surviving the First Year of Motherhood*, Bloomsbury, 1999

Jackson, Deborah. *Mother & Child: The Secret Wisdom of Pregnancy, Birth and Motherhood*, Duncan Baird Publishers, 2001
Three in a Bed : The Benefits of Sleeping with Your Baby, Bloomsbury, 1999

Jones, Dr Nick. *The Mini Rough Guide to Travel Health*, Rough Guides, 2001

Karmel, Annabel. *Annabel Karmel's New Complete Baby and Toddler Meal Planner: Over 200 Quick, Easy and Healthy Recipes*, Ebury Press, 2001

Kitzinger, Sheila. *The Year After Childbirth: Surviving the First Year of Motherhood*, Oxford Paperbacks, 1994
The Year After Childbirth: Enjoying your body, your relationships and yourself in your baby's first year, Prentice Hall & IBD, 1996

Larson, Signe & Osborn, Kevin. *The Complete Idiot's Guide to Bringing Up Baby*, Alpha Books, 1997

Leach, Penelope. *Your Baby and Child*, Penguin Books, 1997
Babyhood, Penguin Books, 1988

Lewis, Sara. *Feeding Your Baby*, Lorenz Books, 2002

Martyn, Elizabeth. *Baby Shock*, Vermilion, 2001

Merry, Emma. *First Names: The Definitive Guide to Popular names in England and Wales*, The Stationery Office Books, 1995

Mindell, Dr Earl L. *Parents' Nutrition Bible: A Guide to Raising Healthy Children*, Hay House, 1992

Morrissey, Sian. *The 'Which?' Guide to Baby Products: How and Where to Buy the Basic Essentials for Your Baby*, Which? Books, 2002

Narter, David. *Don't Name Your Baby...What's Wrong with Every Name in the Book,* Cumberland House Publishing, 2002

Nolan, Mary. Being Pregnant, *Giving Birth: The National Childbirth Trust*, HarperCollins, 1998

Olivier, Suzannah. *What Should I Feed My Baby?: The Complete Nutrition Guide for Babies and Toddlers*, Weidenfeld & Nicolson Illustrated, 1998

Palmer, Gabrielle. *The Politics of Breastfeeding*, Pandora P., March 2003
The Politics of Breastfeeding, Rivers Oram Press/Pandora List, 1993

Parker, Jan & Stimpson, Jan. *Raising Happy Children: What Every Child Needs Their Parents to Know – from 0–7 Years*, Hodder Mobius, 1999

Purves, Libby. *How Not to Be a Perfect Mother: The Crafty Mother's Guide to a Quiet Life*, HarperCollins, 1986

Spock, Dr Benjamin & Parker, Stephen J. *Dr Spock's Baby and Child Care: The One Essential Parenting Book,* Simon & Schuster, 1999

Stoppard, Dr Miriam. *Complete Baby and Childcare*, Dorling Kindersley, 2001
New Baby Care Book: A Practical Guide to the First Three Years, Dorling Kindersley, 1990
Your New Baby, Dorling Kindersley, 2002

Sullivan, Karen. *Commonsense Healthcare for Children*, Piatkus Books, 2000,
Commonsense Healthcare for Children, Piatkus Books, 2001

Thiro, Rosalyn (Ed.), Kitzinger, S., Figes K., Barker R., Hobden J. *Baby and You: The Real Life Guide to Birth and Babies*, Blue Island, 2002

Truskowska, Helen. *Take the Kids Travelling*, Cadogan Guides, 2000

Wilson, Penny. Wipe: *Survival Tactics for Parents with Attitude*, Hodder Mobius, 2002

Index